Philad. Dec: 13. 1753

...ived your Fav.d of the 5th Inst.
...our kind Congratulations .
...me time since, and sent you
...bound Books; the Parcel was
...care of Mr Theyvesandt at
...but it is not yet got to hand.
...Truth give you a good Ac.t
...xcellent Pieces of yours; but where
...had, the best Work comes to the
...I wish the enclos'd were better
...me. — I know nothing
...mention having reverbeen

The Founding Fathers

The Founding Fathers

BENJAMIN FRANKLIN

A Biography in His Own Words

VOLUME 2

Edited by

THOMAS FLEMING

JOAN PATERSON KERR

Picture Editor

NEWSWEEK, New York

ISBN: Clothbound Edition 0-88225-033-7; ISBN: Deluxe Edition 0-88225-034-5
Library of Congress Catalog Card Number 72-75999
Copyright © 1972 by Newsweek, Inc.
All rights reserved. Printed and bound in the United States of America
ENDPAPERS: FRANKLIN TO SAMUEL JOHNSON, DEC. 13, 1753; PRIVATE COLLECTION

A 1787 view of the State House in Philadelphia

Chapter **8**

Spokesman for America

With the Stamp Act repealed, Franklin felt himself on a firmer and broader political foundation than he had ever known before. He was now an unofficial spokesman, not merely for Pennsylvania but for all the Colonies. In the higher levels of the British Government, he had acquired a name that inspired considerable respect, if not always admiration. With peace between the mother country and Colonies seemingly assured, Franklin decided to put this new-found prestige at the service of one of his oldest and most ambitious dreams—the founding of a western colony. The impetus came from his son William Franklin, the Governor of New Jersey. A group of William's friends, notably Samuel Wharton of the important Philadelphia firm of Baynton, Wharton and Morgan, had come up with the idea of petitioning the Crown for a grant of lands in the West to repay them and other traders such as George Croghan for the heavy losses they had suffered during the Indian war known as Pontiac's Uprising, 1763–64. William suggested the idea of petitioning for a colony, rather than a simple grant of land, which the British Government would be more likely to resist. Governor Franklin brought Joseph Galloway into the project, and explained to his father that they hoped to obtain the land from the Indians through the diplomacy of Sir William Johnson, the Indian Superintendent, who was also a secret partner in the company formed to run the colony. Franklin promptly replied on May 10, 1766, that he liked the project "and will forward it to my utmost here." The same day he wrote Galloway that it was "a most desirable measure" and that "the Proposal is much listened to here." In the following letter to William, Franklin discussed the numerous wheels that had begun to turn in pursuit of this scheme. Lord Hillsborough was the new head of the Board of Trade, which had a strong influence in American affairs. General Lyman was Phineas Lyman, a Connecticut soldier who had distinguished himself in the French and Indian War. George Croghan was negotiating with Illinois country Indians on behalf of the British. Lord Adam Gordon was a British soldier and member of Parliament, who had traveled widely in America. "Our friend Sargent" was John Sargent, a London banker.

September 12th, 1766

I have just received Sir William's open letter to Secretary Conway, recommending your plan for a colony in the Ilinois, which I am glad of. I have closed and sent it to him. He is not now in that department; but it will of course go to Lord Shelburne, whose good opinion of it I have reason to hope for; and I think Mr. Conway was rather against distant posts and settlements in America. We have, however, suffered a loss in Lord Dartmouth, who I know was inclined to a grant there in favor of the soldiery, and Lord Hillsborough is said to be terribly afraid of dispeopling Ireland. General Lyman has been long here soliciting such a grant, and will readily join the interest he has made with ours, and I should wish for a body of Connecticut settlers, rather than all from our frontiers. I purpose waiting on Lord Shelburne on Tuesday, and hope to be able to send you his sentiments by Falconer, who is to sail about the twentieth.

A good deal, I imagine, will depend on the account, when it arrives, of Mr. Croghan's negotiation in that country. This is an affair I shall seriously set about, but there are such continual changes here, that it is very discouraging to all applications to be made to the ministry. I thought the last set well established, but they are broken and gone. The present set are hardly thought to stand very firm, and God only knows whom we are to have next.

The plan is I think well drawn, and I imagine Sir William's approbation will go a great way in recommending it, as he is much relied on in all affairs, that may have relation to the Indians. Lord Adam Gordon is not in town, but I shall take the first opportunity of conferring with him. I thank the Company for their willingness to take me in, and one or two others that I may nominate. I have not yet concluded whom to propose it to; but I suppose our friend Sargent should be one. I wish you had allowed me to name more, as there will be in the proposed country, by my reckoning, near sixty-three millions of acres, and therefore enough to content a great number of reasonable people, and by numbers we might increase the weight of interest here.

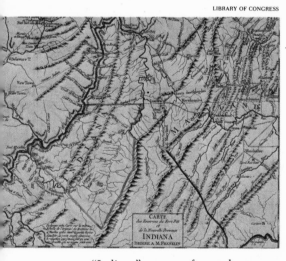

"Indiana" was one of several names suggested for the large western colony assiduously promoted by Franklin.

As always, Franklin found time to maintain a personal correspondence with those he loved. Jane Mecom was one of these, although she was at times a difficult correspondent. She quarreled frequently with her famous brother by mail, taking offense—sometimes theological, sometimes personal—at his opinions and remarks. On his side, Franklin obviously enjoyed discussing religion with her, since she was such a perfect foil for his unorthodox beliefs. In this letter, he tried to relieve the pessimism she felt after having read some harsh criticism of Franklin in American newspapers. His enemies' treatment of him, she said, "makes the world Apear a misereable world to me not withstanding your good opinyon of it."

London, March 2. 1767

Dear Sister

I received your kind Letter of Nov. 8. for which I thank you. It rejoices me to hear that you and your Children continue well. I thank God that I too enjoy a greater Share of Health, Strength and Activity than is common with People of my Years, being now Three-score and one. You mention my Opinion of this being a good sort of World, in which you differ from me. Every one should speak as they find. Hitherto I have found it so, and I should be ungrateful to Providence if I did not own it. As to the Abuses I meet with, which you bring as an Argument against my Opinion, you must know I number them among my Honours. One cannot behave so as to obtain the Esteem of the Wise and Good, without drawing on one's self at the same time the Envy and Malice of the Foolish and Wicked, and the latter is a Testimony of the former. The best Men have always had their Share of this Treatment, and the more of it in proportion to their different and greater degrees of Merit. A Man has therefore some Reason to be asham'd of himself when he meets with none of it. And the World is not to be condemn'd in the Lump because some bad People live in it. Their Number is not great, the Hurt they do is but small, as real good Characters always finally surmount and are established, notwithstanding these Attempts to keep them down. And in the mean time such Enemies do a Man some good; while they think they are doing him harm, by fortifying the Character they would destroy; for when he sees how readily imaginary Faults and Crimes are laid to his Charge, he must be more apprehensive of the Danger of committing real Ones, as he can expect no Quarter, and therefore is more on his Guard to avoid or least to conceal them.

Amore serious personal matter that absorbed Franklin at this time was the marriage of his daughter Sally to Richard Bache. Franklin did not look with favor on the match. English-born, the thirty-year-old Bache had worked with his brother as a merchant in New York in 1765 and in 1766 had moved to Philadelphia, where he opened a dry goods store. He was soon in financial difficulty. Franklin's business friends in Philadelphia told William Franklin that Bache was "a mere Fortune Hunter, who wants to better his Circumstances [by] marrying into a Family that will support him." William confessed that he did not "know what to make of all the different Accounts I hear of him." But he was certain that Bache was involved "in a Load of Debt greatly more than he is worth, and that if Sally marries him they must both be entirely dependent on you for Subsistence." A prudent man, William concluded his letter, "Do burn this." Though his father also made some frosty comments on Bache, he had enough confidence in Deborah's judgment to leave the final decision to her.

London, June 22. 1767

It seems now as if I should stay here another Winter, and therefore I must leave it to your Judgment to act in the Affair of your Daughter's Match as shall seem best. If you think it a suitable one, I suppose the sooner it is compleated, the better. In that case, I would only advise that you do not make an expensive feasting Wedding, but conduct every thing with Frugality and Oeconomy, which our Circumstances really now require to be observed in all our Expences; For since my Partnership with Mr. Hall is expired, a great Source of our Income is cut off; and if I should lose the Post Office, which among the many Changes here is far from being unlikely, we should be reduc'd to our Rent and Interest of Money for a Subsistence, which will by no means afford the chargeable Housekeeping and Entertainments we have been used to; for my own Part I live here as frugally as possible not to be destitute of the Comforts of Life, making no Dinners for any body, and contenting myself with a single Dish when I dine at home; and yet such is the Dearness of Living here in every Article, that my Expences amaze me. I see too by the Sums you have received in my Absence, that yours are very great, and I am very sensible that your Situation naturally brings you a great many Visitors which occasion an Expence not easily to be avoided, especially when one has been long in the Practice and Habit of it: But when People's Incomes are lessened, if they cannot proportionably lessen their Outgoings, they must come to Poverty. If we were young enough to begin Business again, it might be another Matter; but I doubt we are past it; and Business not well managed ruins one faster than no Business. In short, with Frugality and prudent Care we may subsist decently on what we have, and leave it entire to our Children: but without such Care, we shall not be able to keep it together; it will melt away like Butter in the Sunshine; and we may live long enough to feel the miserable Consequences of our Indiscretion.

I know very little of the Gentleman or his Character, nor can I at this Distance. I hope his Expectations are not great of any Fortune to be had with our Daughter before our Death. I can only say, that if he proves a good Husband to her, and a good Son to me, he shall find me as good a Father as I can be: but at present I suppose you would agree with me that we cannot do more than fit her out handsomely in Cloaths and Furniture, not exceeding in the whole Five Hundred Pounds, of Value. For the rest, they must depend as you and I did, on their own Industry and Care: as what remains in our Hands will be barely sufficient for our Support, and not enough for them when it comes to be divided at our Decease.

Franklin's daughter, Sarah Franklin Bache, in a portrait by John Hoppner

A few weeks later Franklin wrote again about the impending marriage, suggesting that it might be best to delay it for a time, while Sally visited England. But this advice was ignored, and Sally and Richard Bache were married in the fall of 1767. Meanwhile, the confused state of English politics gave Franklin little peace of mind. In a letter to Joseph Galloway he acutely analyzed Parliament's drift toward another clash with America.

London, Aug 8. 1767

The Confusion among our Great Men still continues as great as ever, and a melancholy thing it is to consider, that instead of employing the present Leisure of Peace in such Measures as might extend our Commerce, pay off our Debts, secure Allies, and encrease the Strength and Ability of the Nation to support a future War, the whole Time seems wasted in Party Contentions about Power and Profit, in Court Intrigues and Cabals, and in abusing one another.

There has lately been an Attempt to make a kind of Coalition of Parties in a new Ministry; but it is fallen through, and the present Set is like to continue for some time longer, which I am rather pleas'd with, as some of

Joseph Galloway

those who were propos'd to be introduc'd, are profess'd Adversaries to America, which is now made one of the Distinctions of Party here; those who in the two last Sessions have shown a Disposition to favor us, being called by Way of Reproach *Americans;* while the others, Adherents to Grenville and Bedford, value themselves on being true to the Interest of Britain, and zealous for maintaining its Dignity and Sovereignty over the Colonies. This Distinction will, it is apprehended, be carried much higher in the next Session, for the political Purpose of influencing the ensuing Election. It is already given out, that the Compliance of New York in providing for the Quarters, without taking Notice of its being done in Obedience to the Act of Parliament, is evasive and unsatisfactory: that it is high time to put the Right and Power of this Country to tax the Colonies, out of dispute, by an Act of Taxation effectually carried into Execution, and that all the Colonies should be oblig'd explicitly to acknowledge that Right. Every Step is taking to render the Taxing of America a popular Measure, by continually insisting on the Topics of our Wealth and flourishing Circumstances, while this Country is loaded with Debt, great Part of it incurr'd on our Account the Distress of the Poor here by the Multitude and Weight of Taxes, &c. &c. And tho' the Traders and Manufacturers may possibly be kept in our Interest, the Idea of an American Tax is very pleasing to the landed Men, who therefore readily receive and propagate these Sentiments wherever they have Influence. If such a Bill should be brought in, it is hard to say what would be Event of it, or what would be the Effects. Those who oppose it, tho' they should be strong enough to throw it out, would be stigmatiz'd at the next Election as Americans, Betrayers of Old England, &c.—and perhaps our Friends by this means being excluded, a Majority of our Adversaries may get in, and then the Act infallibly passes the following Session. To avoid the Danger of such Exclusion, perhaps little or no Opposition will be given, and then it passes immediately. I know not what to advise on this Occasion, but that we should all do our Endeavours on both sides the Water, to lessen the present Unpopularity of the American Cause; conciliate the Affections of the People here towards us; increase by all possible Means the Number of our Friends, and be careful not to weaken their Hands and strengthen those of our Enemies, by rash Proceedings on our side, the Mischiefs of which are inconceivable.

Meanwhile, Franklin's interest in the western colony remained strong. In a letter to William Franklin he told of further efforts with Lord Shelburne, the Secretary of State for American Affairs.

London, August 8, 1767.

Last week I dined at Lord Shelburne's, and had a long conversation with him and Mr. Conway (there being no other company), on the subject of reducing American expence. They have it in contemplation to return the management of Indian affairs into the hands of the several provinces on which the nations border, that the colonies may bear the charge of treaties, &c. which they think will then be managed more frugally, the treasury being tired with the immense drafts of the superintendants, &c. I took the opportunity of urging it as one means of saving expence in supporting the outposts, that a settlement should be made in the Illinois country; expatiated on the various advantages, viz. furnishing provisions cheaper to the garrisons, securing the country, retaining the trade, raising a strength there which on occasion of a future war, might easily be poured down the Missisippi upon the lower country, and into the Bay of Mexico, to be used against Cuba, or Mexico itself, &c. I mentioned your plan, its being approved by Sir William Johnson, the readiness and ability of the gentlemen concerned to carry the settlement into execution with very little expence to the crown, &c. &c. The Secretaries appeared finally to be fully convinced, and there remained no obstacle but the Board of Trade, which was to be brought over privately before the matter should be referred to them officially. . . .

Du Guerchy the French Ambassador is gone home, and Monsieur Durand is left Minister Plenipotentiary. He is extremely curious to inform himself in the affairs of America; pretends to have a great esteem for me, on account of the abilities shown in my examination; has desired to have all my political writings, invited me to dine with him, was very inquisitive, treated me with great civility, makes me visits, &c. I fancy that intriguing nation would like very well to meddle on occasion, and blow up the coals between Britain and her colonies;

Sir William Johnson

but I hope we shall give them no opportunity.

I write this in a great hurry, being setting out in an hour on another journey with my steady good friend Sir John Pringle. We propose to visit Paris. Durand has given me letters of recommendation to the Lord knows who. I am told I shall meet with great respect there; but winds change and perhaps it will be full as well if I do not. We shall be gone about six weeks.

Franklin returned from France to find another tempest brewing between England and the Colonies. Charles Townshend, Chancellor of the Exchequer in the rather disorganized Ministry nominally headed by William Pitt, now Lord Chatham, decided to take the Americans at their word when they claimed to have no objection to external taxes. He proceeded to impose duties on glass, lead, painters' colors, tea, and paper—all imported in large amounts by the Colonies. The Americans responded by reviving the boycott on imports that had proved successful against the Stamp Act. The turmoil resulted in a Cabinet reshuffle that eliminated Lord Shelburne, who had been in favor of the Franklins' new colony. Wills Hill, Lord Hillsborough, became Secretary of State for Colonies, and he was inclined to take a negative view of all things American. He was particularly opposed to a new colony, because he feared it might depopulate Ireland, where he had vast estates. Hillsborough's attitude and the continued American agitation over the Townshend Acts produced a distinct change in Franklin's thinking. He discussed the change in this letter. The "Farmer's letters" are a reference to John Dickinson's tract, *Letters from a Farmer in Pennsylvania,* which argued that the Townshend Acts were unconstitutional because they were designed not to regulate trade but to raise revenue, and hence were in the same category as the Stamp Act. Later in the year Franklin wrote a preface for the English edition. The letter also reveals the strong concern Franklin felt for his son's career. But the final paragraphs, with their harsh criticism of England, are perhaps most important. The love affair between Franklin and the mother country was already beginning to sour.

London, March 13, 1768.

My Lord H. mentioned the Farmer's letters to me, said he had read them, that they were well written, and he believed he could guess who was the author, looking in my face at the same time as if he thought it was me. He censured the doctrines as extremely wild, &c. I have read them as far as No. 8. I know not if any more have been published. I should have thought they had been written by Mr. Delancey, not having heard any mention of the others you point out as joint authors. I am not yet master of the idea these and the New England writers

A view of Hayes Place in Kent, the seat of William Pitt, Lord Chatham

have of the relation between Britain and her colonies. I know not what the Boston people mean by the "subordination" they acknowledge in their Assembly to Parliament, while they deny its power to make laws for them, nor what bounds the Farmer sets to the power he acknowledges in Parliament to "regulate the trade of the colonies," it being difficult to draw lines between duties for regulation and those for revenue, and if the Parliament is to be the judge, it seems to me that establishing such principles of distinction will amount to little. The more I have thought and read on the subject the more I find myself confirmed in opinion, that no middle doctrine can be well maintained, I mean not clearly with intelligible arguments. Something might be made of either of the extremes; that Parliament has a power to make *all laws* for us, or that it has a power to make *no laws* for us; and I think the arguments for the latter more numerous and weighty than those for the former. Supposing that doctrine established, the colonies would then be so many separate states, only subject to the same King, as England and Scotland were before the Union. And then the question would be, whether a union like that with Scotland would or would not be advantageous to *the whole*. I should have no doubt of the affirmative, being fully persuaded that it would be best for *the whole,* and that though particular parts might find particular disadvantages in it, they would find greater advantages in the security arising to every part from the increased strength of the whole. But such union is not likely to take place, while the nature of our present relation is so little understood on both sides the water, and sentiments concerning it remain so widely different. As to the Farmers' combating, as you say they intend to do, my opinion, that the Parliament might lay duties though not impose internal taxes, I shall not give myself the trouble to defend it. Only to you, I may say, that not only the Parliament of Britain, but every state in Europe claims and exercises a right of laying duties on the exportation of its own commodities to foreign countries. A duty is paid here on coals exported to Holland, and yet England has no right to lay an internal tax on Holland. All goods brought out of France to England, or any other country, are charged with a small duty in France, which the consumers pay, and yet France has no right to tax other countries. And in my opinion the grievance is not that Britain puts duties upon her own manufactures exported to us, but that she forbids us to buy the like manufactures from any other country. This she does however in virtue of her allowed right to regulate the commerce of the whole empire, allowed I mean by the Farmer, though I think whoever would dispute that right might stand upon firmer ground and make much more of the argument: but my reasons are too many and too long for a letter.

Mr. Grenville complained in the House that the Governor of New Jersey, New Hampshire, East and West Florida, had none of them obeyed the orders sent them, to give an account of the manufactures carried on in their respective provinces. Upon hearing this I went, after the House was up and got a sight of the reports made by the other governors. They are all much in the same strain, that there are no manufactures of any consequence; in Massachusetts, a little coarse woollen only made in families for their own wear: glass and linen have been tried and failed. Rhode Island, Connecticut, and New York much the same. Pennsylvania has tried a linen manufactory but it is dropped, it being imported cheaper; there is a glass-house in Lancaster county, but it makes only a little coarse wear for the country neighbours. Maryland is clothed all with English manufactures. Virginia the same, except that in their families, they spin a little cotton of their own growing. South Carolina and Georgia none. All speak of the dearness of labour that makes manufactures impracticable. Only the Governor of North Carolina parades with a large manufacture in his country that may be useful to Britain of *pine boards;* they having fifty saw mills on one river. These accounts are very satisfactory here, and induce the parliament to despise and take no notice of the Boston resolutions. I wish you would send your account before the meeting of next parliament. You have only to report a glass-house for coarse window glass and bottles, and some domestic manufactures of linen and woollen for family use that do not half clothe the inhabitants, all the finer goods coming from England and the like. I believe you will be puzzled to find any other, though I see great puffs in the papers.

The parliament is up and the nation in a ferment with

the new elections. Great complaints are made that the natural interests of country gentlemen in their neighbouring boroughs, is overborne by the monied interest of the new people who have got sudden fortunes in the Indies, or as contractors, &c. £4000 is now the market price for a borough. In short this whole venal nation is now at market, will be sold for about Two Millions; and might be bought out of the hands of the present bidders (if he would offer half a million more) by the very devil himself....

I am your affectionate father,

B. FRANKLIN

As a wise man and a loving father, Franklin was sensible enough to reconcile himself to the marriage his daughter had entered against his better judgment. In a letter to Richard Bache he began to thaw.

London, Aug. 13. 1768

Loving Son,

I received yours of May 20, as also the preceding Letters mentioned in it. You must have been sensible that I thought the Step you had taken, to engage yourself in the Charge of a Family, while your Affairs bore so unpromising an Aspect with Regard to the probable Means of maintaining it, a very rash and precipitate one. I could not therefore but be dissatisfy'd with it, and displeas'd with you whom I look'd upon as an Instrument of bringing future Unhappiness on my Child, by involving her in the Difficulty and Distress that seem'd connected with your Circumstances, you having not merely Nothing beforehand, but being besides greatly in Debt. In this Situation of my Mind, you should not wonder that I did not answer your Letters. I could say nothing agreable: I did not chuse to write, what I thought, being unwilling to give Pain where I could not give Pleasure. Time has made me easier. I hope too, that the Accounts you give me of your better Prospects are well-founded, and that by an industrious Application to Business you may retrieve your Losses. I can only add at present, that my best Wishes attend you, and that if you prove a good Husband & Son, you will find in me an Affectionate Father,

B FRANKLIN

My Love to Sally. I have sent her by Mr. Coleman, who left us this Day, a new Watch & Buckles.

Richard Bache by John Hoppner

Politics continued to be Franklin's main absorption. In a letter to Joseph Galloway he all but abandoned hope for the mission that brought him to England—ousting the Penns from Pennsylvania. The shift from Pennsylvania agent to American spokesman was becoming more and more pronounced. Jeffery Amherst, mentioned in the closing lines, was the British commander in chief in America during the French and Indian War. He was much admired by the Americans, who considered him one of their staunchest supporters in England. He had been made Governor of Virginia and Colonel of the 60th (Royal American) Regiment, both sinecures that enabled him to remain in England while the Colony was ruled by a lieutenant governor and the regiment was run by a lieutenant colonel.

London, August 20. 1768

I wrote a pretty long Letter to you by Falconer, in which I acquainted you with what had heretofore pass'd between Lord Hillsborough and myself relating to the Change of our Government; and that I proposed waiting on him again in a few Days, in consequence of an Intimation I had received that he was now disposed to favour the Petition. I have accordingly been with him, and had a long Audience of him upon the Subject, the Particulars of which I cannot at present give you, but the Conclusion was, that we parted without agreeing on any thing, the Advice he gave us in order to obtain the Change, being such as I assur'd him we could not take. I shall therefore move the Matter no farther during the Administration of a Minister that appears to have a stronger Partiality for Mr Penn than any of his Predecessors. I stay however a little longer here, till I see what Turn American Affairs are like to take. The next News from America, which is anxiously expected, will probably enable us to judge. A Party is now growing in our Favour, which I shall endeavour to increase and strengthen by every Effort of Tongue and Pen. Possibly by our united Endeavours (I wish I could say *probably*) the Repeal of the late offensive Duties may be obtained. If it should be resolv'd by the Ministry to make us easy, I know not but I may still return this Fall. But otherwise, I shall stay the Session, to see if the new Parliament can be brought to disapprove of the violent Measures talked of, and to repeal the Act. Sir Jeffery Amherst's being stript of his Offices, gives great Offence to all the Military People here, and tho' the Measure of requiring a chief Governor to reside in his Government was not in itself a wrong thing, yet Advantage is taken of it by the Opposition, to arraign the

Conduct of Lord Hillsborough, and render him odious. Please to present my best Respects and Duty to the Assembly, and assure them of my most faithful Services.

The struggle over the Townshend Acts did not reach a climax, in the pattern of the Stamp Act crisis. But the British Government finally reacted to the nonimportation agreements, which Americans were maintaining with considerable determination. Franklin rushed news to America of a major shift in the British position. The letter went to Noble Wimberly Jones, Speaker of the Georgia House of Representatives. The Colony had appointed Franklin its agent in 1768.

London, June 7, 1769

I did myself the Honour of Writing to you on the 3d. of the last Month, since when the Parliament has risen without repealing the Duties that have been so generally complain'd of. But we are now assured by the Ministry, that the Affairs of America have been lately considered in Council; that it was the unanimous Opinion no new Acts for the purpose of Raising a Revenue in America should be made here; and that it was the full Intention of his Majesty's Servants to propose early in the ensuing Session the Repeal of the Duties on Glass, Paper, and Painters Colours. Believing this News would be agreable to our Friends, I take the first Opportunity of communicating it to you; and hope that nothing will happen in the mean time, to change the favourable Sentiments towards us, which apparently begin to take place in the Minds of his Majesty and his Ministers. Possibly we may not at first obtain all we desire, or all that ought to be granted to us; but the giving Ground to us in some degree has a good Aspect, and affords room to hope that gradually every Obstruction to that cordial Amity so necessary for the Welfare of the whole Empire, will be removed. Indeed I wish, as I think it would be best, that this could be done at once: But 'tis perhaps too much to expect, considering the Pride natural to so great a Nation, the Prejudices that have so universally prevailed here with regard to the Point of Right, and the Resentment at our disputing it.

The opposition of Lord Hillsborough completely stalled plans for the western colony, as conceived by William Franklin and his American friends. Finally, in 1769, taking Benjamin Franklin's advice, they reorganized the company with a British base, retaining most of the

American partners but opening up shares to many more British partners. Franklin joined forces with banker Thomas Walpole, nephew of a former prime minister, and together they shrewdly selected a cross section of the British establishment, representing all parties and shades of political opinion. In this letter Franklin invited Grey Cooper, one of the Secretaries of the Treasury, to join the group.

> Craven Street, Tuesday July 11. 1769
> An Application being about to be made for a Grant of Lands in the Territory on the Ohio lately purchased of the Indians, I cannot omit acquainting you with it, and giving you my Opinion, that they will very soon be settled by People from the neighbouring Provinces, and be of great Advantage in a few Years to the Undertakers. As you have those fine Children, and are likely to have many more, I wish for their Sakes, you may incline to take this Opportunity of making a considerable Addition to their future Fortunes, as the Expence will be a Trifle. If therefore you will give me leave, I shall put your Name down among us for a Share (40,000 Acres). Your Neighbour Mr Dagge will call upon you some Day and explain the Particulars more fully.

Franklin's letters during these years reflect a steady growth toward a conviction that America must become independent of England. This letter informed Samuel Cooper, pastor of Boston's Brattle Square Church, that the Townshend duties—as a reaction to Colonial non-importation agreements—had been limited to tea. The quartering of British troops in America remained a disputed issue.

> London, June 8, 1770.
> I received duly your favour of March 28. With this I send you two Speeches in Parliament on our Affairs by a Member that you know. The Repeal of the whole late Act would undoubtedly have been a prudent Measure, and I have reason to believe that Lord North was for it, but some of the other Ministers could not be brought to agree to it. So the Duty on Tea, with that obnoxious Preamble, remains to continue the dispute. But I think the next Session will hardly pass over without repealing them; for the Parliament must finally comply with the Sense of the Nation. As to the Standing Army kept up among us in time of Peace, without the Consent of our Assemblies, I am clearly of Opinion that it is not agreable to the Constitution. Should the King by the Aid of his Parliaments in Ireland and the Colonies, raise an Army

Thomas Walpole

and bring it into England, quartering it here in time of Peace without the Consent of the Parliament of Great Britain, I am persuaded he would soon be told that he had no Right so to do, and the Nation would ring with Clamours against it. I own that I see no Difference in the Cases. And while we continue so many distinct and separate States, our having the same Head or Sovereign, the King, will not justify such an Invasion of the separate Right of each State to be consulted on the Establishment of whatever Force is proposed to be kept up within its Limits, and to give or refuse its Consent as shall appear most for the Public Good of that State. That the Colonies originally were constituted distinct States, and intended to be continued such, is clear to me from a thorough Consideration of their original Charters, and the whole Conduct of the Crown and Nation towards them until the Restoration. Since that Period, the Parliament here has usurp'd an Authority of making Laws for them, which before it had not. We have for some time submitted to that Usurpation, partly thro' Ignorance and Inattention, and partly from our Weakness and Inability to contend. I hope when our Rights are better understood here, we shall, by prudent and proper Conduct be able to obtain from the Equity of this Nation a Restoration of them. And in the mean time I could wish that such Expressions as, *The Supreme Authority of Parliament; The Subordinacy of our Assemblies to the Parliament* and the like, (which in Reality mean nothing if our Assemblies with the King have a true Legislative Authority) I say, I could wish that such Expressions were no more seen in our publick Pieces. They are too strong for Compliment, and tend to confirm a Claim [of] Subjects in one Part of the King's Dominions to be Sovereigns over their Fellow-Subjects in another Part of his Dominions; when [in] truth they have no such Right, and their Claim is founded only on Usurpation, the several States having equal Rights and Liberties, and being only connected, as England and Scotland were before the Union, by having one common Sovereign, the King. This kind of Doctrine the Lords and Commons here would deem little less than Treason against what they think their Share of the Sovereignty over the Colonies. To me those Bodies seem to have been long encroaching on the Rights of their and our Sovereign, assuming too much of his

Drawing of Number 7 Craven Street,
where Franklin lived in London

Authority, and betraying his Interests. By our Constitution he is, with [his] Plantation Parliaments, the sole Legislator of his American Subjects, and in that Capacity is and ought to be free to exer[cise] his own Judgment unrestrain'd and unlimited by his Parliament here. And our Parliaments have right to grant him Aids without the Consent of this Parliament, a Circumstance which, by the [way] begins to give it some Jealousy. Let us therefore hold fast [our] Loyalty to our King (who has the best Disposition towards us, and has a Family-Interest in our Prosperity); as that steady Loyalty is the most probable Means of securing us from the arbitrary Power of a corrupt Parliament, that does not like us, and conceives itself to have an Interest in keeping us down and fleecing us. If they should urge the *Inconvenience* of an Empire's being divided into so many separate States, and from thence conclude that we are not so divided; I would answer, that an Inconvenience proves nothing but itself. England and Scotland were once separate States, under the same King. The Inconvenience found in their being separate States, did not prove that the Parliament of England had a right to govern Scotland. A formal Union was thought necessary, and England was an hundred Years soliciting it, before she could bring it about. If Great Britain now think such a Union necessary with us, let her propose her Terms, and we may consider of them. Were the general Sentiments of this Nation to be consulted in the Case, I should hope the Terms, whether practicable or not, would at least be equitable: for I think that except among those with whom the Spirit of Toryism prevails, the popular Inclination here is, to wish us well, and that we may preserve our Liberties.

Polly Stevenson married Dr. William Hewson early in July, 1770. In September, Mrs. Stevenson took a trip to the country, and Polly and her husband came to Craven Street to run the house. To amuse himself and his friends, Franklin composed *The Craven Street Gazette,* a delightful burlesque of contemporary British newspapers. Miss Franklin was a young English cousin who spent much of her time at Craven Street. The *"great* person" was, of course, Benjamin Franklin himself.

Saturday, Sept. 22. 1770
This Morning Queen Margaret, accompanied by her first Maid of Honour, Miss Franklin, set out for Rochester. Immediately on their Departure, the whole street was

in tears—from a heavy Shower of Rain.

It is whispered, that the new Family Administration which took place on her Majesty's Departure, promises, like all other new Administrations, to govern much better than the old one.

We hear that the *great* person (so called from his enormous Size), of a certain Family in a certain Street, is grievously affected at the late Changes, and could hardly be comforted this Morning, tho' the new Ministry promised him a roasted Shoulder of Mutton, and Potatoes, for his dinner.

It is said, that the same *great* Person intended to pay his Respects to another great Personage this Day, at St. James's, it being Coronation-Day; hoping thereby a little to amuse his grief; but was prevented by an accident, Queen Margaret, or her Maid of Honour having carried off the Key of the Drawers, so that the Lady of the Bedchamber could not come at a laced Shirt for his Highness. Great Clamours were made on this Occasion against her Majesty.

Other Accounts say, that the Shirts were afterwards found, tho' too late, in another Place. And some suspect, that the Wanting a Shirt from those Drawers was only a ministerial Pretence to excuse Picking the Locks, that the new Administration might have every thing at Command.

We hear that the Lady Chamberlain of the Household went to Market this Morning by her own self, gave the Butcher whatever he ask'd for the Mutton, and had no Dispute with the Potatoe Woman—to their great Amazement—at the Change of Times!

It is confidently asserted, that this Afternoon, the Weather being wet, the great *Person* a little chilly, and no body at home to find fault with the Expence of Fuel, he was indulg'd with a Fire in his Chamber. It seems the Design is, to make him contented, by Degrees, with the Absence of the Queen.

A Project has been under Consideration of Government, to take the Opportunity of her Majesty's Absence, for doing a Thing she was always averse to, viz. Fixing a new Lock on the Street Door, or getting a Key made to the old one; it being found extreamly inconvenient, that one or other of the Great Officers of State, should, whenever the Maid goes out for a Ha'p worth of Sand or

"Cries of London," a series of water colors painted in 1759 by Paul Sandby, included an inkseller (top), cane chair weaver, and shrimp girl.

226

a Pint of Porter, be obliged to attend the Door to let her in again. But Opinions, being divided, which of the two Expedients to adopt, the Project is for the present laid aside.

We have good Authority to assure our Readers, that a Cabinet Council was held this Afternoon at Tea; the Subject of which was a Proposal for the Reformation of Manners, and a more strict Observation of the Lord's Day. The Result was a unanimous Resolution, that no Meat should be dress'd tomorrow; whereby the Cook and the first Minister will both be at Liberty to go to Church, the one having nothing to do, and the other no Roast to rule. It seems the cold Shoulder of Mutton, and the Apple pye, were thought sufficient for Sunday's Dinner. All pious People applaud this Measure, and 'tis thought the new Ministry will soon become popular....

Sunday, Sept. 23.

It is now found by sad Experience, that good Resolutions are easier made than executed. Notwithstanding yesterday's solemn Order of Council, no body went to Church to day. It seems the *great* Person's broad-built-bulk lay so long abed, that Breakfast was not over 'till it was too late to dress. At least this is the Excuse. In fine, it seems a vain thing to hope Reformation from the Example of our great Folks. The Cook and the Minister, however, both took Advantage of the Order so far, as to save themselves all Trouble, and the Clause of *cold Dinner* was enforc'd, tho' the *going to Church* was dispens'd with; just as the common working People observe the Commandments; *the seventh day thou shalt rest,* they think a sacred Injunction; but the other *Six Days shalt thou labour* is deem'd a mere Piece of Advice, which they may practise when they want Bread and are out of Credit at the Alehouse, and may neglect whenever they have Money in their Pockets. It must nevertheless be said in justice to our Court, that whatever Inclination they had to Gaming, no Cards were brought out to Day....

Monday, Sept. 24.

We are credibly informed, that the *great* Person dined this Day with the Club at the Cat-and-Bagpipes in the City, on cold Round of boil'd Beef. This, it seems, he was under some Necessity of Doing (tho' he rather dislikes Beef) because truly the Ministers were to be all abroad somewhere to dine on hot roast Venison. It is thought

The hot pudding- (top), green vegetable-, and mop-venders, as drawn by Sandby, were all familiar London street sights to Franklin.

that if the Queen had been at home, he would not have been so slighted. And tho' he shows outwardly no Marks of Dissatisfaction, it is suspected that he begins to wish for her Majesty's Return....

This evening there was high Play at the Groom Porter's in Cravenstreet House. The Great Person lost Money. It is supposed the Ministers, as is usually supposed of all Ministers, shared the Emoluments among them.

Tuesday, Sept. 25.

This morning the good Lord Hutton call'd at Cravenstreet House, and enquired very respectfully & affectionately concerning the Welfare of the absent Queen. He then imparted to the big Man a Piece of Intelligence important to them both, which he had just received from Lady Hawkesworth, viz. That [the] amiable and excellent Companion Miss Dorothea Blount had made a Vow to marry absolutely him of the two, whose Wife should first depart this Life. It is impossible to express with Words the various Agitations of Mind appearing in both their Faces on this Occasion. *Vanity* at the Preference given them to the rest of Mankind; *Affection* to their present Wives; *Fear* of losing them; *Hope,* (if they must lose them) to obtain the propos'd Comfort; *Jealousy* of each other, in case both Wives should die together; &c. &c. &c. all working at the same time, jumbled their Features into inexplicable Confusion. They parted at length with Professions & outward Appearances indeed of ever-during Friendship; but it was shrewdly suspected that each of them sincerely wished Health & long Life to the other's Wife; & that however long either of these Friends might like to live himself, the other would be very well pleas'd to survive him....

The Publick may be assured, that this Morning a certain *great Person* was ask'd very complaisantly by the Mistress of the Household, if he would chuse to have the Blade Bone of Saturday's Mutton that had been kept for his Dinner to Day, *broil'd* or *cold.* He answer'd gravely, *If there is any Flesh on it, it may be broil'd; if not, it may as well be cold.* Orders were accordingly given for broiling it. But when it came to Table, there was indeed so very little Flesh, or rather none, (Puss having din'd on it yesterday after Nanny) that if our new Administration had been as good Oeconomists as they would be thought, the Expence of Broiling might well have been saved to

227

the Publick, and carried to the Sinking Fund. It is assured the great Person bears all with infinite Patience. But the Nation is astonish'd at the insolent Presumption, that dares treat so much Mildness in so cruel a manner.

A terrible Accident had *like to have happened* this Afternoon at Tea. The Boiler was set too near the End of the little square Table. The first Ministress was sitting at one End of the Table to administer the Tea; the great Person was about to sit down at the other End where the Boiler stood. By a sudden Motion, the Lady gave the Table a Tilt. Had it gone over, the great *person* must have been scalded; perhaps to Death. Various are the Surmises and Observations on this Occasion. The Godly say, it would have been a just Judgment on him, for preventing, by his Laziness, the Family's going to Church last Sunday. The Opposition do not stick to insinuate that there was a Design to scald him, prevented only by his quick Catching the Table. The Friends of the Ministry give out, that he carelessly jogg'd the Table himself, & would have been inevitably scalded had not the Ministress sav'd him. It is hard for the Publick to come at the Truth in these Cases.

At six o'Clock this Afternoon News came by the Post, that her Majesty arrived safely at Rochester on Saturday Night. The Bells immediately rang—for Candles, to illuminate the Parlour; the Court went into Cribbidge, and the Evening concluded with every other Demonstration of Joy....

We hear that from the Time of her Majesty's leaving Craven Street House to this Day, no Care is taken to file the Newspapers; but they lie about in every Room, in every Window, and on every Chair, just where the Doctor lays them when he reads them. It is impossible Government can long go on in such Hands.

From America came news that Franklin had become a grandfather. Sally had given birth to a boy, who was named Benjamin Franklin Bache. In this letter Franklin responded with some good-humored advice to Deborah on the art of grandmothership.

London, October 3, 1770

My dear Child,

I received your kind Letter of Aug. 16, which gave me a great deal of Satisfaction. I am glad your little Grandson recovered so soon of his Illness, as I see you are quite in

Love with him, and your Happiness wrapt up in his; since your whole long Letter is made up of the History of his pretty Actions. It was very prudently done of you not to interfere when his Mother thought fit to correct him; which pleases me the more, as I feared, from your Fondness of him, that he would be too much humoured, and perhaps spoiled. There is a Story of two little Boys in the Street; one was crying bitterly; the other came to him to ask what was the Matter? I have been, says he, "for a pennyworth of Vinegar, and I have broke the Glass, and spilt the Vinegar, and my Mother will whip me." *No, she won't whip you* says the other. Indeed, she will, says he. *What,* says the other, *have you then got ne'er a Grandmother?*

From Boston came even more unexpected news. Thanks largely to the letter he had written to Samuel Cooper on June 8, 1770, Franklin had been appointed the agent of Massachusetts. In reply to Cooper's letter telling him of this action, Franklin called the appointment "one of the greatest honours." But it was in many respects also a profound embarrassment to him. Since Boston was regarded as the most radical and troublesome of the Colonies, whoever represented it was almost *de facto* out of favor with the British Ministry. Moreover, Franklin was only the agent of the Assembly. The Governor, Thomas Hutchinson, and his Council, retained other agents in London to represent their views, which sharply differed from those of the Assembly. A month after Franklin wrote to Cooper accepting the appointment, the new agent wrote another letter, describing the reception he received from Lord Hillsborough when he attempted to inform that stiff-necked noble of his appointment.

London, Feb. 5. 1771

I have just received your kind Favour of January 1 by Mr. Bowdoin, to whom I should be glad to render any Service here. I wrote to you some Weeks since in Answer to yours of July and November, expressing my Sentiments without the least Reserve on Points that require free Discussion, as I know I can confide in your Prudence not to hurt my Usefulness here, by making me more obnoxious than I must necessarily be from that known Attachment to the American Interest, which my Duty as well as Inclination demands of me.

In the same Confidence I send you the inclosed Extract from my Journal, containing a late Conference between the Secretary and your Friend, in which you will see a little of his Temper: It is one of the many Instances of his Behaviour and Conduct, that have given me the very mean Opinion I entertain of his Abilities and Fitness for his Station. His Character is Conceit, Wrongheadedness, Obstinacy, and Passion. Those, who would speak most favourably of him, allow all this; they only add, that he is an honest Man, and means well. If that be true, as perhaps it may, I wish him a better Place, where only Honesty and Well-meaning are required, and where his other Qualities can do no harm. Had the War taken place, I have reason to believe he would have been removed. He had, I think, some Apprehensions of it himself at the Time I was with him. I hope, however, that our Affairs will not much longer be perplex'd and embarass'd by his perverse and senseless Management. I have since heard, that his Lordship took great Offence at some of my last Words, which he calls extreamly rude and abusive. He assured a Friend of mine, that they were equivalent to telling him to his Face, that the Colonies could expect neither Favour nor Justice during his Administration. I find he did not mistake me.

It is true, as you have heard, that some of my Letters to America have been echo'd back hither; but that has not been the Case with any that were written to you. Great Umbrage was taken, but chiefly by Lord Hillsborough, who was disposed before to be angry with me, and therefore the Inconvenience was the less; and, whatever the Consequences are of his Displeasure, putting all my Offences together, I must bear them as well as I can. Not but that, if there is to be War between us, I shall do my best to defend myself and annoy my Adversary, little regarding the story of the Earthen Pot and Brazen Pitcher. One encouragement I have, the knowledge, that he is not a whit better lik'd by his Colleagues in the Ministry, than he is by me, that he cannot probably continue where he is much longer, and that he can scarce be succeeded by anybody, who will not like me the better for his having been at Variance with me....

Minutes of the Conference mentioned in the preceeding Letter.

Wednesday, January 16, 1771.

I went this morning to wait on Lord Hillsborough. The porter at first denied his Lordship, on which I left my name and drove off. But, before the coach got out of the square, the coachman heard a call, turned, and went back to the door, when the porter came and said, "His Lordship will see you, Sir." I was shown into the levee I have lately made a Tour thro' Ireland and Scotland. room, where I found Governor Bernard, who, I understand, attends there constantly. Several other gentlemen were there attending, with whom I sat down a few minutes, when Secretary Pownall came out to us, and said his Lordship desired I would come in.

I was pleased with this ready admission and preference, having sometimes waited three or four hours for my turn; and, being pleased, I could more easily put on the open, cheerful countenance, that my friends advised me to wear. His Lordship came towards me and said, "I was dressing in order to go to court; but, hearing that you were at the door, who are a man of business, I determined to see you immediately." I thanked his Lordship, and said that my business at present was not much; it was only to pay my respects to his Lordship, and to acquaint him with my appointment by the House of Representatives of Massachusetts Bay to be their agent here, in which station if I could be of any service —(I was going on to say—"to the public, I should be very happy;" but his Lordship, whose countenance changed at my naming that province, cut me short by saying, with something between a smile and a sneer,)

L. H.   I must set you right there, Mr. Franklin, you are not agent.

B. F.   Why, my Lord?

L. H.   You are not appointed.

B. F.   I do not understand your Lordship; I have the appointment in my pocket.

L. H.   You are mistaken; I have later and better advices. I have a letter from Governor Hutchinson; he would not give his assent to the bill.

B. F.   There was no bill, my Lord; it was a vote of the House.

L. H.   There was a bill presented to the governor for the purpose of appointing you and another, one Dr. Lee, I think he is called, to which the governor refused his assent.

B. F.   I cannot understand this, my Lord; I think there must be some mistake in it. Is your Lordship quite sure that you have such a letter?

Wills Hill, Lord Hillsborough

L. H. I will convince you of it directly. (*Rings the bell.*) Mr. Pownall will come in and satisfy you.

B. F. It is not necessary, that I should now detain your Lordship from dressing. You are going to court. I will wait on your Lordship another time.

L. H. No, stay; he will come immediately. (*To the servant.*) Tell Mr. Pownall I want him.

(*Mr. Pownall comes in.*)

L. H. Have not you at hand Governor Hutchinson's letter, mentioning his refusing his assent to the bill for appointing Dr. Franklin agent?

Sec. P. My Lord?

L. H. Is there not such a letter?

Sec. P. No, my Lord; there is a letter relating to some bill for the payment of a salary to Mr. De Berdt, and I think to some other agent, to which the governor had refused his assent.

L. H. And is there nothing in the letter to the purpose I mention?

Sec. P. No, my Lord.

B. F. I thought it could not well be, my Lord; as my letters are by the last ships, and they mention no such thing. Here is the authentic copy of the vote of the House appointing me, in which there is no mention of any act intended. Will your Lordship please to look at it? (*With seeming unwillingness he takes it, but does not look into it.*)

L. H. An information of this kind is not properly brought to me as Secretary of State. The Board of Trade is the proper place.

B. F. I will leave the paper then with Mr. Pownall to be—

L. H. (*Hastily.*) To what end would you leave it with him?

B. F. To be entered on the minutes of that Board, as usual.

L. H. (*Angrily.*) It shall not be entered there. No such paper shall be entered there, while I have any thing to do with the business of that Board. The House of Representatives has no right to appoint an agent. We shall take no notice of any agents, but such as are appointed by acts of Assembly, to which the governor gives his assent. We have had confusion enough already. Here is one agent appointed by the Council, another by the House of Representatives. Which of these is agent for the

Portrait of Governor Thomas Hutchinson by Edward Truman

province? Who are we to hear in provincial affairs? An agent appointed by act of Assembly we can understand. No other will be attended to for the future, I can assure you.

B. F.   I cannot conceive, my Lord, why the consent of the governor should be thought necessary to the appointment of an agent for the people. It seems to me that —

L. H.   (*With a mixed look of anger and contempt.*) I shall not enter into a dispute with YOU, Sir, upon this subject.

B. F.   I beg your Lordship's pardon; I do not presume to dispute with your Lordship; I would only say, that it seems to me, that every body of men, who cannot appear in person, where business relating to them may be transacted, should have a right to appear by an agent. The concurrence of the governor does not seem to me necessary. It is the business of the people, that is to be done; he is not one of them; he is himself an agent.

L. H.   (*Hastily.*) Whose agent is he?

B. F.   The King's, my Lord.

L. H.   No such matter. He is one of the corporation by the province charter. No agent can be appointed but by an act, nor any act pass without his assent. Besides, this proceeding is directly contrary to express instructions.

B. F.   I did not know there had been such instructions. I am not concerned in any offence against them, and —

L. H.   Yes, your offering such a paper to be entered is an offence against them. (*Folding it up again without having read a word of it.*) No such appointment shall be entered....

B. F.   (*Reaching out his hand for the paper, which his Lordship returned to him.*) I beg your Lordship's pardon for taking up so much of your time. It is, I believe, of no great importance whether the appointment is acknowledged or not, for I have not the least conception that an agent can *at present* be of any use to any of the colonies. I shall therefore give your Lordship no further trouble. (*Withdrew.*)

Around this time Franklin wrote a song, "The Mother Country," which summed up in an amusing and ironic way his complex feelings toward England.

We have an old Mother that peevish is grown,
She snubs us like Children that scarce walk alone;
She forgets we're grown up and have Sense of our own;
      Which nobody can deny, deny,
        Which nobody can deny.
If we don't obey Orders, whatever the Case;
She frowns, and she chides, and she loses all Patience,
  and sometimes she hits us a Slap in the Face,
      Which nobody can deny, &c.
Her Orders so odd are, we often suspect
That Age has impaired her sound Intellect:
But still an old Mother should have due Respect,
      Which nobody can deny, &c.
Let's bear with her Humours as well as we can:
But why should we bear the Abuse of her Man?
When Servants make Mischief, they earn the Rattan,
      Which nobody can deny, &c.
Know too, ye bad Neighbours, who aim to divide
The Sons from the Mother, that still she's our Pride;
And if ye attack her we're all of her side,
      Which nobody can deny, &c.
We'll join in her Lawsuits, to baffle all those,
Who, to get what she has, will be often her Foes:
For we know it must all be our own, when she goes,
      Which nobody can deny, deny,
        Which nobody can deny.

Meanwhile, at Craven Street, Polly Stevenson Hewson had given birth to a son; Franklin was his godfather. The "Place" he mentioned in the first line of this letter to her was the Yorkshire home of his son-in-law, Richard Bache, who had come to England to meet Franklin.

Preston, Nov. 25, 1771.

Dear Friend,

I came to this Place on Saturday night, right well, and untir'd with a 70 miles' Journey that day. I met with your and my Dolly's joint Letter, which would have refreshed me with its kindness, if I had been ever so weary....

I thank you for your Intelligence about my Godson. I believe you are sincere, when you say you think him as fine a Child as you wish to see. He had cut two Teeth, and three, in another Letter, make five; for I know you never write Tautologies. If I have over-reckon'd, the Number will be right by this Time. His being like me in so many Particulars pleases me prodigiously; and I am persuaded there is another, which you have omitted, tho' it must have occurr'd to you while you were putting them down. Pray let him have every thing he likes; I think it of great Consequence while the Features of the Countenance are forming; it gives them a pleasant Air, and, that being once become natural and fix'd by Habit, the Face is ever after the handsomer for it, and on that much of a Person's good Fortune and Success in Life may depend. Had I been cross'd as much in my Infant Likings and Inclinations as you know I have been of late Years, I should have been, I was going to say, not near so handsome; but as the Vanity of that Expression would offend other Folk's Vanity, I change it, out of regard to them, and say, a great deal more homely.

Eighteenth-century "Irish Cabbin"

Franklin's visit to Ireland made a deep impression on him. He saw in grisly detail what happened to a country that totally surrendered its independence to another nation. In a letter to Dr. Joshua Babcock, postmaster of Westerly, Rhode Island, he gave a vivid description of Ireland's degradation.

London, Jan. 13. 1772

I have lately made a Tour thro' Ireland and Scotland. In those Countries a small Part of the Society are Landlords, great Noblemen, and Gentlemen, extreamly opulent, living in the highest Affluence and Magnificence: The Bulk of the People Tenants, extreamly poor, living in the most sordid Wretchedness, in dirty Hovels of Mud and Straw, and cloathed only in Rags.

I thought often of the Happiness of New England, where every Man is a Freeholder, has a Vote in publick Affairs, lives in a tidy, warm House, has plenty of good Food and Fewel, with whole cloaths from Head to Foot, the Manufacture perhaps of his own Family. Long may they continue in this Situation! But if they should ever envy the Trade of these Countries, I can put them in a Way to obtain a Share of it. Let them with three fourths of the People of Ireland live the Year round on Potatoes and Buttermilk, without Shirts, then may their Merchants export Beef, Butter, and Linnen. Let them, with the Generality of the Common People of Scotland, go Barefoot, then may they make large Exports in Shoes and Stockings: And if they will be content to wear Rags, like the Spinners and Weavers of England, they may

An Irish day laborer

235

make Cloths and Stuffs for all Parts of the World.

Farther, if my Countrymen should ever wish for the honour of having among them a gentry enormously wealthy, let them sell their Farms & pay rack'd Rents; the Scale of the Landlords will rise as that of the Tenants is depress'd, who will soon become poor, tattered, dirty, and abject in Spirit. Had I never been in the American Colonies, but was to form my Judgment of Civil Society by what I have lately seen, I should never advise a Nation of Savages to admit of Civilization: For I assure you, that, in the Possession & Enjoyment of the various Comforts of Life, compar'd to these People every Indian is a Gentleman: And the Effect of this kind of Civil Society seems only to be, the depressing Multitudes below the Savage State that a few may be rais'd above it.

Franklin fought a war on two fronts with Lord Hillsborough, the Secretary of State for Colonies. He opposed Hillsborough's policy of repression and severity toward America in general, and behind the scenes he lobbied intensively for the western colony, which Hillsborough was blocking. Negotiations for the colony reached a climax when Hillsborough, as president of the Board of Trade, issued a report against it. Franklin and his friends demanded a hearing before the Privy Council; and Samuel Wharton, who had come over to England to assist Franklin in pushing the plan, made a long speech that reads as though it was composed by Franklin, or written under his direction and advice. The Privy Council rejected the Board of Trade's decision and declared in favor of the colony. Hillsborough, mortified, had no alternative but to resign. The Council's decision was undoubtedly affected by the presence among its members of several sharers in the Grand Ohio Company, as the founding organization was now called. In these letters to his son William, Franklin carefully restrained his exultation over this triumph. One reason may well have been his knowledge that his letters were being opened by the Ministry.

London, August 17, 1772.

At length we have got rid of Lord Hillsborough, and Lord Dartmouth takes his place, to the great satisfaction of all the friends of America. You will hear it said among you, I suppose, that the interest of the Ohio planters has ousted him; but the truth is, what I wrote you long since, that all his brother ministers disliked him extremely, and wished for a fair occasion of tripping up his heels; so, seeing that he made a point of defeating our scheme, they made another of supporting it, on purpose to mortify him, which they knew his pride could not bear. I do not mean they would have done this, if they had thought our proposal bad in itself, or his opposition well founded; but I believe, if he had been on good terms with them, they would not have differed with him for so small a matter. The King, too, was tired of him and of his administration, which had weakened the affection and respect of the colonies for a royal government, of which (I may say it to you) I used proper means from time to time that his Majesty should have due information and convincing proofs. More of this when I see you.

The King's dislike made the others more firmly united in the resolution of disgracing Hillsborough, by setting at nought his famous report. But, now that business is done, perhaps our affair may be less regarded in the cabinet and suffered to linger, and possibly may yet mis-carry. Therefore let us beware of every word and action, that may betray a confidence in its success, lest we render ourselves ridiculous in case of disappointment....

I am writing by Falconer, and therefore in this only add, that I am ever your affectionate father,

B FRANKLIN

P.S. The regard Lord Dartmouth has always done me the honour to express for me, gives me room to hope being able to obtain more in favour of our colonies upon occasion, than I could for some time past.

Engraving of Lord Dartmouth after a portrait by Sir Joshua Reynolds

London, August 19, 1772.

As to my situation here, nothing can be more agreeable, especially as I hope for less embarrassment from the new minister; a general respect paid me by the learned, a number of friends and acquaintance among them, with whom I have a pleasing intercourse; a character of so much weight, that it has protected me when some in power would have done me injury, and continued me in an office they would have deprived me of; my company so much desired, that I seldom dine at home in winter, and could spend the whole summer in the country-houses of inviting friends, if I chose it. Learned and ingenious foreigners, that come to England, almost all make a point of visiting me; for my reputation is still higher abroad than here. Several of the foreign ambassadors have assiduously cultivated my acquaintance, treating me as one of their *Corps,* partly I believe from the desire they have, from time to time, of hearing something of American

ŒUVRES
DE
M. FRANKLIN,
DOCTEUR ÈS LOIX,

MEMBRE DE L'ACADÉMIE ROYALE DES SCIENCES
de Paris, des Sociétés Royales de Londres & de Gottingue,
des Sociétés Philosophiques d'Edimbourg & de Rotterdam,
Président de la Société Philosophique de Philadelphie,
& Résident à la Cour de la Grande Bretagne pour plusieurs
Colonies Britanniques Américaines.

TRADUITES DE L'ANGLOIS SUR LA QUATRIEME ÉDITION.
PAR M. BARBEU DUBOURG.
AVEC DES ADDITIONS NOUVELLES
ET des Figures en Taille douce.

TOME PREMIER.

À PARIS,

QUILLAU l'aîné, Librairie, rue Christine, au Magasin Littéraire,
Chez ESPRIT, Libraire de Mgr. le Duc de Chartres, au Palais Royal,
Et l'Auteur, rue de la Bucherie, aux Ecoles de Médecine.

M. DCC. LXXIII.
Avec Approbation & Permission du Roi.

*A French edition of Franklin's works,
published in 1773, lists him as
a member of the Royal Academy.*

affairs, an object become of importance in foreign courts, who begin to hope Britain's alarming power will be diminished by the defection of her colonies; and partly that they may have an opportunity of introducing me to the gentlemen of their country who desire it. The King, too, has lately been heard to speak of me with great regard.

These are flattering circumstances, but a violent longing for home sometimes seizes me, which I can no otherwise subdue but by promising myself a return next spring or next fall, and so forth. As to returning hither, if I once go back, I have no thoughts of it. I am too far advanced in life to propose three voyages more....

August 22d.—I find I omitted congratulating you on the honour of your election into the Society for propagating the Gospel. There you match indeed my Dutch honour. But you are again behind, for last night I received a letter from Paris, of which the enclosed is an extract, acquainting me that I am chosen *Associé Etranger* [foreign member] of the Royal Academy there. There are but eight of these *Associés Etrangers* in all Europe, and those of the most distinguished names of science. The vacancy I have the honour of filling was made by the death of the late celebrated Van Swieten of Vienna. This mark of respect from the first academy in the world, which Abbé Nollet, one of its members, took so much pains to prejudice against my doctrines, I consider as a kind of victory without ink-shed, since I never answered him. I am told he has but one of his sect now remaining in the Academy. All the rest, who have in any degree acquainted themselves with electricity, are as he calls them *Franklinists.*

Although Franklin himself, earlier in his life, had owned one or two slaves, who worked for him as house servants, he very soon imbibed a deep detestation for slavery from his close association with Philadelphia's Quakers. In this letter to Anthony Benezet, a Quaker who devoted his life to the abolition of the slave trade, Franklin linked the origins of slavery to British imperial policy.

London, August 22: 1772.
I made a little extract from yours of April 27, of the number of slaves imported and perishing, with some close remarks on the hypocrisy of this country, which encourages such a detestable commerce by laws for promoting the Guinea trade; while it piqued itself on its virtue, love

of liberty, and the equity of its courts, in setting free a single negro. This was inserted in the *London Chronicle,* of the 20th of June last.

I thank you for the Virginia address, which I shall also publish with some remarks. I am glad to hear that the disposition against keeping negroes grows more general in North America. Several pieces have been lately printed here against the practice, and I hope in time it will be taken into consideration and suppressed by the legislature. Your labours have already been attended with great effects. I hope, therefore, you and your friends will be encouraged to proceed.

On the whole, Franklin was in a buoyant mood in 1772. The western colony seemed within his grasp, and something close to a détente seemed to prevail between England and America. In this sunny atmosphere, he tossed off one of his most delightful letters to Georgiana Shipley, daughter of Jonathan Shipley, the Bishop of St. Asaph. It was at the Shipleys' country home, in the village of Twyford, that Franklin wrote the first part of his autobiography. Mungo was an American squirrel whom Franklin had given to the Shipleys. He escaped from their garden and was killed by a neighbor's dog.

London, September 26, 1772.

I LAMENT with you most sincerely the unfortunate end of poor MUNGO. Few squirrels were better accomplished; for he had had a good education, had travelled far, and seen much of the world. As he had the honour of being, for his virtues, your favourite, he should not go, like common skuggs, without an elegy or an epitaph. Let us give him one in the monumental style and measure, which, being neither prose nor verse, is perhaps the properest for grief; since to use common language would look as if we were not affected, and to make rhymes would seem trifling in sorrow.

EPITAPH.

Alas! poor Mungo!
Happy wert thou, hadst thou known
Thy own felicity.
Remote from the fierce bald eagle,
Tyrant of thy native woods,
Thou hadst nought to fear from his piercing talons,
Nor from the murdering gun
Of the thoughtless sportsman.
Safe in thy wired castle,

Georgiana Shipley

GRIMALKIN never could annoy thee.

Daily wert thou fed with the choicest viands,
By the fair hand of an indulgent mistress;
But, discontented,
Thou wouldst have more freedom.
Too soon, alas! didst thou obtain it;
And wandering,
Thou art fallen by the fangs of wanton, cruel RANGER!

Learn hence,
Ye who blindly seek more liberty,
Whether subjects, sons, squirrels or daughters,
That apparent restraint may be real protection;
Yielding peace and plenty
With security.

You see, my dear Miss, how much more decent and proper this broken style is, than if we were to say, by way of epitaph,

Here SKUGG
Lies snug,
As a bug
In a rug.

and yet, perhaps, there are people in the world of so little feeling as to think that this would be a good-enough epitaph for poor Mungo.

Suddenly the pace of politics quickened. The British Government became deeply entangled in the problems of the East India Company. In a letter written to William Franklin around this time, Franklin almost mordantly discussed "how the continued refusal of North America to take tea" had come close to wrecking the company. Numerous bankruptcies, caused by the abrupt plunge of the company's stock, had given "such a shock to credit" as England had not experienced since the collapse of the great speculation known as the South Sea Bubble about fifty years earlier. Manufacturers in turn were forced to lay off thousands of hands, and there was serious unrest in the manufacturing towns. "Blessed effects of pride, pique and passion in government, which should have no passions," Franklin said. This turmoil did not augur much progress for the western colony. In this letter to Joseph Galloway, Franklin discussed these and other matters.

London, April 6, 1773.

The Parliament is busy about India Affairs, and as yet see no End of the Business. It is thought they will sit till the End of June. An Alliance with France and

Spain is talk'd of; and a War with Prussia. But this may blow over. A War with France and Spain would be of more Advantage to American Liberty; Every Step would then be taken to conciliate our Friendship, our Grievances would be redress'd, and our Claims allow'd. And this will be the Case sooner or later. For as the House of Bourbon is most vulnerable in its American Possessions, our hearty Assistance in a War there must be of the greatest Importance.

The Affair of the Grant goes on but slowly. I do not yet clearly see Land. I begin to be a little of the Sailor's Mind when they were handing a Cable out of a Store into a Ship, and one of 'em said: "Tis a long, heavy Cable. I wish we could see the End of it." "D—n me," says another, "if I believe it has any End; somebody has cut it off."

In Boston, the political pot also began to boil again. A town meeting, organized by Samuel Adams, produced a report summarizing all the irritations and grievances that existed between England and America. Governor Thomas Hutchinson called it "a declaration of independency" and convened the General Court (or Massachusetts Assembly) to answer it. Franklin's low opinion of Hutchinson was part of the reason why he took a step that was to have enormous consequences both for him and for America. Early in 1773, a friend showed him some letters that Hutchinson and Lieutenant Governor Andrew Oliver had written to Thomas Whately, an undersecretary in the British Cabinet and a political follower of George Grenville. The letters had been stolen from Whately's files after his death. In these letters, Hutchinson and Oliver recommended a severe policy of repression to handle the unrest in Boston. Franklin forwarded copies of these explosive missives to Boston, with the proviso that they should be shown only to a small circle of leading men. The more radical Boston leaders decided to ignore this prohibition, and the letters were soon published, edited to make Governor Hutchinson and Lieutenant Governor Oliver appear in the most odious light possible. In this letter to Samuel Cooper, Franklin discussed the motives he had for sending the letters to Boston.

London, July 25, 1773.

I am glad to know your Opinion, that those Letters came seasonably, and may be of public Utility. I accompanied them with no Restriction relating to myself. My duty to the Province, as their Agent, I thought required the Communication of them, as far as I could. I was sensible I should make Enemies there, and perhaps might offend government here; but those Apprehensions I disregarded. I did not expect and hardly still expect that my sending them could be kept a Secret; but since it is so hitherto, I now wish it may continue so, because the Publication of the Letters, contrary to my Engagement, has changed the Circumstances. If they serve to diminish the Influence and demolish the Power of the Parties, whose Correspondence has been, and would probably have continued to be so mischievous to the Interest and Rights of the Province, I shall on that Account be more easy under any inconveniences I may suffer, either here or there; and shall bear, as well as I can, the Imputation of not having taken sufficient Care to insure the Performance of my Promise.

The situation in Boston made Franklin very touchy about his relationship with Crown officials. In this letter to William Franklin, he also revealed a significant turn in his thinking about the causes of the trouble between England and America. Lord North was First Minister in the reorganized British Cabinet.

London, July 14, 1773.

I am glad to find by yours of May 4 that you have been able to assist Josiah Davenport a little, but vex'd that he and you should think of putting me upon a Solicitation, which it is impossible for me to engage in. I am not upon Terms with Lord North, to ask any such Favour from him. Displeased with something he said relating to America, I have never been at his Levees, since the first. Perhaps he has taken that amiss. For the last Week we met occasionally at Lord Le Despencer's, in our Return from Oxford, where I had been to attend the Solemnity of his Installation, and he seemed studiously to avoid speaking to me. I ought to be asham'd to say that on such occasions I feel myself to be as proud as anybody. His Lady indeed was more gracious. She came, and sat down by me on the same Sopha, and condescended to enter into a Conversation with me agreably enough, as if to make some Amends. Their Son and Daughter were with them. They staied all Night, so that we din'd, supp'd, and breakfasted together, without exchanging three Sentences. But had he ever so great a Regard for me, I could not ask that Office, trifling as it is, for any Relation of mine. And detesting as I do the whole System of American Customs, believing they will one Day bring on a Breach, through the Indiscretion and Insolence of those

Andrew Oliver

Lord North, after a Ramsay portrait

concern'd in the Collection, I should never wish to see one so near to me in that Business....I am glad you stand so well with Lord Dartmouth. I am likewise well with him, but he never spoke to me of augmenting your Salary. He is truly a good Man, and wishes sincerely a good Understanding with the Colonies, but does not seem to have Strength equal to his Wishes. Between you and I, the late Measures have been, I suspect, very much the King's own, and he has in some Cases a great Share of what his Friends call *Firmness.* Yet, by some Painstaking and proper Management, the wrong Impressions he has received may be removed, which is perhaps the only Chance America has for obtaining *soon* the Redress she aims at. This entirely to yourself.

A few weeks later Franklin wrote to William about a more personal matter. In England before his marriage, William—himself illegitimate—had fathered an illegitimate son, whom he had named William Temple Franklin. Benjamin Franklin had paid for the boy's education in a school outside of London, and Temple had grown up thinking he was a distant relation of the Franklin family. By now the boy was almost thirteen and he no doubt knew who his father was. Lord le Despencer, whose gardens Franklin was enjoying, was head of the British Post Office. The buttons his son had sent him were actually pebbles from a beach near Philadelphia that Franklin had dubbed "Button-mold Bay."

West Wycombe, Lord le Despencer's,
Aug. 3. 1773.

Temple is just return'd to School from his Summer Vacation. He always behaves himself so well, as to encrease my Affection for him every time he is with me.

As you are like to have a considerable Landed Property, it would be well to make your Will, if you have not already done it, and secure that Property to him. Our Friend Galloway will advise you in the Manner. Whatever he may come to possess, I am persuaded he will make a good Use of it, if his Temper and Understanding do not strangely alter.

I am in this House as much at my Ease as if it was my own; and the Gardens are a Paradise. But a pleasanter Thing is the kind Countenance, the facetious and very intelligent Conversation of mine Host, who having been for many Years engaged in publick Affairs, seen all Parts of Europe, and kept the best Company in the World, is himself the best existing.

I wear the Buttons (for which I thank you) on a suit of light gray which matches them. All the *connoisseurs* in natural Productions are puzzeled with them, not knowing any thing similar.

Throughout these years Franklin continued to campaign in the newspapers on behalf of America. Scarcely a month passed without one of his essays appearing. Most of them debated with the numerous critics of America, who were also busy writing to the papers. But in 1773, as a new storm brewed between England and America, Franklin abruptly shifted his tone from vigorous debate to savage satire. On September 11, 1773, the *Public Advertiser* published an essay, "Rules by which a Great Empire May be Reduced to a Small One." Addressed to "All ministers who have the management of extensive dominions," it laid down twenty rules that were guaranteed to destroy a great empire, all of which, it soon became obvious to the reader, the British Ministry was already faithfully following. Eleven days later, the *Public Advertiser* published another essay, "An Edict by the King of Prussia." Both essays caused something of a sensation in England. The "Edict" was far more popular, and in fact sold out the paper.

Dantzic, Sept. 5, [1773]

"FREDERICK, by the grace of God, King of Prussia, &c. &c. &c., to all present and to come, (*à tous présens et à venir,*) Health. The peace now enjoyed throughout our dominions, having afforded us leisure to apply ourselves to the regulation of commerce, the improvement of our finances, and at the same time the easing our domestic subjects in their taxes: For these causes, and other good considerations us thereunto moving, we hereby make known, that, after having deliberated these affairs in our council, present our dear brothers, and other great officers of the state, members of the same, we, of our certain knowledge, full power, and authority royal, have made and issued this present Edict, viz.

"Whereas it is well known to all the world, that the first German settlements made in the Island of Britain, were by colonies of people, subject to our renowned ducal ancestors, and drawn from their dominions, under the conduct of Hengist, Horsa, Hella, Uff, Cerdicus, Ida, and others; and that the said colonies have flourished under the protection of our august house for ages past; have never been emancipated therefrom; and yet have hitherto yielded little profit to the same: And whereas we ourself have in the last war fought for and defended the said colonies, against the power of France, and thereby enabled them to make conquests from the said power of America, for which we have not yet received adequate compensation: And whereas it is just and expedient that a revenue should be raised from the said colonies in Britain, towards our indemnification; and that those who are descendants of our ancient subjects, and thence still owe us due obedience, should contribute to the replenishing of our royal coffers as they must have done, had their ancestors remained in the territories now to us appertaining: We do therefore hereby ordain and command, that, from and after the date of these presents, there shall be levied and paid to our officers of the *customs,* on all goods, wares, and merchandizes, and on all grain and other produce of the earth, exported from the said Island of Britain, and on all goods of whatever kind imported into the same, a duty of four and a half per cent *ad valorem,* for the use of us and our successors. And that the said duty may more effectually be collected, we do hereby ordain, that all ships or vessels bound from Great Britain to any other part of the world, or from any other part of the world to Great Britain, shall in their respective voyages touch at our port of Koningsberg, there to be unladen, searched, and charged with the said duties.

"And whereas there hath been from time to time discovered in the said island of Great Britain, by our colonists there, many mines or beds of iron-stone; and sundry subjects, of our ancient dominion, skilful in converting the said stone into metal, have in time past transported themselves thither, carrying with them and communicating that art; and the inhabitants of the said island, presuming that they had a natural right to make the best use they could of the natural productions of their country for their own benefit, have not only built furnaces for smelting the said stone into iron, but have erected plating-forges, slitting-mills, and steel-furnaces, for the more convenient manufacturing of the same; thereby endangering a diminution of the said manufacture in our ancient dominion;—we do therefore hereby farther ordain, that, from and after the date hereof, no mill or other engine for slitting or rolling of iron, or any plating-forge to work with a tilt-hammer, or any furnace for making steel, shall be erected or continued in the said island of Great Britain: And the Lord Lieutenant of

A serene view of West Wycombe, home of Lord and Lady le Despencer, where Franklin was "as much at my Ease as if it were my own."

every county in the said island is hereby commanded, on information of any such erection within his county, to order and by force to cause the same to be abated and destroyed; as he shall answer the neglect thereof to us at his peril. But we are nevertheless graciously pleased to permit the inhabitants of the said island to transport their iron into Prussia, there to be manufactured, and to them returned; they paying our Prussian subjects for the workmanship, with all the costs of commission, freight, and risk, coming and returning; any thing herein contained to the contrary notwithstanding.

"We do not, however, think fit to extend this our indulgence to the article of wool; but, meaning to encourage, not only the manufacturing of woollen cloth, but also the raising of wool, in our ancient dominions, and to prevent both, as much as may be, in our said island, we do hereby absolutely forbid the transportation of wool from thence, even to the mother country, Prussia; and that those islanders may be farther and more effectually restrained in making any advantage of their own wool in the way of manufacture, we command that none shall be carried out of one country into another; nor shall any worsted, bay, or woollen yarn, cloth, says, bays, kerseys, serges, frizes, druggets, cloth-serges, shalloons, or any other drapery stuffs, or woollen manufactures whatsoever, made up or mixed with wool in any of the said counties, be carried into any other county, or be waterborne even across the smallest river or creek, on penalty of forfeiture of the same, together with the boats, carriages, horses, &c., that shall be employed in removing them. Nevertheless, our loving subjects there are hereby permitted (if they think proper) to use all their wool as manure for the improvement of their lands....

"And, lastly, being willing farther to favor our said colonies in Britain, we do hereby also ordain and command, that all the *thieves,* highway and street robbers, house-breakers, forgerers, murderers, s—d—tes, and villains of every denomination, who have forfeited their lives to the law in Prussia; but whom we, in our great clemency, do not think fit here to hang, shall be emptied out of our gaols into the said island of Great Britain, for the better peopling of that country.

"We flatter ourselves, that these our royal regulations and commands will be thought just and reasonable by our much-favoured colonists in England; the said regulations being copied from their statutes of 10 and 11 William III. c. 10, 5 Geo. II. c. 22, 23, Geo. II. c. 29, 4 Geo. I. c. 11, and from other equitable laws made by their parliaments; or from instructions given by their Princes; or from resolutions of both Houses, entered into for the good government of their *own colonies in Ireland and America. . . ."*

In a letter to his son, Franklin discussed the impact of his satires and included a vivid account of how totally the "Edict" fooled his English friends. But the letter is more important for an early paragraph in which Franklin stated his conclusion on the essential quarrel with England —and noted the ominous fact that his son did not agree with him.

London, October 6, 1773.

From a long and thorough consideration of the subject, I am indeed of opinion, that the parliament has no right to make any law whatever, binding on the colonies; that the king, and not the king, lords, and commons collectively, is their sovereign; and that the king, with their respective parliaments, is their only legislator. I know your sentiments differ from mine on these subjects. You are a thorough government man, which I do not wonder at, nor do I aim at converting you. I only wish you to act uprightly and steadily, avoiding that duplicity, which in Hutchinson, adds contempt to indignation. If you can promote the prosperity of your people, and leave them happier than you found them, whatever your political principles are, your memory will be honoured.

I have written two pieces here lately for the *Public Advertiser,* on American affairs, designed to expose the conduct of this country towards the colonies in a short, comprehensive, and striking view, and stated, therefore, in out-of-the-way forms, as most likely to take the general attention. The first was called *"Rules by which a Great Empire may be reduced to a small one;"* the second, *"An Edict of the King of Prussia."* I sent you one of the first, but could not get enough of the second to spare you one, though my clerk went the next morning to the printer's, and wherever they were sold. . . .

I am not suspected as the author, except by one or two friends; and have heard the latter spoken of in the highest terms, as the keenest and severest piece that has appeared here for a long time. Lord Mansfield, I hear, said of it, that it *was very* ABLE *and very* ARTFUL *indeed*; and would do mischief by giving here a bad impression of the measures of government; and in the colonies, by encouraging them in their contumacy....

What made it the more noticed here was, that people in reading it were, as the phrase is, *taken in,* till they had got half through it, and imagined it a real edict, to which mistake I suppose the King of Prussia's *character* must have contributed. I was down at Lord Le Despencer's, when the post brought that day's papers. Mr. Whitehead was there, too, (Paul Whitehead, the author of "Manners,") who runs early through all the papers, and tells the company what he finds remarkable. He had them in another room, and we were chatting in the breakfast parlour, when he came running in to us, out of breath, with the paper in his hand. Here! says he, here's news for ye! *Here's the King of Prussia, claiming a right to this kingdom!* All stared, and I as much as anybody; and he went on to read it. When he had read two or three paragraphs, a gentleman present said, *Damn his impudence, I dare say, we shall hear by next post that he is upon his march with one hundred thousand men to back this.* Whitehead, who is very shrewd, soon after began to smoke it, and looking in my face said, *I'll be hanged if this is not some of your American jokes upon us.* The reading went on, and ended with abundance of laughing, and a general verdict that it was a fair hit: and the piece was cut out of the paper and preserved in my Lord's collection.

Violent events now led one to another in England and America. The uproar over the Hutchinson letters caused a tremendous reaction inside the British Government. When the Massachusetts General Court directed Franklin to submit a petition to the King, asking for the removal of Hutchinson and Oliver, the issue swiftly spread to the newspapers and aroused vigorous debate. William Whately, brother of the man who had received the letters, accused John Temple, an American friend of Franklin's, of stealing them. Temple, who had been a customs commissioner in Boston, returned to England to defend himself against accusations of favoring American smugglers and challenged Whately to a duel, which took place in Hyde Park and left Whately slightly wounded. Franklin, hearing that Whately intended to renew the combat as soon as he recovered, published the following letter on Christmas Day, 1773, admitting that he was the man who had sent the letters to Boston. Franklin later noted, as a kind of footnote to this letter, that Hutchinson had "the same idea of *duty* when he procured copies of Dr. Franklin's letters to the Assembly, and sent them to the Ministry of England."

[London, December 25, 1773]

Finding that two gentlemen have been unfortunately engaged in a duel about a transaction and its circumstance, of which both of them are totally ignorant and innocent; I think it incumbent upon me to declare (for the prevention of farther mischief, as far as such a declaration may contribute to prevent it), that I alone am the person who obtained and transmitted to Boston the letters in question. Mr. W. could not communicate them, because they were never in his possession; and for the same reason, they could not be taken from him by Mr. T. They were not of the nature of *private* letters between friends. They were written by public officers to persons in public stations, on public affairs, and intended to procure public measures; they were therefore handed to other public persons who might be influenced by them to produce those measures. Their tendency was to incense the mother country against her colonies and, by the steps recommended, to widen the breach; which they effected. The chief caution expressed with regard to privacy was, to keep their contents from the colony agents, who, the writers apprehended, might return them, or copies of them to America. That apprehension was, it seems, well founded; for the first agent who laid his hands on them, thought it his duty to transmit them to his constituents.

A
FAITHFUL ACCOUNT
OF THE
Whole of the Transactions
RELATING TO A LATE
AFFAIR OF HONOUR
BETWEEN
J. TEMPLE, and W. WHATELY, Esqrs.
CONTAINING
A particular History of that unhappy Quarrel,
LIKEWISE,
The whole of their LETTERS that passed on that Occasion, with those signed *Antenor, An Enemy to Villains of every Denomination,* &c. &c.

LONDON:
Printed for R. SNAGG, in Pater-noster-Row; and T. AXTELL, at the Royal-Exchange.
M DCC LXXIV.
[Price One Shilling.]

A 1774 account of the duel between John Temple and William Whately

Fourteen days later, Franklin was mildly astonished to discover that the petition of the Massachusetts Assembly was to receive a formal hearing before the Privy Council's Committee for Plantation Affairs on the following Tuesday, January 11. At the hearing it became evident that the British Government was determined to support Hutchinson. Alexander Wedderburn, an ambitious Scot who had recently become Solicitor General in the North Ministry, had been "hired" to defend Governor Hutchinson and Lieutenant Governor Oliver. Faced with such formidable opposition, Franklin asked for an adjournment to seek the advice of counsel. Then came news that fanned the already inflamed tempers of the British Ministry into an uncontrollable conflagration. On January 19, 1774; the British ship *Hayley* reached Dover from Boston, and three days later *The St. James's Chronicle* printed a complete description of the Boston Tea Party. The following day the ship *Polly* docked at Gravesend with its cargo of tea, rejected at Philadelphia, still in the hold. On Thursday, January 27, Governor Hutchinson's official report of the assault on British property arrived in London, and Lord North and his Cabinet met that evening to ponder the crisis. They decided, as a first step, to make an example of Benjamin Franklin. In this excerpt from his long letter to Thomas Cushing of Boston, Franklin narrated the experience in the Cockpit, the Privy Council's meeting place, that ended his love affair with England forever.

London, February 15, 1774

The transactions relating to the tea had increased and strengthened the torrent of clamour against us. No one had the least expectation of success to the petition; and, though I had asked leave to use counsel, I was half inclined to waive it, and save you the expense; but Mr. Bollan was now strongly for it, as they had refused to hear him. And, though fortified by his opinion, as he had long experience in your affairs, I would at first have ventured to deviate from the instructions you sent me in that particular, supposing you to allow some discretionary liberty to your agents; yet, now that he urged it as necessary, I employed a solicitor, and furnished him with what materials I could for framing a brief. . . .

The briefs being prepared and perused by our counsel, we had a consultation at Mr. Dunning's chambers in Lincoln's Inn. I introduced Mr. Arthur Lee, as my friend and successor in the agency. The brief, as you will see by a copy I send you, pointed out the passages of the letters, which were applicable in support of the particular charges contained in the resolutions and petition. But the counsel observed, we wanted evidence to prove those passages false; the counsel on the other side would say, they were true representations of the state of the country; and, as to the political reflections of the writers, and their sentiments of government, their aims to extend and enforce the power of Parliament and diminish the privileges of their countrymen, though these might appear in the letters and need no other proof, yet they would never be considered here as offences, but as virtues and merits. The counsel therefore thought it would answer no good end to insist on those particulars; and that it was more advisable to state as facts the general discontent of the people, that the governors had lost all credit with them, and were become odious, &c.; facts of which the petition was itself full proof, because otherwise it could not have existed; and then show that

BRITISH MUSEUM

The issue of The St. James's Chronicle *that described the Boston Tea Party*

A nineteenth-century engraving depicting Franklin's ordeal before the Lords in Council in Whitehall

it must in such a situation be necessary for his Majesty's service, as well as the peace of the province, to remove them. By this opinion, great part of the brief became unnecessary.

Notwithstanding the intimations I had received, I could not believe that the solicitor-general would be permitted to wander from the question before their Lordships into a new case, the accusation of another person for another matter, not cognizable before them, who could not expect to be there so accused, and therefore could not be prepared for his defence. And yet all this happened, and in all probability was preconcerted; for all the courtiers were invited, as to an entertainment, and there never was such an appearance of privy counsellors on any occasion, not less than thirty-five, besides an immense crowd of other auditors.

The hearing began by reading my letter to Lord Dartmouth, enclosing the petition, then the petition itself, the resolves, and lastly the letters, the solicitor-general making no objections, nor asking any of the questions he had talked of at the preceding board. Our counsel then opened the matter, upon their general plan, and acquitted themselves very handsomely; only Mr. Dunning, having disorder on his lungs that weakened his voice exceedingly, was not so perfectly heard as one could have wished. The solicitor-general then went into what he called a history of the province for the last ten years, and bestowed plenty of abuse upon it, mingled with encomium on the governors. But the favorite part of his discourse was levelled at your agent, who stood there the butt of his invective ribaldry for near an hour, not a single Lord adverting to the impropriety and indecency of treating a public messenger in so ignominious a manner, who was present only as the person delivering your petition, with the consideration of which no part of *his* conduct had any concern. If he had done a wrong, in obtaining and transmitting the letters, that was not the tribunal where he was to be accused and tried. The cause was already before the Chancellor. Not one of their Lordships checked and recalled the orator to the business before them, but, on the contrary, a very few excepted, they seemed to enjoy highly the entertainment, and frequently burst out in loud applauses. This part of his speech was thought so good, that they have since printed

251

it, in order to defame me everywhere, and particularly to destroy my reputation on your side of the water; but the grosser parts of the abuse are omitted, appearing, I suppose, in their own eyes, too foul to be seen on paper....

The reply of Mr. Dunning concluded. Being very ill, and much incommoded by standing so long, his voice was so feeble, as to be scarce audible. What little I heard was very well said, but appeared to have little effect.

Their Lordship's Report, which I send you, is dated the same day. It contains a severe censure, as you will see, on the petition and the petitioners; and, as I think, a very unfair conclusion from my silence, that the charge of surreptitiously obtaining the letters was a true one; though the solicitor, as appears in the printed speech, had acquainted them that the matter was before the Chancellor; and my counsel had stated the impropriety of my answering there to charges then trying in another court. In truth I came by them honourably, and my intention in sending them was virtuous, if an endeavour to lessen the breach between two states of the same empire be such, by showing that the injuries complained of by one of them did not proceed from the other, but from traitors among themselves.

It may be supposed, that I am very angry on this occasion, and therefore I did purpose to add no reflections of mine on the treatment the Assembly and their agent have received, lest they should be thought the effects of resentment and a desire of exasperating. But, indeed, what I feel on my own account is half lost in what I feel for the public. When I see, that all petitions and complaints of grievances are so odious to government, that even the mere pipe which conveys them becomes obnoxious, I am at a loss to know how peace and union are to be maintained or restored between the different parts of the empire. Grievances cannot be redressed unless they are known; and they cannot be known but through complaints and petitions. If these are deemed affronts, and the messengers punished as offenders, who will henceforth send petitions? And who will deliver them? It has been thought a dangerous thing in any state to stop up the vent of griefs. Wise governments have therefore generally received petitions with some indulgence, even when but slightly founded. Those, who think themselves injured by their rulers, are sometimes, by a mild and prudent answer, convinced of their error. But where complaining is a crime, hope becomes despair.

The day following I received a written notice from the secretary of the general postoffice, that his Majesty's postmaster-general *found it necessary* to dismiss me from my office of deputy postmaster-general in North America.

In these same tense weeks, Franklin wrote two sharply contrasting letters to his son. The first, on February 2, only three days after his ordeal in the Cockpit, reflected the anger he was still feeling. The second displayed a cooler, more dispassionate view of the affair.

London, February 2, 1774.

This Line is just to acquaint you that I am well, and that my Office of Deputy-Postmaster is taken from me. As there is no Prospect of your being ever promoted to a better Government, and that you hold has never defray'd its Expenses, I wish you were well settled in your farm. 'Tis an honester and a more honourable, because a more independent Employment. You will hear from others the Treatment I have receiv'd. I leave you to your own Reflections and Determinations upon it....

February 18, 1774

Some tell me that it is determined to displace you likewise, but I do not know it as certain. I only give you the hint, as an Inducement to you to delay awhile your removal to Amboy, which in that Case would be an Expense and Trouble to no purpose. Perhaps they may expect that your Resentment of their Treatment of me may induce you to resign, and save them the shame of depriving you when they ought to promote. But this I would not advise you to do. Let them take your place if they want it, though in truth I think it is scarce worth your Keeping, since it has not afforded you sufficient to prevent your running every year behindhand with me. But one may make something of an Injury, nothing of a Resignation.

William Franklin by Mather Brown

Meanwhile, the British Ministry proceeded to espouse the policy of repression recommended by Governor Thomas Hutchinson. In a letter to Thomas Cushing, Franklin described and discussed some of the bills—the so-called Punitive, or Coercive, Acts; in America called the Intolerable Acts—being proposed to punish Boston for the Tea Party.

London, April 16, 1774.

The Torrent is still violent against America. A Bill is brought in to alter the Charter appointing the Council by the Crown, giving Power to the Governors to nominate and commission Magistrates without Consent of Council, and Forbidding any Town Meeting to be held in the Province...without the Permission of the Governor, and for that Business only for which such Permission shall be requested. The Manner of appointing Jurors is likewise to be altered. And another Bill is to provide for the Security of Persons who may be concern'd in executing or enforcing Acts of Parliament there, by directing their Trials for any thing done by them to be in some neighbouring Province or in Great Britain at the Discretion of the Governor. I hope to get the Breviates of these Bills in time to send by this Ship. They will meet with Opposition in both Houses; but there is little Hope that they will not pass, we having very few Friends in Parliament at present. The House will probably sit 'till some time in June, perhaps longer, and till they hear the Effect of these Measures in America. I think to stay here as long as they sit....

General Gage has been hastily commission'd and sent away to be your Governor. It is given out that Copies of several Letters of mine to you are sent over here to the Ministers, and that their Contents are treasonable, for which I should be prosecuted if Copies could be made Evidence. I am not conscious of any treasonable Intention, and I know that much Violence must be us'd with my Letters before they can be construed into Treason, yet having lately seen two of my Actions, one my Endeavour to lessen the Differences between the two Countries, the other to stop a dangerous Quarrel between Individuals, and which I should have thought and still think to be good Actions, condemn'd as bad ones by high Authority, I am not to wonder if less than a small Lump in my Forehead is voted a Horn. And you will not wonder if my future Letters contain mere Relations of Facts, without any of my Sentiments upon them, which perhaps I have been too forward in offering. With the greatest Respect I have the honour to be, Sir....

In the midst of this political turmoil came a personal blow that Franklin felt almost as keenly as the Stevensons did. He told about it in a letter to Deborah.

London, May 5, 1774

Our Family here is in great Distress. Poor Mrs Hewson has lost her Husband, and Mrs Stevenson her Son-in-law. He died last Sunday Morning of a Fever which baffled the Skill of our best Physicians. He was an excellent young Man, ingenious, industrious, useful, and beloved by all that knew him. She is left with two young Children, and a third soon expected. He was just established in a profitable growing Business, with the best Prospects of bringing up his young Family advantageously. They were a happy Couple!

In America the First Continental Congress met on September 5, 1774, in Philadelphia to discuss the political crisis. In a letter to Thomas Cushing, Franklin reported on the impact that the calling of this assembly, as a demonstration of American unity, had in England.

London, Sept. 3. 1774

It is a long time since I have been favoured by a Line from you. I suppose you thought me on my return to America, & that your Letters would probably not reach me here: But I have been advised by our Friends to stay till the Result of your Congress should arrive. The Coolness, Temper, & Firmness of the American Proceedings; the Unanimity of all the Colonies, in the same Sentiments of their Rights, & of the Injustice offered to Boston; and the Patience with which those Injuries are at Present borne, without the least Appearance of Submission; have a good deal surprized and disappointed our Enemies, and the Tone of Publick Conversation, which has been violently against us, begins evidently to turne; so that I make no doubt that before the meeting of Parliament it will be as general in our Favour. All who know well the State of things here, agree, that if the Non Consumption Agreement should become general, and be firmly adhered to, this Ministry must be ruined, and our Friends succeed them, from whom we may hope a great Constitutional Charter to be confirmed by King, Lords, & Commons, whereby our Liberties shall be recognized and established, as the only sure Foundation of that Union so necessary for our Common welfare. You will see a stronger Opposition in our Favour at the next Meeting of Parliament than appear'd in the last: But as I have said in former Letters, we should depend chiefly upon ourselves.

A few days later, Franklin wrote his last letter—although he did not realize it at the time—to his wife Deborah. Some six months earlier she had suffered a stroke, which had considerably impaired her physically and mentally. Apparently Franklin's son and daughter decided not to tell him about her condition, hoping no doubt that he would soon return, as he had assured William he planned to do. But she died in December, 1774, without seeing her husband again. For some fifteen of their forty-four-year married life, they had been separated.

Deborah Franklin

London, September 10, 1774

It is now nine long Months since I received a Line from my dear Debby. I have supposed it owing to your continual Expectation of my Return; I have feared that some Indisposition had rendered you unable to write; I have imagined any thing rather than admit a Supposition that your kind Attention towards me was abated. And yet when so many other old Friends have dropt a Line to me now and then at a Venture, taking the Chance of its finding me here or not as it might happen, why might I not have expected the same Comfort from you, who used to be so diligent and faithful a Correspondent, as to omit scarce any Opportunity?

The Continental Congress was an extralegal gathering, upon which no royal official could look with favor. It inevitably put a strain on the relationship between Franklin and his son. In the following letter, he was more than a little curt in his discussion of Governor Franklin's alternative suggestion, a congress of royal governors who would mediate the quarrel.

London, Sept. 7, 1774

You say my Presence is wish'd for at the Congress, but no Person besides in America has given me the least Intimation of such a Desire; and it is thought by the great Friends of the Colonies here, that I ought to stay till the Result of the Congress arrives, when my Presence here may be of Use. In my Opinion all depends on the Americans themselves. If they make, & keep firm Resolutions not to consume British Manufactures till their Grievances are redress'd and their Rights acknowledged, this Ministry must fall, and the aggrieving Laws be repeal'd. This is the Opinion of all wise men here.

I hear nothing of the Proposal you have made for a Congress of Governors etc. I do not so much as you do wonder that the Massachusetts have not offered Payment for the Tea: 1. Because of the uncertainty of the Act, which gives them no surety that the Port shall be opened on their making that Payment. 2, no specific Sum is demanded. 3, no one knows what will satisfy the Custom-house Officers, nor who the "others" are, that must be satisfied; nor what will satisfy them. And 4, after all they are in the King's Power, how much of the Port shall be opened. As to "doing Justice before they ask it," that should have been thought of by the Legislature here, before they demanded it of the Bostonians. They have extorted many Thousand Pounds from America uncon-stitutionally, under Colour of Acts of Parliament, and with an armed Force. Of this Money they ought to make Restitution. They might first have taken out Payment for the Tea, &c. and return'd the Rest. But you, who are a thorough Courtier, see every thing with Government Eyes.

It has become almost a historical cliché to picture Franklin as a voice of moderation and compromise. But in these months before the outbreak of the Revolution, he spoke with a voice that was far from temperate. What he had seen and experienced in England enraged him. Most of the time, he was able to mask this rage, but sometimes in letters to intimate correspondents it blazed out. No better example of his fury and his essential toughness exists than this letter to his Boston cousin, Jonathan Williams, Sr.

London, September 28, 1774

Cousin Jonathan showed me last night the Letters he had just received from you and his Mother. The Firmness they express, under your present Difficulties, gave me great Pleasure. The Unanimity and Resolution of the Colonies, astonishes their Enemies here, being totally unexpected. By its Continuance, you will undoubtedly carry all your Points: by giving way you will lose every thing. Strong Chains will be forged for you, and you will be made to pay for both the Iron and the Workmanship. I rejoice to see the Zeal with which your Cause is taken up by the other Colonies. But were they all to desert New England, she ought in my Opinion to hold the same Determination of defending her Rights, even if all Europe were to league with Britain in attempting to enslave her. And I think she would finally succeed; for it is incon-ceivable what a small, virtuous, determined People may affect, with the Blessing of God, in defence of their Liberty, against Millions of Adversaries. History gives us many Instances of this kind.

I did once wish the destroyed Tea to be voluntarily paid for, before this or any compulsory Act should be formed. But now my Opinion is, that you should state an Account, charge Government here with all the Tea Duties, and other unconstitutional Revenue Duties that have been extorted from you by an armed Force under colour of Acts of Parliament, from the Commencement of those Acts; then give Credit for the Tea, and strike a Ballance. If it be against you, offer to pay it. If for you, demand it. . . .

The Cry against America here is greatly abated; new Advocates for her are daily arising. The Manufacturers and Merchants begin to have their Apprehensions, and will soon begin to feel what they apprehend; they will then bestir themselves in Opposition to these absurd Measures. You have only to be firm, united, and persevering.

Hutchinson, I hear, flatters the Ministry with Assurances that you will soon be tired of the Contest and submit, and he is supposed to be well acquainted with your Temper and Meanness of Spirit. . . .

If you should ever tamely submit to the Yoke prepared for you, you cannot conceive how much you will be despised here, even by those who are endeavoring to impose it on you: your very Children and Grandchildren will curse your Memories for entailing Disgrace upon them and theirs; and making them ashamed to own their Country. If you continue on the contrary to make a virtuous, firm and steady Resistance, your very Enemies will honour you, endeavour to reconcile themselves with you, and court your Friendship: and your Friends will almost adore you. Poltroons are neither regarded by Friends or Foes. They are fit only to bear Burthens, and be paid with Contempt. They deserve no better Treatment.

Franklin's London calling card

This brief note, written to Edmund Burke, who was not only a leader of the opposition in Parliament but also agent for New York, succinctly described Franklin's final role in England—ambassador without portfolio for the yet-unformed American nation.

Craven Street, Monday, Dec. 19, 1774
Having just received a Petition from the American Congress to the King, with a Letter directed to the North-American Agents among whom you are named;

this is to request you would be pleased to meet the other Agents to-morrow Noon, at Waghom's Coffeehouse, Westminster, in order to consider the said Letter, and agree upon the time and manner of presenting the Petition.

A letter to Jonathan Shipley revealed Franklin's deep commitment to America. "The Speech" to which he referred was a denunciation of British policy and an unequivocal statement of support for the American cause, which Shipley had made in mid-1774. Franklin had had it printed and widely distributed in both England and America.

London, January 7, 1775

I find it impossible to visit my dear Friend at Twyford.... My Time is totally engrossed by Business.

The Petition from the Congress has been presented to the King by Lord Dartmouth to whom we delivered it for that purpose. The Answer we received was, that his Majesty had been pleased to receive it very graciously, and had commanded him to tell us, "it contained Matters of such Importance that he should as soon as they met lay it before his two Houses of Parliament." We have been advised not to let it be printed till it has been communicated to Parliament as an immediate Publication might be deemed disrespectful to the King. But I inclose a Copy for your Perusal. It will fall short of what you wish in the Manner, not equalling the admirable Remonstrances of the French Parliaments or the *Cour des Aides;* but having made some Allowances for unpolished America, you will not I hope think it much amiss. When I consider that Congress, as consisting of Men, the free, unbiased, unsollicited Choice of the Free-holders of a great Country, selected from no other Motives than the general Opinion of their Wisdom and Integrity, to transact Affairs of the greatest Importance to their Constituents, and indeed of as great Consequence as any that have come under Consideration in any great Council for Ages past; and that they have gone through them with so much Coolness, though under great Provocations to Resentment; so much Firmness, under Cause to apprehend Danger; and so much Unanimity, under every Endeavour to divide and sow Dissensions among them; I cannot but look upon them with great Veneration. And I question whether I should be so proud of any Honour any King could confer upon me, as I am of that

Jonathan Shipley

259

I received by only having my Health drank by that Assembly.

In America, some of Franklin's friends were moving in the opposite political direction. Joseph Galloway had presented a plan of union to the Continental Congress, calling for an American Parliament that would be subordinate to England's Parliament. It was narrowly defeated, six Colonies to five. Deeply offended by this rejection, and by personal attacks on his loyalty, Galloway withdrew from Congress and sent the plan to Franklin, who replied in two letters. The first, on February 5, 1775, was moderate in tone. "I cannot but lament with you the impending calamities Britain and her colonies are about to suffer from great imprudencies on both sides," he said. "Those arising there, are more in your view; these here, which I assure you are very great, in mine." His second letter, written three weeks later, was more critical. It reflected the downward spiral of his last-ditch negotiations with the British Ministry to prevent war.

London, Feb. 25, 1775.

In my last per Falconer I mention'd to you my showing your Plan of Union to Lords Chatham and Camden. I now hear, that you had sent it to Lord Dartmouth. Lord Gower I believe alluded to it, when in the House he censur'd the Congress severely, as first resolving to receive a Plan for uniting the Colonies to the Mother Country, and afterwards rejecting it, and ordering their first Resolution to be eras'd out of their Minutes. Permit me to hint to you, that it is whisper'd here by ministerial People, that yourself and Mr. Jay of New York are Friends to their Measures, and give them private Intelligence of the Views of the Popular or Country Party in America. I do not believe this; but I thought it a Duty of Friendship to acquaint you with the Report.

I have not heard what Objections were made to the Plan in the Congress, nor would I make more than this one, that, when I consider the extream Corruption prevalent among all Orders of Men in this old rotten State, and the glorious publick Virtue so predominant in our rising Country, I cannot but apprehend more Mischief than Benefit from a closer Union. I fear they will drag us after them in all the plundering Wars, which their desperate Circumstances, Injustice, and Rapacity, may prompt them to undertake; and their wide-wasting Prodigality and Profusion is a Gulph that will swallow up every Aid we may distress ourselves to afford them.

Here Numberless and needless Places, enormous

Salaries, Pensions, Perquisites, Bribes, groundless Quarrels, foolish Expeditions, false Accounts or no Accounts, Contracts and Jobbs, devour all Revenue, and produce continual Necessity in the Midst of natural Plenty. I apprehend, therefore, that to unite us intimately will only be to corrupt and poison us also.... However, I would try any thing, and bear any thing that can be borne with Safety to our just Liberties, rather than engage in a War with such near relations, unless compelled to it by dire Necessity in our own Defence.

But, should that Plan be again brought forward, I imagine, that, before establishing the Union, it would be necessary to agree on the following preliminary Articles.

1. The Declaratory Act of Parliament to be repeal'd.

2. All Acts of Parlt, or Parts of Acts, laying Duties on the Colonies to be repeal'd.

3. All Acts of Parlt altering the Charters, or Constitutions, or Laws of any Colony, to be repeal'd.

4. All Acts of Parlt restraining Manufacturers to be repeal'd.

5. Those Parts of the Navigation Acts, which are for the Good of the whole Empire, such as require that Ships in the Trade should be British or Plantation built, and navigated by 3/4 British Subjects, with the Duties necessary for regulating Commerce, to be reënacted by both Parliaments.

6. Then, to induce the Americans to see the regulating Acts faithfully executed, it would be well to give the Duties collected in each Colony to the Treasury of the Colony, and let the Govr and Assembly appoint the Officers to collect them, and proportion their Salaries. Thus the Business will be cheaper and better done, and the Misunderstandings between the two Countries, now created and fomented by the unprincipled Wretches, generally appointed from England, be entirely prevented.

These are hasty Thoughts submitted to your Consideration.

You will see the new Proposal of Lord North, made on Monday last, which I have sent to the Committee. Those in Administration, who are for violent Measures, are said to dislike it. The others rely upon it as a means of *dividing,* and by that means subduing us. But I cannot

Franklin's staunch friend, Edmund Burke, conferred with him about a speech on conciliating the Colonies just before Franklin sailed for home.

conceive that any Colony will undertake to grant a Revenue to a Government, that holds a Sword over their Heads with a Threat to strike the moment they cease to give, or do not give so much as it is pleas'd to expect. In such a Situation, where is the Right of giving our own Property freely, or the Right to judge of our own Ability to give? It seems to me the Language of a Highwayman, who, with a Pistol in your Face, says, "Give me your Purse, and then I will not put my Hand into your Pocket. But give me all your Money, or I will shoot you through the Head."

In clubs and in private homes during his last weeks in England, Franklin heard almost incredible contempt and scorn heaped on America. William Strahan came to him with a story about a Scottish sergeant in Boston who had captured forty American militiamen singlehanded. In a debate in the House of Lords, Franklin heard the spokesman for the Ministry make "base reflections on American courage, religion, understanding &c." Americans were condemned as "the lowest of mankind, and almost of a different species from the English of Britain." Franklin became so angry that he drew up a blazing memorial, which he considered presenting to Lord Dartmouth. It was a fiery attack on the Punitive Acts, in which he demanded "satisfaction" for damage the laws had done to Massachusetts and New England. Friends, such as Thomas Walpole, warned him that it might be considered "a national affront" and persuaded him not to submit it. By this time Franklin had reserved a cabin aboard the Pennsylvania packet and was within a few days of departing. On one of his last days in London, Franklin conferred with Edmund Burke, who was planning to make a major speech on conciliating the Colonies and wanted to take as realistic a position as possible from an American point of view. Throughout these last weeks, Franklin had been negotiating with the Ministry through intermediaries such as his Quaker friend, Dr. John Fothergill. Not long after Burke left Craven Street, Franklin received a letter from the honest doctor urging him to warn Americans—and particularly well-meaning Philadelphia Quakers— "that whatever specious pretenses are offered, (by the Ministry) they are all hollow; and that to get a larger field on which to fatten a herd of worthless parasites is all that is regarded." War was very close and Franklin knew it. On his last day in London he spent several hours with his scientist friend Joseph Priestley, going over newspapers recently arrived from America. Franklin selected articles that might win sympathy for the American cause if they were reprinted in English papers. This last attempt to play the propagandist on America's behalf, a role in which he had tragically failed, overwhelmed him. "He was frequently not able to proceed for the tears literally running down his cheeks," Priestley later said.

Chapter **9**

The Oldest Revolutionary

At sea, en route to Philadelphia, Franklin wrote the longest letter of his life — a ninety-seven-page report detailing his futile attempt to negotiate a reconciliation between England and America. It began with two very significant words: "Dear Son." Nothing underscores more clearly Franklin's growing fear that he and William were on a collision course. When he reached Philadelphia on May 5, 1775, war had already begun. On April 19, fighting had broken out at Lexington and Concord, and the British army was now besieged inside Boston by an impromptu gathering of New England militiamen. The first letter Franklin wrote upon his arrival was also to William. While there is no evidence that they had met by this time, the letter seems to carry on an argument that had already begun. William refused to resign as Royal Governor of New Jersey, claiming that he felt obligated to the Ministry because they had not dismissed him. One thing is evident, Franklin believed that William should have resigned the moment he heard the news about Lexington.

> May 7, 1775.
>
> I don't understand it as any favour to me or to you, the being continued in an office by which, with all your prudence, you cannot void running behind-hand, if you live suitably to your Station. While you are in it I know you will execute it with fidelity to your master, but I think independence more honourable than any service, and that in the state of American Affairs which, from the present arbitrary measures is likely soon to take place, you will find yourself in no comfortable Situation, and perhaps wish you had soon disengaged yourself.

The next letter Franklin wrote was to Joseph Galloway, probably the person — after his son — he most cared about in America. Galloway had been elected to the Second Continental Congress, which was gathering in Philadelphia at this time. But he had declined to serve.

Monday, May 8, 1775

I am much obliged by your kind Congratulations. I am concerned at your Resolution of quitting public Life at a time when your Abilities are so much wanted. I hope you will change that Resolution. I hear my Son is to be at Burlington this day Week to meet his Assembly. I had purposed (if he could not conveniently come hither) to meet him there, and in my Return to visit you at Trevose. I shall know in a Day or two, how that will be. But being impatient to see you, I believe I shall accept the kind Offer of your Carriage, and come to you directly. If I conclude upon that, I shall let you know. At present I am so taken up with People coming in continually, that I cannot stir, and can scarce think what is proper or practicable.

Franklin promptly began communicating with influential friends in England, a practice he continued throughout the war. This letter to Edmund Burke made sarcastic use of the anti-American propaganda that Franklin—and Burke—had heard so often in Parliament.

Philadelphia, May 15, 1775

You will see by the Papers that Gen. Gage call'd his Assembly to propose Lord North's pacific Plan, but before they could meet drew the Sword, and began the War. His Troops made a vigorous Retreat, 20 Miles in 3 Hours, scarce to be parallell'd in History: The feeble Americans, who pelted them all the Way, could scarce keep up with them.

All People here feel themselves much oblig'd by your Endeavours to serve them. I hear your propos'd Resolves were negativ'd by a great Majority; which was denying the most notorious Truths; and a kind of rational Lying, of which they may be convicted by their own Records.

The Congress is met here, pretty full. I had not been here a Day before I was return'd a Member. We din'd together on Saturday, when your Health was among the foremost.

William Temple Franklin had come to America with his grandfather. Meeting his father and stepmother for the first time, the handsome sixteen-year-old charmed and delighted the childless William Franklins. He was soon spending most of his time at the opulent new mansion that the province of New Jersey had had built for Governor Franklin in Perth Amboy. Franklin, busy in the Continental Congress, tried to keep in touch with his grandson by mail. The "young Gentlemen" referred to were Benjamin Franklin Bache and William Bache, Sally's oldest sons.

Philada, June 13, 1775.

My dear Billy,

I wonder'd it was so long before I heard from you. The Packet it seems was brought down to Philadelphia, and carry'd back to Burlington before it came hither. I am glad to learn by your Letters that you are happy in your new Situation, and that tho' you ride out sometimes, you do not neglect your Studies. You are now in that time of Life which is the properest to store your Mind with such Knowledge as is hereafter to be ornamental and useful to you. I confide that you have too much Sense to let the Season slip. The Ancients painted *Opportunity* as an old Man with Wings to his Feet & Shoulders, a great Lock of Hair on the forepart of his Head, but bald behind; whence comes our old Saying, *Take Time by the Forelock*; as much as to say, when it is past, there is no means of pulling it back again; as there is no Lock behind to take hold of for that purpose. —

I am sorry your Things have suffered so much Damage in their Way to you; and I fear if I send the Glass you write for, it may likewise be hurt in the Carriage, as I have no Convenience at present of packing it safely, and the Boatmen and Waggoners are very careless People. If you want to use a Glass, your Father has a better, which he will lend you. But a Perspective Glass is not so good as the Eye for Prospects, because it takes in too small a Field. It is only useful to discern better some particular Objects. So, as I expect you here after the Vacation, to go to the College, I think it best to keep the Glass for you till you come, when you will find it in your Desk and Book Case with your little Beginning of a Library; and I hope about the same time your Books and Things from London will be arrived.

I have received a long Letter from Mrs. Stevenson. It is a kind of Journal for a Month after our Departure, written on different Days, & of different Dates, acquainting me who has call'd, and what is done, with all the small News. In four or five Places, she sends her Love to her dear Boy, hopes he was not very sick at Sea, &c., &c. Mrs. Hewson and the Children were well. She was

Contemporary German engraving of the Battle of Lexington, April 19, 1775.

Greene homestead in Warwick, R.I., where Jane Mecom was sheltered

afraid, she says, to see some of your Friends, not knowing how to excuse your not taking leave of them.

Your shirts will go by to-morrow's Stage. They are in a little Trunk, and I hope will get safe to hand. Mr & Mrs Bache send their Love to you. The young Gentlemen are well and pleas'd with your remembring them. Will has got a little Gun, marches with it, and whistles at the same time by way of Fife. I am ever, Your affectionate Grandfather

B FRANKLIN

The situation in Boston deeply concerned Franklin, from a personal as well as a political point of view. Many of his friends and relatives had been forced to flee into the country as refugees. Of particular concern was the fate of his sister Jane, who was sixty-four and in ill health. He received a letter from her early in June, telling in plaintive terms how she left town with only a few bits of furniture and clothing piled on a wagon. Franklin's old friend Catherine Ray Greene had taken Jane into her Warwick, Rhode Island, home, in spite of the fact that the house was already crowded with other refugee relatives. In the following letter Franklin replied to Jane.

Philada June 17, 1775

I wrote to you some time since, having heard from one of the Delegates that you were at Warwick, and I supposed it must be with that good Family, so I directed my Letter to you there; I hope you receiv'd it. I have since received your kind Letter of May 14. with one from dear Mrs Green. I sympathise most sincerely with you and the People of my native Town & Country. Your Account of the Distresses attending their Removal affects me greatly. I desired you to let me know if you wanted any thing, but have not since heard from you. I think so many People must be a great Burthen to that hospitable House; and I wish you to be other wise provided for as soon as possible, and I wish for the Pleasure of your Company, but I know not how long we may be allowed to continue in Quiet here if I stay here, nor how soon I may be ordered from hence; nor how convenient or inconvenient it may be for you to come hither, leaving your Goods as I suppose you have in Boston. My son tells me he has invited you to Amboy: Perhaps that may be a Retreat less liable to Disturbance than this: God only knows, but you must judge. Let me know however if I can render you any Service; and in what way. You know it will give me Pleasure.

No portrait of Jane is known to exist; reproduced here is the last page of her manuscript "Book of Ages."

On the day Franklin wrote to Jane, the Battle of Bunker Hill was fought on Charlestown Heights outside of Boston. In the course of the battle, the town of Charlestown, a handsome village of about three hundred houses opposite Boston, was almost totally destroyed by hot shot fired from British warships. Bunker Hill aroused new rage in Franklin, and he vented it on his old friend William Strahan, who was bombarding him with letters urging him to play a conciliatory role. In this short, pungent paragraph Franklin summed up—and, perhaps, released—much of his anger. On reflection, he decided not to send the letter. But he later made use of it as a propaganda piece in the newspapers.

Philada July 5, 1775

Mr. Strahan,

You are a Member of Parliament, and one of that Majority which has doomed my Country to Destruction.—You have begun to burn our Towns, and murder our People.—Look upon your Hands! They are stained with the Blood of your Relations!—You and I were long Friends:—You are now my Enemy,—and I am

Yours,

B Franklin

Early in October, Franklin paid his last visit to Massachusetts. But it was not on the peaceful business of postmaster nor to see old friends and relations. The Continental Congress appointed him, Benjamin Harrison of Virginia, and Thomas Lynch of South Carolina to confer with George Washington on reorganizing and supplying the American army. From Washington's headquarters in Cambridge, Franklin wrote to Richard Bache.

Cambridge Headquarters, October 19, 1775

Dear Son

We hear you have had an Alarm at Philadelphia. I hope no ill consequences have attended it. I wonder I had no Line from you. I make no doubt of our People's defending their City and Country bravely, on the most trying Occasions.

I hear nothing yet of Mr Goddard, but suppose he is on the Road. I suppose we shall leave this Place next Week. I shall not return in Company with the other Delegates, as I call for my Sister, and we shall hardly be able to travel so fast, but I expect to be at Philadelphia within a few Days of them.

There has been a plentiful Year here as well as with us: And there are as many chearful Countenances among those who are driven from House and Home at Boston or lost their All at Charlestown, as among other People.

Cartoon of the Battle of Bunker Hill

Not a Murmer has yet been heard, that if they had been less zealous in the Cause of Liberty they might still have enjoyed their Possessions. For my own Part though I am for the most prudent Parsimony of the publick Treasure, I am not terrified by the Expence of this War, should it continue ever so long. A little more Frugality, or a little more Industry in Individuals will with Ease defray it. Suppose it 100,000 £ a Month or 1,200,000 £ a Year: If 500,000 Families will each spend a Shilling a Week less, or earn a Shilling a Week more; or if they will spend 6 pence a Week less and earn 6 pence a Week more, they may pay the whole Sum without otherwise feeling it. Forbearing to drink Tea saves three fourths of the Money; and 500,000 Women doing each threepence Worth of Spinning or Knitting in a Week will pay the rest.* I wish nevertheless most earnestly for Peace, this War being a truly unnatural and mischievous one: but we have nothing to expect from Submission but Slavery, and Contempt. I am ever Your affectionate Father

B. F.

[*Postscript:*] Love to dear Sally and the Children.

PS. Oct. 24.   We purpose setting out homewards tomorrow. Here is a fine healthy Army, wanting nothing but some Improvement in its Officers, which is daily making.

*How much more then may be done by the superior Frugality and Industry of the Men?

Franklin was not the man to remain passive in the face of British attempts to prevent the Americans from getting European aid. Congress appointed him to the Secret Committee of Foreign Correspondence, and since he had more contacts abroad than any other American, he was soon acting as the chairman. In this role, he wrote the instructions for Silas Deane, the first American agent to be sent to Europe.

Philadelphia, March 2, 1776
On your arrival in France you will for some little Time be engaged in the Business of providing goods for the Indian Trade. This will give good Countenance to your appearing in the Character of a Merchant, which we wish you continually to retain among the French in general, it being probable that the Court of France may not like it should be known publickly, that any Agent from the Colonies is in that Country.

When you come to Paris, by delivering Doctor Franklin's

Letters to Monsr Le Roy—and Monsr Dubourg, you will be introduced to a Set of acquaintance, all friends to the American cause. By conversing with them, you will have a good Opportunity of learning the Parisian French and you will find in Monsr. Dubourgh, a Man prudent, faithful, secret, intelligent in Affairs, and capable of giving you very sage advice. It is scarce necessary to pretend any other business at Paris, than the gratifying of that Curiosity which draws Numbers thither yearly, merely to see so famous a City.

With the assistance of Monsr Dubourg, who understands English, you will be able to make immediate Application to Monsr de Vergennes, Minister &c. either personally or by a Letter, if Monsr Dubourg advises that method, acquainting him, that you are in France upon Business for the American Congress in the Character of a Merchant. That having something to communicate to him that may be mutually beneficial to France and the Colonies, you request an Audience of him, and that he would be pleased to appoint the Time and place.

At this Audience, if agreed to, it may be well to show him first your Letter of Credence, and then acquaint him, that the Congress finding that in the common course of Commerce, it was not practicable to furnish the Continent of America with the Quantities of Arms and Ammunition necessary for its defence (the Ministry of Great Britain having been extremely industrious to prevent it) you have been dispatched by their Authority to apply to some European power for a supply.

That France had been pitched on for the first Application, from an Opinion that if we should, (as there is great Appearance we shall) come to a total Separation from Great Britain, France would be looked upon as the Power, whose Friendship it would be fittest for us to obtain and cultivate. That the Commercial Advantages, Britain had enjoyed with the Colonies had contributed greatly to her late Wealth and Importance.

That it is likely great part of our Commerce will naturally fall to the Share of France, especially if she favors us in this Application, as that will be a means of gaining and securing the friendship of the Colonies. And, that as our Trade rapidly increasing with our Increase of People and in a greater proportion, her part of it will be extremely valuable.

First American agent sent to Europe

That the Supply we at present want is Cloathing and Arms for 25,000 Men, with a suitable Quantity of Ammunition, and 100 field pieces. That we mean to pay for the same by Remittances to France, Spain, Portugal and the French Islands, as soon as our Navigation can be protected by ourselves or Friends and that we shall besides want great Quantities of Linens and Woolens, with other Articles for the Indian Trade, which you are now actually purchasing, and for which you ask no Credit; and that the whole (if France should grant the other supplies) would make a Cargoe, which it might be well to secure by a Convoy of two or three Ships of War.

If you should find Monsr. De Vergennes reserved and not inclined to enter into free conversation with you, it may be well to shorten your Visit, request him to consider what you have proposed, acquaint him with your place of lodging; that you may yet stay some time at Paris and that knowing how precious his Time is, you do not presume to ask another Audience.

But that if he should have any Commands for you, you will upon the least Notice, immediately wait upon him.

If at a future Conference, he should be more free and you find a Disposition to favor the Colonies, it may be proper to acquaint him, that they must necessarily in your Opinion be anxious to know the disposition of France on certain points, which with his Permission, you would mention. Such as, whether, if the Colonies should form themselves into an Independent State, France would probably acknowledge them as such, receive their Ambassadors, enter into any Treaty or Alliance with them, for Commerce, or defence, or both? If so, on what principal Conditions? Intimating, that you shall speedily have an Opportunity of sending to America, if you do not immediately return.

And that he may be assured of your fidelity and Secrecy in transmitting carefully any thing he would wish to convey to the Congress on that Subject.

In subsequent Conversations, you may as you find it convenient, enlarge on these Topics that have been the Subject of our Conferences with you, to which you may add occasionally, the well known substantial Answers; we usually give to the several Calumnies thrown out against us.

If these Supplies on the Credit of the Congress should

be refused, you are to endeavor the obtaining a permission of purchasing those Articles, or as much of them, as you can find credit for.

You will keep a daily Journal of all your material Transactions and particularly of what passes in your conversation with great personages; and you will by every safe Opportunity furnish us with such Information, as may be important....

> B. Franklin.
> B. Harrison.
> John Dickinson.
> Robt Morris.
> John Jay.

Congress next sought Franklin's help in a crisis on another front. The American war effort in Canada was faltering. Congress appointed Franklin, Charles Carroll, and Samuel Chase of Maryland to investigate the situation and if possible persuade the French Canadians to support the American cause. En route, Franklin paused to mail an angry letter to another Englishman he knew was sympathetic to the American cause, Anthony Todd, Secretary of the Post Office. The sentence about "Allen and his People, with Lovell," referred to the fate of Ethan Allen, captured with several of his men while assaulting Montreal and shipped to England in chains, and James Lovell, who was imprisoned by the British and taken with them to Halifax when they evacuated Boston.

New York, March 29, 1776

Dear Sir....

How long will the *Insanity* on your side the Water continue? Every day's plundering of our Property and Burning our Habitations, serves but to exasperate and unite us the more: The Breach between you and us grows daily wider and more difficult to heal. Britain without us can grow no stronger; without her we shall become a tenfold greater and mightier people. Do you choose to have so increasing a Nation of Enemies? Do you think it prudent by your Barbarities to fix us in a rooted hatred of your Nation, and make all our innumerable Posterity detest you? Yet this is the way in which you are now proceeding. Our Primers begin to be printed with Cutts of the Burning of Charlestown, of Falmouth, of James-Town, of Norfolk, with the Flight of Women and Children from these defenceless Places, some falling by Shot in their Flight. Allen and his People, with Lovell an amiable Character and a Man

of Letters all in CHAINS on board your Ships;* while
we treat your People that are our Prisoners with the
utmost Kindness and Humanity. Your Ministers may
imagine that we shall soon be tired of this, and submit, but they are mistaken, as you may recollect they
have been hitherto in every Instance, in which I told
you at the time that they were mistaken. And I now
venture to tell you, that though this War may be a long
one (and I think it will probably last beyond my Time)
we shall with God's Help finally get the better of you;
the Consequences I leave to your Imagination....

P.S.   Since writing the above I have been riding round
the Skirts of this Town to view the Works, they are but
lately begun but prodigiously forward, all Ranks of
People working at them as Volunteers with the greatest
Alacrity and without pay, to have them ready for the
Reception of Genl. Howe, who having finished his Visit
to Boston is daily expected here.

What will you do with this Spirit? You can have no
Conception of Merchants and Gentlemen working with
Spades and Wheelbarrows among Porters and Negroes.
I suppose you will scarce believe it.

[*In the margin:*] *Is any body among you weak enough
to imagine that these *Mischiefs* are neither to be paid
for nor be revenged?

The trip to Canada proved to be an exhausting experi-
ence for a man of seventy. Only the hospitality of Philip Schuyler and his
family, first at Albany and then at their country home in Saratoga, enabled
Franklin to survive. For a few days he was so weak that he felt death was
imminent, and he wrote farewell letters, such as this one to Josiah Quincy
of Boston. His son Josiah Quincy, Jr., had visited Franklin in London in late
1774, and had died on the voyage home. The letter is perhaps most interesting because of Franklin's comments on the steady progress toward a declaration of independence in the Continental Congress—progress to which he
lent all his influence, from the day he landed in Philadelphia. "Troublesome
neighbors" was a reference to the British army, which had evacuated Boston
on March 17, 1776.

Saratoga, April 15, 1776.
I am here on my way to Canada, detained by the present
state of the Lakes, in which the unthawed ice obstructs
navigation. I begin to apprehend that I have undertaken
a fatigue, that, at my time of life, may prove too much

for me; so I sit down to write to a few friends by way of farewell.

I congratulate you on the departure of your late troublesome neighbours. I hope your country will now for some time have rest, and that care will be taken so to fortify Boston, as that no force shall be able again to get footing there. Your very kind letter of November 13th, enclosing Lord Chatham's and Lord Camden's speeches, I duly received. I think no one can be more sensible than I am of the favours of corresponding friends, but I find it impossible to answer as I ought. At present I think you will deem me inexcusable, and therefore I will not attempt an apology. But if you should ever happen to be at the same time oppressed with years and business, you may then extenuate a little for your old friend.

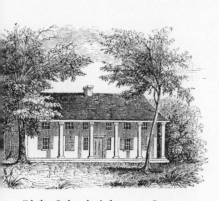

Philip Schuyler's home in Saratoga

LOSSING, *Pictorial Fieldbook of the Revolution*

The notes of the speeches taken by your son, whose loss I shall ever deplore with you, are exceedingly valuable, as being by much the best account preserved of that day's debate.

You ask, "When is the Continental Congress by *general consent* to be formed into a supreme legislature; alliances, defensive and offensive, formed; our ports opened; and a formidable naval force established at the public charge?" I can only answer at present, that nothing seems wanting but that "general consent." The novelty of the thing deters some, the doubt of success, others, the vain hope of reconciliation, many. But our enemies take continually every proper measure to remove these obstacles, and their endeavours are attended with success, since every day furnishes us with new causes of increasing enmity, and new reasons for wishing an eternal separation; so that there is a rapid increase of the formerly small party, who were for an independent government.

Canada was brutally cold and unpleasant, and it was evident to Franklin and his fellow commissioners that the situation was hopeless. The French Canadians had no interest in siding with the Protestant Americans, the British had reinforced Quebec, and the American army was on the brink of disintegration. Franklin left his fellow commissioners to do what they could, and went home. Exhausted and ill, Franklin took little part in the feverish politicking in the Continental Congress that preceded the Declaration of Independence. Gout may not have been the only reason for his nonattendance. On June 17, Governor William Franklin of New Jersey was arrested and arraigned before a committee of the New Jersey

Assembly as "a virulent enemy of this country." Refusing to sign a parole, which would have permitted him to live unmolested on his farm near Burlington, New Jersey, William was sent to jail in Connecticut. Franklin did not, of course, mention his personal embarrassment in this letter to George Washington.

> Philadelphia, June 21. 76
>
> I am much obliged by your kind Care of my unfortunate Letter, which at last came safe to Hand. —I see in it a Detail of the Mighty Force we are threatened with; which however I think is not certain will ever arrive; and I see more certainly the Ruin of Britain if she persists in such expensive distant Expeditions, which will probably prove more disastrous to her than anciently her Wars in the Holy Land. —
>
> I return Gen. Sulivan's Letter enclos'd: Am glad to find him in such Spirits. —and that the Canadians are returning to their regard for us. —I am just recovering from a severe Fit of the Gout, which has kept me from Congress & Company almost ever since you left us, so that I know little of what has pass'd there, except that a Declaration of Independence is preparing.

Although Franklin was a member of the committee directed to prepare a declaration of independence, he changed only a few minor words in Jefferson's draft. There is no clear historical evidence that he said, as he signed it, "We must all hang together, or we will all hang separately." But the tradition is a strong one, and the expression was current in Congress at the time. Not many days after the Declaration was voted, Franklin received a letter from Richard Lord Howe, who had come to America in the dual role of peace commissioner and commander in chief of the British navy. His brother, General Sir William Howe, was in command of the British army. Lord Howe had been one of the unofficial spokesmen for the Government in the fruitless negotiations Franklin conducted in London to prevent the war. In America, Howe declared the purpose of his mission was the "establishment of lasting peace and union with the colonies." He hoped the "deep-rooted prejudices of America, and the necessity of preventing her trade from passing into foreign channels" would not "keep us still a divided people." Franklin's tough reply was not calculated to raise his Lordship's hopes.

> Philadelphia, July 30th, 1776.
>
> My Lord,
>
> I receiv'd safe the Letters your Lordship so kindly forwarded to me, and beg you to accept my thanks.
>
> The official dispatches, to which you refer me, contain

nothing more than what we had seen in the Act of Parliament, viz. Offers of Pardon upon Submission, which I was sorry to find, as it must give your Lordship Pain to be sent upon so fruitless a Business.

Directing Pardons to be offered to the Colonies, who are the very Parties injured, expresses indeed that Opinion of our Ignorance, Baseness, and Insensibility, which your uninform'd and proud Nation has long been pleased to entertain of us; but it can have no other effect than that of increasing our Resentments. It is impossible we should think of Submission to a Government, that has with the most wanton Barbarity and Cruelty burnt our defenceless Towns in the midst of Winter, excited the Savages to massacre our Peacefull Farmers, and our Slaves to murder their Masters, and is even now bringing foreign Mercenaries to deluge our Settlements with Blood. These atrocious Injuries have extinguished every remaining Spark of Affection for that Parent Country we once held so dear; but, were it possible for *us* to forget and forgive them, it is not possible for *you* (I mean the British Nation) to forgive the People you have so heavily injured. You can never confide again in those as Fellow Subjects, and permit them to enjoy equal Freedom, to whom you know you have given such just Cause of lasting Enmity. And this must impel you, were we again under your Government, to endeavour the breaking our Spirit by the severest Tyranny, and obstructing, by every Means in your Power, our growing Strength and Prosperity.

But your Lordship mentions "the King's paternal solicitude of promoting the Establishment of lasting *Peace* and Union with the Colonies." If by Peace is here meant a Peace to be entered into between Britain and America, as distinct States now at War, and his Majesty has given your Lordship Powers to treat with us of such a Peace, I may venture to say, though without Authority, that I think a Treaty for that purpose not yet quite impracticable, before we enter into foreign Alliances. But I am persuaded you have no such Powers. Your nation, though, by punishing those American Governors, who have fomented the Discord, rebuilding our burnt Towns, and repairing as far as possible the mischiefs done us, might yet recover a great Share of our Regard, and the greatest Part of

Lord Howe by H. Singleton

Center section of the State House in Philadelphia, as it looked when Congress was in session during 1776

our growing Commerce, with all the Advantage of that additional Strength to be derived from a Friendship with us; but I know too well her abounding Pride and deficient Wisdom, to believe she will ever take such salutary Measures. Her Fondness for Conquest, as a warlike Nation, her lust of Dominion, as an ambitious one, and her wish for a gainful Monopoly, as a commercial One, (none of them legitimate Causes of war,) will all join to hide from her Eyes every view of her true Interests, and continually goad her on in those ruinous distant Expeditions, so destructive both of Lives and Treasure, that must prove as pernicious to her in the End, as the Crusades formerly were to most of the Nations in Europe.

I have not the Vanity, my Lord, to think of intimidating by thus predicting the Effects of this War; for I know it will in England have the Fate of all my former Predictions, not to be believed till the Event shall verify it.

Long did I endeavour, with unfeigned and unwearied Zeal, to preserve from breaking that fine and noble China Vase, the British Empire; for I knew, that, being once broken, the separate Parts could not retain even their Shares of the Strength and Value that existed in the Whole, and that a perfect Reunion of those Parts could scarce ever be hoped for. Your Lordship may possibly remember the tears of Joy that wet my Cheek, when, at your good Sister's in London, you once gave me Expectations that a Reconciliation might soon take Place. I had the Misfortune to find those Expectations disappointed, and to be treated as the Cause of the Mischief I was laboring to prevent. My Consolation under that groundless and malevolent Treatment was, that I retained the Friendship of many wise and good Men in that country, and, among the rest, some Share in the Regard of Lord Howe.

The well-founded Esteem, and, permit me to say, Affection, which I shall always have for your Lordship, makes it Painful to me to see you engaged in conducting a War, the great Ground of which, as expressed in your Letter, is "the necessity of preventing the American trade from passing into foreign Channels." To me it seems, that neither the Obtaining or Retaining of any trade, how valuable soever, is an Object for which men may justly spill each other's Blood; that the true and sure Means of extending and securing Commerce is the goodness and Cheapness of Commodities; and that the profit of no trade can ever be equal to the Expence of compelling it, and holding it, by Fleets and Armies.

I consider this War against us, therefore, as both unjust and unwise; and I am persuaded, that cool, dispassionate Posterity will condemn to Infamy those who advised it; and that even Success will not save from some Degree of Dishonor those, who voluntarily engaged to Conduct it. I know your great motive in coming hither was the hope of being Instrumental in a Reconciliation; and I believe, when you find *that* to be impossible on any Terms given you to propose, you will relinquish so odious a Command, and return to a more honourable private Station.

With her husband in jail, Elizabeth Franklin wrote tearful letters to Temple, in Philadelphia, telling how the local American troops were abusing her and plundering the Governor's property. Temple received permission from his grandfather to visit his stepmother. Meanwhile the British army, in their campaign to seize New York, was moving toward a clash with George Washington's Americans. A battle began on Long Island at dawn on the day that Franklin wrote this letter. The "dear little Girl" Franklin mentions was Sally Bache's short-lived fourth child, born December 1, 1775.

Philadelphia, August 27, 1776

Dear Grandson

Your Letter acquainting us with your safe Arrival was very agreable to us all. But as you are near the Scene of Action, we wish to hear from you by every Post, and to have all the News. It will cost you but little Trouble to write, and will give us much Satisfaction.

The Family has been in great Grief, from the Loss of our dear little Girl. She suffer'd much: but is now at Rest. Will is to come home to-morrow; he will help to comfort us.

Give my Love to your Mother, and let me know what you hear from your Father.

I am, Your affectionate Grand Father

B FRANKLIN

[*Postscript:*] Say how you spend your time; I hope in some Improvement.

All sorts of requests and calls for help from soldiers and citizens rained in upon Franklin. In Congress, meanwhile, he struggled in vain to persuade his fellow Americans to make the compromises necessary to create a confederacy. Yet he remained optimistic. As he wrote this letter to Anthony Wayne, replying to his request for aid for the Pennsylvania troops stationed at Ticonderoga, Franklin did not know that by this time the American army on Long Island had been badly beaten and driven into its entrenchments on Brooklyn Heights.

Philadelphia, August 28, 1776

I have received two of your Favours, which were immediately communicated to the Board of War, who are in Committee of Congress appointed to take Care of every thing in that Department, and who will I make no doubt take the necessary Measures for supplying your Wants. But as America is new in the Business of Providing for Armies, there must be for a time Deficiencies that are very inconvenient to the Troops, and which Experience only can bring us into the Mode of Preventing. I am pleas'd to find your People bear them with a Soldierly Spirit, and I hope they will soon be remedied.

A general Action is every day expected at New York. If the Enemy is beaten, it will probably be decisive as to them; for they can hardly produce such another Armament for another Campaign: But our growing Country can bear considerable Losses, and recover them, so that a Defeat on our part will not by any means occasion our giving up the Cause. Much depends on the Bravery of you who are posted at Ticonderoga. If you prevent the Junction of the two Armies, their Project for this Year will be broken, the Credit of the British Arms thro'out Europe and of the Ministry in England will be demolish'd, and the Nation grow sick of the Contest.

I am much oblig'd by your Draft of the Situation of our Troops, and of the Defences. I pray heartily for your Success, not doubting you will deserve it.

The greatest Unanimity continues in the Congress. The Convention of this Province is sitting, engag'd in framing a new Government. The greatest Part of our Militia are in New Jersey. Arms and Ammunition are daily arriving, the French Government having resolv'd to wink at the Supplying of us: So that in another Year our People throughout the Continent will be both better arm'd and better disciplin'd, as most of them will have some Experience of a Camp Life and actual Service.

Meanwhile, Franklin had to cope with a loyalist uprising in his own family. William Temple Franklin asked for permission to visit his father, to carry a letter from his stepmother to him. This did not justify the trip in Franklin's opinion. Temple apparently wrote a rather angry reply to his grandfather, defending his projected trip and showing the strong influence of his loyalist stepmother. In his reply, Franklin tried to avoid a quarrel. Jonathan Trumbull was chief executive of Connecticut.

Philada Sept. 22. 1776

Dear Grandson,

You are mistaken in imagining that I am apprehensive of your carrying dangerous Intelligence to your Father; for while he remains where he is, he could make no use of it were you to know and acquaint him with all that passes. You would have been more in the right if you would have suspected me of a little tender Concern for your Welfare, on Acct of the Length of the Journey, your Youth and Inexperience, the Number of Sick returning on that Road with the Infectious Camp Distemper, which makes the Beds unsafe, together with the Loss of Time in your Studies, of which I fear you begin to grow tired. To send you on such a Journey merely to avoid the being oblig'd to Govr Trumbull for so small a Favour as the forwarding a Letter, seems to me inconsistent with your Mothers usual Prudence. I rather think the Project takes its rise from your own Inclination to a Ramble, & Disinclination for Returning to College, join'd with a Desire I do not blame of seeing a Father you have so much Reason to love, — They send to me from the Office for my Letter, so I cannot add more than to acquaint you, I shall by next post if desired send several Frank'd Covers directed to Govr Trumbull, for Mrs. F. to use as she has occasion. I write to him in the first now sent, to introduce her Request. She may desire her Husband to send his Letters to her under Cover to me. It will make but 2 Days odds. The Family is well & join in Love to her & you,

Your affectionate Grandfather

B Franklin

Franklin's friend Josiah Wedgwood, an American sympathizer, made these three medallions of Franklin (left, above), his son William, and his grandson William Temple (above).

Six days later, Franklin wrote a cryptic note to Temple, which settled the unspoken argument about the young man's political destiny. The "something offering" was the opportunity to accompany Franklin to France as his secretary. The Congress had appointed Franklin, Silas Deane, and Thomas Jefferson (later replaced by Arthur Lee) commissioners to negotiate a treaty of alliance with France.

Philadelphia, September 28, 1776

Dear Temple,

I hope you will return hither immediately, and that your Mother will make no Objection to it, something offering here that will be much to your Advantage if you are not out of the Way. I am so hurried that I can only add Ever your affectionate Grandfather.

B FRANKLIN

[Postscript:] My Love to her.

On the eve of Franklin's departure for France, the prospects for America's future seemed grim. Washington's army had suffered two serious defeats at New York and had abandoned the city. Congress was in disarray, unable to agree on articles of confederation, because the small states feared the power of the large states. Yet Franklin remained undaunted. As a last gesture of defiance and determination, he pledged his property in Philadelphia and raised four thousand pounds, which he lent to Congress. On the day before he sailed, he wrote the following letter to an unknown correspondent, probably in Boston. The fragment of the letter was later communicated to the Massachusetts Council.

Philadelphia, October 25, 1776

BEING once more ordered to Europe, and to embark this day, I write this line, etc.

As to our public affairs, I hope our people will keep up their courage. I have no doubt of their finally succeeding by the blessing of God, nor have I any doubt that so good a cause will fail of that blessing. It is computed that we have already taken a million sterling from the enemy. They must soon be sick of their piratical project. No time should be lost in fortifying three or four posts on our extended coast as strong as art and expense can make them. Nothing will give us greater weight and importance in the eyes of the commercial states than a conviction that we can annoy, on occasion, their trade and carry our prizes into safe harbours; and whatever expense we are at in such fortifying will be soon repaid by the encouragement and success of privateering.

Chapter **10**

Bonhomme Richard

In spite of the optimistic reports that Franklin had received while he was in America, the mood of the French Government was far from the whole-hearted support that the American Revolution so desperately needed. The French people instinctively sympathized with the Americans, but King Louis XVI and many of his advisers feared that France lacked the financial resources to fight a war with England. They espoused a wait-and-see policy. If the Americans successfully resisted the English, and made it clear they were an ally worth having in a war, France would consider joining them. Franklin had barely landed in the little fishing village of Auray, than he went to work to convince the French that the Americans were more than holding their own. This letter was written to Barbeu Dubourg, translator of many of Franklin's writings.

Auray in Brittany, December 4, 1776.
My dear good friend will be much surprised to receive a letter from me dated in France, when neither of us had been expecting such a thing. I left Philadelphia the 26th of October, on a vessel of war, belonging to Congress, and in thirty days dropped anchor in Quiberon Bay. On our voyage we captured two British vessels and brought them with us. Our ship is destined for Nantes, but the wind being unfavourable to entering the Loire, we waited some days in Quiberon Bay, until becoming impatient to put my feet on land, I availed myself of a boat to get here, whence I shall go by land to Nantes, where I shall probably rest for a few days. Learning that the post leaves here this evening, I seize the opportunity to salute you, as well as my dear Madame Dubourg and Mesdlles. Prehesson and Basseport, whom I hope soon to have the pleasure of finding in good health.

The port of Auray, where Franklin landed on his arrival in France

I suppose that Messrs. Deane and Morris have the honour of being known to you, and as I do not know their address, I take the liberty of addressing each of them a word under your cover, and beg you to transmit it to them. I shall see to the reimbursement of your expenses.

I see that you have had bad news of our affairs in America, but they are not true. The British, with the assistance of their ships, have gained a footing in two islands, but they have not extended their foothold on the continent, where we hold them at a respectful distance. Our armies were one or two miles apart when I left, and both entrenched. In different skirmishes which had occurred lately between parties of five hundred and a thousand men on each side, we have always had the advantage, and have driven them from the field with loss, our fire being more destructive than theirs. On the sea we have seriously molested their commerce, taking large numbers of their ships in the West Indies, which are daily brought to our ports. But I do not care to dwell upon these subjects until I shall have the pleasure of seeing you.

Franklin had brought with him not only William Temple Franklin, but also Sally's son, seven-year-old Benjamin Franklin Bache. In a journal Franklin kept of their trip, most of which has been lost, he recorded the journey from Auray to Nantes in the following words: "The carriage was a miserable one, with tired horses, the evening dark, scarce a traveler but ourselves on the road; and to make it more *comfortable,* the driver stopped near a wood we were to pass through, to tell us that a gang of eighteen robbers infested that wood, who but two weeks ago had robbed and murdered some travelers on that very spot." In Nantes Franklin wrote to Silas Deane, who had been in Paris more than six months, working for the American Government.

Nantes, December 7, 1776

I wrote a Line to you on Wednesday last, from Auray (where I landed out of the Ship of War that brought me over) acquainting you with my Arrival and with our Appointment (jointly with Mr Arthur Lee) to negotiate a Treaty of Commerce and Friendship with the Court of France, for which I have with me ample Instructions. I have acquainted no one here with this Commission, continuing incog. as to my publick Character; because not being sufficiently acquainted with the Disposition and present Circumstances of this Court, relative to our

Contest with GB. I cannot judge whether it would be agreable to her at this time to receive publickly Ministers from the Congress as such, and I think we should not embarras her unnecessarily on the one hand, nor subject ourselves to the Hazard of a disgraceful Refusal on the other. I therefore send you herewith a Copy of our Commission, that you may have time to consider and advise upon it before my Arrival at Paris, for which Place I shall set out as soon as I can, being oblig'd to wait here a little for my Baggage, which continues on board the Ship, and the Wind has not yet been favourable to bring her from Quiberon Bay into this River. We are impowered by a Vote of Congress, to live in such a Stile at Paris, as we shall find proper. A Cargo, suppos'd to the Value of 3000£ Sterling brought in the Ship with me is to be sold by our Merchants here, and the Produce is to be subject to the Drafts of the Commissioners towards their Expences. And the Committee have Orders to add to the Fund, till they make it up 10,000 £. *I requested you to provide me a Lodging. If in the same Hotel with you, it will be the more agreable.* I have with me two Grandsons; one about 16, who will serve me as a private Secretary; the other a Child of 7, whom I purpose to place in some Boarding School, that he may early learn the French Language. One Bed in the meantime may serve them both; but I must have them in the same Lodging with me till I can place the young one. M. Penet talks of accompanying me to Paris. I suppose we may set out about the Middle of next Week, but cannot be certain, because it depends on my receiving my Baggage, and that depends on the Winds. In the mean time it would be a vast Satisfaction to me to hear from you, or meet you, but I do not see how it can be manag'd.

The Count de Vergennes

Soon settled in the Hôtel de Hambourg with Silas Deane Franklin lost no time going to work on his diplomatic business. The first letter was to the French Foreign Minister, the Count de Vergennes, the second to the Committee of Secret Correspondence.

Paris, December 23, 1776.

I beg leave to acquaint your Excellency that we are appointed and fully empowered by the Congress of the United States of America to propose and negotiate a treaty of amity and commerce between France and the United States. The just and generous treatment their trading ships have received by a free admission into the ports of this kingdom, with other considerations of respect, has induced the Congress to make this offer first to France. We request an audience of your Excellency, wherein we may have an opportunity of presenting our credentials, and we flatter ourselves that the propositions we are authorized to make are such as will not be found unacceptable.

 With the greatest regard, we have the honour to be,

Your Excellency's most obedient

and most humble servants,

B FRANKLIN,

SILAS DEANE,

ARTHUR LEE.

Arthur Lee by John Trumbull

Paris, January 4, 1777

I arrived here about two weeks since, where I found Mr. Deane. Mr. Lee has since joined us from London. We have had an Audience of the Minister Count De Vergennes, and were respectfully received. We left for his consideration a sketch of the proposed treaty. We are to wait upon him to-morrow with a strong memorial, requesting the aids mentioned in our instructions. By his advice, we had an Interview with the Spanish ambassador, Count d'Aranda, who seems well disposed towards us, and will forward copies of our memorials to his court, which will act, he says, in perfect concert with this. Their fleets are said to be in fine order, manned and fit for the sea. The cry of this nation is for us, but the court, it is thought, views an approaching war with reluctance. The press continues in England. As soon as we can receive a positive answer from these courts we shall despatch an express with it.

At the same time, Franklin did not forget his friends. One of the first letters he wrote to England went to Polly Stevenson Hewson. The marten fur cap was an item that Franklin had picked up on his trip to Canada. He wore it in Paris, partly because a scalp irritation made wearing a wig uncomfortable. Another, stronger reason was the striking effect it had on the Parisians, who regarded it as an example of American simplicity and boldness. For a Frenchman, defiance of fashion was the height of courage. It was for such shrewd propaganda strokes—and the popularity of his book, *The Way to Wealth*—that Franklin became known throughout France as Bonhomme Richard.

Paris, Jan. 12, 1777

My dear, dear Polly,

Figure to yourself an old Man, with grey Hair Appearing under a Martin Fur Cap, among the Powder'd Heads of Paris. It is this odd Figure that salutes you, with handfuls of Blessings on you and your dear little ones.

On my Arrival here, Mlle. Biheron gave me great Pleasure in the Perusal of a Letter from you to her. It acquainted me that you and yours were well in August last. I have with me here my young Grandson, Benja. Franklin Bache, a special good Boy. I give him a little French Language and Address, and then send him over to pay his Respects to Miss Hewson. My Love to all that love you, particularly to dear Polly. I am ever, my dear Friend, your affectionate

B Franklin

P.S.   Temple, who attends me here, presents his Respects. I must contrive to get you to America. I want all my Friends out of that wicked Country. I have just seen in the Papers 7 Paragraphs about me, of which 6 were Lies.

A few days later, Franklin said farewell to that English dream that had absorbed so much of his time and attention—the western colony. In this letter to Thomas Walpole, he also seized the opportunity to do a little propagandizing with that influential Englishman, who was in close touch with many leading politicians. Major Trent was William Trent, one of the American partners in the Grand Ohio Company.

Paris, January 12, 1777

I left Major Trent well. He had Thoughts of applying to Congress relating to the Lands of our Purchase, but was dissuaded by Mr Galloway. I had some Information that Virginia, which claims all the Crown Lands within its Boundary, will not dispute that Purchase with us, but expects the Purchase-Money to be paid into their Treasury. It may be long before these Matters can be adjusted; and longer still before we shall see Peace. Had Lord Chatham's first wise Motion for withdrawing the Troops, been attended to by your mad Ministry; or his Plan of Accommodation been accepted and carried into Execution, all this Mischief might have been prevented. If that great Man be yet living, I pray you to present my affectionate Respects to him, and also to Lord Camden.

As the Money I left with your good Brother cannot now be of any Use to me in England, I request a Letter of

Credit for the Amount on some Banker here: I mean the Money for my two Shares.

About this time Franklin wrote a less important but more interesting letter to Julianna Ritchie, wife of Philadelphia merchant William Ritchie. Writing from Cambrai, where she was living as a governess to five wealthy young Englishwomen who were studying in France, she had warned Franklin that he was surrounded by spies—which was nothing less than the truth. Franklin's reply reveals his keen insight into the nature of his mission. He had already seen that the more the British learned about the French Government's clandestine aid to America, the more likely they were to declare war on France.

Paris, Jan. 19, 1777.

I am much oblig'd to you for your kind Attention to my Welfare in the Information you give me. I have no doubt of its being well founded. But as it is impossible to discover in every case the Falsity of pretended Friends who would know our Affairs; and more so to prevent being watch'd by Spies, when interested People may think proper to place them for that Purpose; I have long observ'd one Rule which prevents any Inconvenience from such Practices. It is simply this, to be concern'd in no Affairs that I should blush to have made publick, and to do nothing but what Spies may see & welcome. When a Man's Actions are just & honourable, the more they are known, the more his Reputation is increas'd & establish'd. If I was sure therefore that my Valet de Place was a Spy, as probably he is, I think I should not discharge him for that, if in other Respects I lik'd him. The various Conjectures you mention concerning my Business here must have their Course. They amuse those that make them, & some of those that hear them; they do me no harm, and therefore it is not necessary that I should take the least Pains to rectify them.

A few days later, Franklin wrote in a far sterner tone to Joseph Priestley. The "Fix'd Air" to which he referred was oxygen, which Priestley had discovered in 1772.

Paris, Jan. 27, 1777.

I received your very kind Letter of Feby last, some time in September. Major Carleton, who was so kind as to forward it to me, had not an Opportunity of doing it sooner. I rejoice to hear of your continual Progress in those useful Discoveries; I find that you have set all the

Philosophers of Europe at Work upon Fix'd Air; and it is with great Pleasure I observe how high you stand in their Opinion; for I enjoy my Friends' fame as my own.

The Hint you gave me jocularly, that you did not quite despair of the Philosopher's Stone, draws from me a Request, that, when you have found it, you will take care to lose it again; for I believe in my conscience, that Mankind are wicked enough to continue slaughtering one another as long as they can find Money to pay the Butchers. But, of all the Wars in my time, this on the part of England appears to me the wickedest; having no Cause but Malice against Liberty, and the Jealousy of Commerce. And I think the Crime seems likely to meet with its proper Punishment; a total loss of her own Liberty, and the Destruction of her own Commerce.

I suppose you would like to know something of the state of Affairs in America. In all Probability we shall be much stronger the next campaign than we were in the last; better arm'd, better disciplin'd, and with more Ammunition. When I was at the camp before Boston, the Army had not 5 Rounds of Powder a Man. This was kept a Secret even from our People. The World wonder'd that we so seldom fir'd a Cannon; we could not afford it; but we now make Powder in Plenty.

To me it seems, as it has always done, that this War must end in our favour, and in the Ruin of Britain, if she does not speedily put an end to it. An English Gentleman here the other day, in Company with some French, remarked, that it was folly in France not to make War immediately; *And in England,* reply'd one of them, *not to make Peace.*

Do not believe the reports you hear of our internal Divisions. We are, I believe, as much united as any People ever were, and as firmly.

Meanwhile, Franklin kept the pressure on the French. This letter, signed by the three American commissioners, was aimed at forcing France to abandon its policy of watchful waiting. The promise of no separate peace exceeded the commissioners' instructions from Congress, but they had jointly decided it was worth the risk.

Paris, Feb. 2d. 1777.

It is considered that in the present situation of things at the Courts of France and Spain, we find no probability of obtaining any effectual aid, alliance or declaration of war against Great Britain, without the following stipulation; therefore

We the Commissioners plenipotentiary from the Congress of the United States of America, are unanimously of Opinion, that if France and Spain should conclude a Treaty of Amity and Commerce with our States, and enter into a War with Great Britain in consequence of that, or of open aid given to our States; it will be right and proper for us, or in absence of the others, for any one of us, to stipulate and agree that the United States shall not separately conclude a Peace, nor aid Great Britain against France or Spain, nor intermit their best exertions against Great Britain during the continuance of such War. Provided always that France and Spain, do on their part enter into a similar stipulation, with our States.

Good news from America—Washington's Christmas Day victory at Trenton—inspired Franklin to reach for his pen and write one of his best satires, directed at the British policy of hiring Hessians. It was addressed from the Count de Schaumbergh to the Baron Hohendorf, commanding the Hessian troops in America.

Rome, February 18, 1777.
On my return from Naples, I received at Rome your letter of the 27th December of last year. I have learned with unspeakable pleasure the courage our troops exhibited at Trenton, and you cannot imagine my joy on being told that of the 1950 Hessians engaged in the fight, but 345 escaped. There were just 1605 men killed, and I cannot sufficiently commend your prudence in sending an exact list of the dead to my minister in London. This precaution was the more necessary, as the report sent to the English ministry does not give but 1455 dead. This would make 483,450 florins instead of 643,500 which I am entitled to demand under our convention. You will comprehend the prejudice which such an error would work in my finances, and I do not doubt you will take the necessary pains to prove that Lord North's list is false and yours correct.

The court of London objects that there were a hundred wounded who ought not to be included in the list, nor paid for as dead; but I trust you will not overlook my instructions to you on quitting Cassel, and that you will not have tried by human succor to recall the life of the unfortunates whose days could not be lengthened but by the loss of a leg or an arm. That would be making them a

BOTH: ANNE S. K. BROWN MILITARY COLLECTION

pernicious present, and I am sure they would rather die than live in a condition no longer fit for any service. I do not mean by this that you should assassinate them; we should be humane, my dear Baron, but you may insinuate to the surgeons with entire propriety that a crippled man is a reproach to their profession, and that there is no wiser course than to let every one of them die when he ceases to be fit to fight.

I am about to send to you some new recruits. Don't economize them. Remember glory before all things. Glory is true wealth. There is nothing degrades the soldier like the love of money. He must care only for honour and reputation, but this reputation must be acquired in the midst of dangers. A battle gained without costing the conqueror any blood is an inglorious success, while the conquered cover themselves with glory by perishing with their arms in their hands. Do you remember that of the 300 Lacedaemonians who defended the defile of Thermopylae, not one returned? How happy should I be could I say the same of my brave Hessians!

It is true that their king, Leonidas, perished with them: but things have changed, and it is no longer the custom for princes of the empire to go and fight in America for a cause with which they have no concern. And besides, to whom should they pay the thirty guineas per man if I did not stay in Europe to receive them? Then, it is necessary also that I be ready to send recruits to replace the men you lose. For this purpose I must return to Hesse. It is true, grown men are becoming scarce there, but I will send you boys. Besides, the scarcer the commodity the higher the price.

Above and opposite, groups of Hessian soldiers in America

Requests for letters of recommendation from Frenchmen eager to try their luck in America were a constant torment to Franklin. In a cooler moment, Franklin attacked the problem with humor and wrote one of his more famous compositions, "Model of a Letter of Recommendation of a Person You Are Unacquainted With." Temple Franklin says that his grandfather actually used it several times in France to shame persons who were making especially indiscreet applications.

Paris, April 2, 1777.

The bearer of this, who is going to America, presses me to give him a Letter of Recommendation, tho' I know nothing of him, not even his name. This may seem extraordinary, but I assure you it is not uncommon here.

Sometimes, indeed one unknown Person brings another equally unknown, to recommend him; and sometimes they recommend one another! As to this Gentleman, I must refer you to himself for his Character and Merits, with which he is certainly better acquainted than I can possibly be. I recommend him however to those Civilities, which every Stranger, of whom one knows no Harm, has a Right to; and I request you will do him all the good Offices, and show him all the Favour that, on further Acquaintance, you shall find him to deserve.

The British, in their vexation and frustration with the Americans, refused to treat captives—especially men captured at sea from American warships and privateers—as prisoners of war. Instead, they crowded them into wretched prisons, threatened them with transportation to British colonies in Asia and Africa, and then cynically offered them the opportunity of volunteering to fight aboard British ships. Franklin protested this treatment in a blazing letter to the British Ambassador Lord Stormont. Stormont returned the letter with a note: "The King's ambassador receives no letters from rebels but when they come to implore His Majesty's mercy."

Paris, April 2, 1777.

We did ourselves the Honour of writing some time since to your Lordship on the Subject of Exchanging Prisoners. You did not condescend to give us any Answer, and therefore we expect none to this. We however take the Liberty of sending you Copies of certain Depositions which we shall transmit to Congress whereby it will be known to your Court that the United States are not unacquainted with the barbarous Treatment their People receive when they have the Misfortune of being your Prisoners here in Europe. And that if your Conduct towards us is not altered it is not unlikely that severe Reprisals may be thought justifiable from the Necessity of putting some Check to such abominable Practices. For the sake of Humanity it is to be wish'd that Men would endeavour to alleviate as much as possible the unavoidable Misseries attending a State of War. It has been said that among the civilized Nations of Europe the ancient Horrors of that State are much diminished. But the Compelling Men by Chains, Stripes & Famine to fight against their Friends and Relations, is a new Mode of Barbarity which your Nation alone has the Honour of inventing. And the sending American Prisoners of War to Africa and Asia remote from all Probability of Exchange and where they can scarce hope ever to hear from their Families even if the Unwholesomeness of the Climate does not put a speedy End to their Lives, is a manner of treating Captives that you can justify by no Precedent or Custom except that of the black Savages of Guinea.

Benjamin Vaughan, a young Englishman who was a close friend of Lord Shelburne and other opposition politicians, became the first of many Englishmen to attempt to persuade Franklin to discuss peace terms. In this letter, Franklin suggested an inconspicuous place to meet.

[Paris] Thursday, September 18, 1777

I shall be very happy to see my dear Friend if it may be without Inconvenience to him; and the sooner the happier. The Duke de Chaulnes, who was with me last Night, has ask'd me to dine with him on Sunday, when he expected you: But that is a long time for me to wait; And I cannot think of another Place where a Meeting with me would not occasion Speculation. Yes: There is *les Bains de Poitevin* a large white wooden Building upon a Boat in the River opposite to the Tuilleries. You may go there in a Hackney Coach; and you will find me there at Six in the Evening precisely. The People know me only by Sight as I go there often to bathe. Ask for an old Englishman with grey Hair.

With all his problems and duties, Franklin did not forget his favorite correspondents, such as his sister Jane. This letter supplies us with a charming description of his new residence, the Hôtel de Valentinois in the village of Passy, outside Paris on the Seine, and of his life there.

Passy, near Paris, Oct. 5, 1777

I enjoy here an exceeding good State of Health. I live in a fine airy House upon a Hill, which has a large Garden with fine Walks in it, about ½ an hours Drive from the City of Paris. I walk a little every Day in the Garden, have a good Appetite & sleep well. I think the French Cookery agrees with me better than the English; I suppose because there is little or no Butter in their sauces: for I have never once had the Heartburn since my being here tho' I eat heartily, which shows that my Digestion is good. I have got into a good Neighborhood, of very agreable People who appear very fond of me; at least they are pleasingly civil: so that upon the whole I live as comfortably as a Man can well do so far from his Home and his Family.

Franklin's grandson Benjamin Franklin Bache made this drawing of the Hôtel de Valentinois.

In the fall of 1777, the news from America was almost all bad. One British army, commanded by General John Burgoyne, was advancing down the lakes from Canada, and had captured the key fortress of Fort Ticonderoga. Another British army, commanded by Sir William Howe, after beating Washington at Brandywine Creek, had moved against Philadelphia. The city fell shortly thereafter—especially bitter news for Franklin. Not only was most of his property in the city, but his family, including his sister Jane Mecom, was there too. Then, on December 4, came the best possible news, brought by Jonathan Loring Austin of Boston. Burgoyne and his entire army had been captured at Saratoga. Franklin immediately prepared the following announcement, translated here from the French, to be circulated throughout Paris.

[Paris, December 4, 1777]

Mail arrived from Philadelphia at Dr. Franklin's home in Passy after 34 days.

On October 14th Bourgoyne had to lay down his arms, 9200 men killed or taken prisoner.

The terms of surrender were brought with Gates.

Besides the General, 4 members of the English Parliament were among the prisoners.

They left Howe in Philadelphia, where he is imprisoned.

All communication with his fleet is cut off.

17 of his ships which wanted to approach were destroyed or captured.

Washington with his army, other generals with detached forces and militia are surrounding the city. General Gates and his victorious army are coming to join them.

Contemporary German engraving of the surrender of General Burgoyne

Franklin's next logical move was to increase the diplomatic pressure on France. The following letter to Vergennes, signed by the three commissioners, but written by Franklin, did that job very neatly.

Passy, December 8, 1777

The Commissioners from the Congress of the United States of America, beg leave to represent to your Excellency, that it is near a year since they had the Honour of putting into your Hands the Propositions of the Congress for a Treaty of Amity and Commerce with this Kingdom, to which, with sundry other Propositions contained in subsequent Memorials, requesting the Aid of Ships of War, and offering Engagements to unite the Forces of the said States with those of France and Spain in acting against the Dominions of Great Britain, and to make no Peace but in Conjunction with those Courts, if Britain should declare War with them; to all which they have yet received no determinate Answer; and apprehending that a Continuance of this State of Uncertainty with regard to those Propositions, together with the Reports that must soon be spread in America of rigorous Treatment met with by our Armed Ships in the Ports of these Kingdoms, may give Advantage to our Enemies in making ill Impressions on the Minds of our People, who, from the Secrecy enjoyn'd us, cannot be informed of the Friendly and essential Aids that have been so generously but privately afforded us; the Commissioners conceive, that, the present Circumstances considered, the compleating such a Treaty at this Time would have the most happy Effect, in raising the Credit of the United States abroad, and strengthening their Resolutions at Home; as well as discouraging their internal Enemies, and confirming their Friends that might otherwise waver: And the Commissioners are further of Opinion that the Aid of Ships desired might at this Juncture be employed to great Advantage in America; which when honour'd with a Conference they could more particularly explain. They therefore request your Excellency most earnestly to resume the Consideration of those Affairs, and appoint them some speedy Day of Audience thereupon.

They also pray that their grateful Acknowledgements may be presented to the King for the additional Aid of three Millions which he has been so graciously pleased to promise them; and that his Majesty may be assured whatever Engagements they may enter into in behalf of the United States, in pursuance of the full Powers they are vested with, will be executed with the most punctual Good Faith by the Congress, who believing their Interests to be the same, and that a secure Increase of the Commerce, Wealth and Strength of France and Spain will be one Consequence of their Success in this Contest, wish for nothing so much, after establishing their own Liberty, as a firm and everlasting Union with these Nations.

Simultaneously, Franklin was supplying his friends in England with information that would, he hoped, bring down the North Ministry and make a negotiated peace possible. The following letter to Thomas Walpole had such a political purpose, evident in the postscript. The medallion

Franklin made this charming sketch of one of the neighboring gardens that he enjoyed while in Passy.

Franklin mentioned was distributed by the thousands across France as part of the propaganda campaign to popularize the American cause. "Dr. B." is Edward Bancroft, the secretary to the American mission, a Connecticut-born physician who spent most of his life in London. He was at the same time on the British payroll as a spy. But as this letter makes clear, he also contributed in a modest way to the American cause.

> Paris, December 11, 1777
>
> I am sorry Lord Chatham's Motion for a Cessation of Arms, was not agreed to. Every thing seems to be rejected by your mad Politicians that would lead to Healing the Breach; and every thing done that can tend to make it everlasting....
>
> From a Sketch Dr. B. had which was drawn by your ingenious and valuable Son, they have made here Medaillons in *terre cuit*. A Dozen have been presented to me, and I think he has a Right to one of them. Please deliver it to him with my Compliments.
>
> With the greatest Esteem and Respect I am ever Dear Sir, Your most obedient humble Servant
>
> B FRANKLIN
>
> [*Postscript:*] My sincere Respects if you please to your noble Friends, Lords Chatham and Cambden.
> Blessed are the Peacemakers.

The French responded positively to Franklin's pressure, and an enormous diplomatic victory seemed to be in sight. At the same time, ironically, Franklin was forced in this letter to Robert Morris to reveal for the first time the mounting acrimony within the American mission in Paris. The "five of us in this City" included the three commissioners—himself, Silas Deane, and Arthur Lee; Arthur's brother William Lee, who had been appointed the commercial agent for the Americans in France; and Ralph Izard, a wealthy South Carolinian who had been appointed Ambassador to Tuscany and was in Paris, awaiting permission to enter the country to which he was accredited. Izard tended to side with the two Lees against Franklin and Deane.

> Paris, December 21, 1777
>
> I remember that long before I was ordered here, you once did me the Honour to say, you should not dislike being sent to France with me. Since my being here, I have frequently wish'd that Appointment had taken place. I think I should have pass'd my time more comfortably. We are now five of us in this City, all honest and capable Men (if I may include myself in that Description) and all meaning well for the Public but our

Medallion of Franklin made by Jean Baptiste Nini, after a sketch done by the son of Thomas Walpole

Tempers do not suit, and we are got into Disputes and Contentions that are not to our Credit, and which I have sometimes feared would go to Extremes. You know the natural Disposition of some of us, how jealous, how captious, how suspicious even of real Friends, and how positive, after suspecting a while, that the Suspicions are certain Truths, *"Confirmations strong, as Proofs from holy Writ."* You will therefore, I am persuaded, if Complaints of one another should come to your hands, make due Allowance for such Tempers, and suffer no Man to be condemn'd unheard. I do not write thus on my own Account, as I am not apprehensive of your receiving any Complaints of me; for tho' it is difficult to live in peace with such Characters, how much soever one esteems them for the Virtues and Abilities they otherwise possess, I have however done it tolerably hitherto; but as I am not sure it can last, I wish most sincerely that we were separated; for our being together seems of no Use, and, as we hinted formerly in a joint Letter, is attended with many Inconveniencies. Such Inconveniencies being formerly experienced by other States, is, I suppose, the Reason, that no Power in Europe, for a Century past, has sent more than one Person to one Court. Possibly this desirable Event may soon take place; for if France and Spain acknowledge us as independent States, the other Courts will follow, and receive our Envoys.

I have the Pleasure to assure you, that all Europe is of our side except the King of England and his Placemen and Pensioners, Contractors and Expecters. There is however a furious Ferment in his Parliament about his Measures; and if you could be fortunate enough to treat Howe as you have done Burgoyne, he would be in danger of two *old Houses* falling on his Head.

The British Ministry, learning through spies such as Edward Bancroft that a treaty with France was imminent, launched a peace offensive of its own, sending Paul Wentworth, chief of the British Secret Service in France, to find out from Franklin if he would accept anything short of independence as peace terms. Franklin toyed with Wentworth, inviting him to dinner and letting him argue his case for more than two hours. Then he told the spy that America was prepared to fight fifty years for independence. Franklin had passed along previous British peace offers to the French Government. He said nothing about Wentworth's visit, although he knew that French spies would instantly report it to the Count de

Vergennes. The French had been hesitating about completing the negotiations for the treaty of alliance and commerce, because Spain declined to join them. Now, they reacted with alarmed alacrity. The French Undersecretary for Foreign Affairs, Conrad Alexandre Gérard, met with Franklin, Deane, and Lee at Deane's lodgings in Paris. Franklin wrote out the following response to Gérard's question. Gérard glanced at it and quietly informed them the King had given his word—the treaty would be signed.

January 8, 1778

Question,   What is necessary to be done to give such Satisfaction to the American Commissioners, as to engage them not to listen to any Propositions from England for a new Connection with that Country?

Answer,   The Commissioners have long since propos'd a Treaty of Amity and Commerce, which is not yet concluded: the immediate Conclusion of that Treaty will remove the Uncertainty they are under with regard to it, and give them such a Reliance on the Friendship of France, as to reject firmly all Propositions made to them of Peace from England, which have not for their Basis the entire Freedom and Independence of America, both in Matters of Government and Commerce.

British spy Edward Bancroft

While the details of the treaty were being worked out with the French, Franklin had to cope with the mounting personal feuds inside the American mission. Ralph Izard was particularly troublesome, feeling that Franklin should have consulted him about certain clauses in the treaty that concerned the trade of the southern states with the French West Indies. Franklin cut him down with the following letter.

Passy, Jan. 29, 1778

I received yours late last Evening. Present Circumstances which I will explain to you when I have the Honr of seeing you, prevent my giving it a full Answer now. The Reasons you offer had before been all under Consideration; but I must submit to remain some days under the Opinion you appear to have form'd not only of my poor Understanding in the general Interests of America, but of my Defects in Sincerity, Politeness & Attention to your Instructions. These offences I flatter myself will admit of fair Excuses [or rather will be found not to have existed]. You mention, that you *feel yourself hurt*. Permit me to offer you a Maxim, which has thro' Life been of Use to me & may be so to you in preventing such imaginary Hurts. It is, always to *suppose* one's Friends *may be right* till one *finds* them wrong; rather than *to suppose them wrong* till one *finds* them right. You have heard and imagined all that can be said or suppos'd on one side of the Question, but not on the other.

The British continued to attempt to stave off the Franco-American alliance. James Hutton, an old Craven Street neighbor of Franklin's ("My Lord Hutton" of *The Craven Street Gazette)* and a leading member of the Moravian Church, visited Franklin in France, no doubt at the instigation of British politicians, to see whether Franklin would discuss peace informally with him. In a letter to Hutton, Franklin opened a campaign to force the British to surrender, as the price of peace, considerably more than the territory ruled by the Thirteen Colonies in revolt.

Passy, February 1, 1778.

You desired, that if I had no Propositions to make, I would at least give my Advice. I think it is Ariosto who says, that all things lost on Earth are to be found in the Moon; on which somebody remarked, that there must be a great deal of good Advice in the Moon. If so, there is a good deal of mine, formerly given and lost in this Business. I will, however, at your Request give a little more, but without the least Expectation that it will be followed; for none but God can at the same time give good Counsel, and Wisdom to make use of it.

You have lost by this mad War, and the Barbarity with which it has been carried on, not only the Government and Commerce of America, and the public Revenues and private Wealth arising from that Commerce, but what is more, you have lost the Esteem, Respect, Friendship, and Affection of all that great and growing People, who consider you at present, and whose Posterity will consider you, as the worst and wickedest Nation upon Earth. A Peace you may undoubtedly obtain by dropping all your Pretensions to govern us; and, by your superior skill in huckstering negotiation, you may possibly make such an apparently advantageous Treaty as shall be applauded in your Parliament; but, if you do not, with the Peace, recover the Affections of that People, it will not be a lasting nor a profitable one, nor will it afford you any part of that Strength, which you once had by your Union with them, and might (if you had been wise enough to take Advice) have still retained.

To recover their Respect and Affection, you must tread back the Steps you have taken. Instead of honouring and rewarding the American Advisers and Pro-

Conrad Alexandre Gérard, French Undersecretary for Foreign Affairs

moters of this War, you should disgrace them; with all those who have inflamed the Nation against America by their malicious Writings; and all the Ministers and Generals who have prosecuted the War with such Inhumanity. This would show a national change of Disposition of what had passed.

In proposing terms, you should not only grant such as the Necessity of your Affairs may evidently oblige you to grant, but such additional ones as may show your Generosity, and thereby demonstrate your good Will. For instance, perhaps you might, by your Treaty, retain all Canada, Nova Scotia and the Floridas. But if you would have a real friendly as well as able Ally in America, and avoid all occasions of future Discord, which will otherwise be continually arising on your American Frontiers, you should throw in those Countries. And you may call it, if you please, an Indemnification for the needless and cruel burning of their Towns, which Indemnification will otherwise be some time or other demanded.

I know your People can not see the Utility of such Measures, and will never follow them, and even call it Insolence and Impudence in me to mention them. I have, however, complied with your Desire, and am, as ever, your affectionate friend,

B FRANKLIN

Engraving of David Hartley,
after a portrait by George Romney

David Hartley was a member of Parliament who had acted on Franklin's plea and laid out money to relieve the distresses of American prisoners in England. Franklin opened this letter by thanking him; but then, in the second paragraph he went on to far more important matters. The day after he wrote this letter, Franklin signed the treaty of alliance and commerce with France. The "certain Person" to whom he referred may have been Lord North, or more probably Lord Chatham, the one man with prestige enough to organize significant opposition to the North Ministry. Insistence on complete control and a refusal to make any political arrangements with allies were Chatham's most notable traits—and they considerably lessened his effectiveness as an English politician.

[Paris,] February 5, 1778

I am exceedingly obliged by your interesting yourself so warmly in behalf of those unhappy people. I understand you advanc'd money: Your bills on that account will be punctually paid. As yet I have heard of none.

Understanding that a certain Person promised to make

proposals for healing a certain Breach, I postpon'd and delayed a material operation till I shou'd hear what those proposals were. I am now told that he will not make them till he finds it in his power to do what he pleases. Therefore Adieu my dear friend; and I bid you all *Good Night.*

On February 6, in the office of the Ministry of Foreign Affairs, Franklin, Deane, and Lee signed the treaty of alliance and commerce with France. The treaty was to have been signed on February 5, but it had been put off because Gérard, the French negotiator, had a cold. On both days, the Americans noticed that Franklin wore the same suit he had worn the day that Wedderburn had abused him at the Cockpit. They asked him why, and he smiled and said, "To give it a little revenge." Panicked, the North Ministry now pushed through Parliament two conciliatory bills that gave the Americans everything that Franklin had demanded in his peace negotiations in 1775. But they were hedged with provisos and qualifications to make them palatable to members of Parliament who wanted to fight to the finish. In this letter to Hartley, Franklin tore the peace proposals apart. Perhaps the most significant part of the letter, however, is the postscript. Once more, Franklin was making it clear that if the North Ministry were to be replaced, peace would be possible.

The 1778 treaty with France, bearing the signatures of Franklin, Deane, and Lee

Passy, Feb. 26, 1778.

I receiv'd yours of the 18th and 20th of this Month, with Lord North's proposed Bills. The more I see of the Ideas and Projects of your Ministry, and their little Arts and Schemes of amusing and dividing us, the more I admire the prudent, manly, and magnanimous Propositions contained in your intended Motion for an Address to the King. What Reliance can we have on an Act expressing itself to be only a Declaration of the *Intention* of Parliament concerning the *Exercise* of the Right of imposing Taxes in America, when, in the Bill itself, as well as in the Title, a Right is suppos'd and claimed, which never existed; and a *present Intention* only is declared not to use it, which may be changed by another Act next Session, with a Preamble, that this *Intention* being found inexpedient, it is thought proper to repeal this Act, and resume the Exercise of *the Right* in its full Extent? If any solid permanent Benefit was intended by this, why is it confin'd to the Colonies of North America, and not extended to the loyal ones in the Sugar Islands? But it is now needless to criticise, as all Acts that suppose your future Government of the Colonies can be no longer significant.

Porcelain statuette of Louis XVI and Franklin, commemorating the signing of the treaty of alliance

In the Act for appointing Commissioners, instead of full Powers to agree upon Terms of Peace and Friendship, with a Promise of ratifying such Treaty as they shall make in pursuance of those Powers, it is declared that their Agreements shall have no force nor Effect, nor be carried into Execution till approved of by Parliament, so that every thing of Importance will be uncertain. But they are allow'd to proclaim a Cessation of Arms, and revoke their Proclamation, as soon as in confidence of it, our Militia have been allowed to go home: They may suspend the Operation of Acts, prohibiting Trade; and take off the Suspension when our Merchants, in consequence of it have been induc'd to send their Ships to Sea; in short, they may do every thing that can have a Tendency to divide and distract us, but nothing that can afford us Security. Indeed, Sir, your Ministers do not yet know us. We may not be quite so cunning as they; but we have really more Sense as well as more Courage than they have ever been willing to give us Credit for: And I am persuaded that these Acts will rather obstruct Peace than promote it, and that they will not in America answer the mischievous and malevolent Ends for which they were intended. In England they may indeed amuse the Public Creditors, give Hopes and Expectations, that shall be of some present use, and continue the Mismanagers a little longer in their Places. *Voilà tout!*

In return for your repeated Advice to us, not to conclude any Treaty with the House of Bourbon, permit me to give (through you) a little Advice to the Whigs in England. Let nothing induce them to join with the Tories, in supporting and continuing this wicked War against the Whigs of America, whose Assistance they may hereafter want to secure their own Liberties, or whose Country they may be glad to retire to for the Enjoyment of them.

If Peace by a Treaty with America, upon equal Terms were really desired, your Commissioners need not go there for it; supposing that as they are impower'd by the Bill "to treat with such Person or Persons, as in their Wisdom and Discretion they shall think meet," they should happen to conceive, that the Commissioners at Paris might be included in that Description. I am ever, dear Sir, &c.

B FRANKLIN

P.S. Seriously, on further thoughts, I am of opinion, that, if wise and honest men, such as Sir George Saville, the Bishop of St. Asaph, and yourself, were to come over here immediately with powers to treat, you might not only obtain peace with America, but prevent a war with France.

To help English credit sink a little faster, Franklin, the previous year, had composed the following catechism relating to the British national debt.

[Paris, spring or summer, 1777?]

Question 1.   Supposing this debt to be only one hundred and ninety-five millions of pounds sterling at present, although it is much more, and that was all to be counted in shillings, that a man could count at the rate of one hundred shillings per minute, for twelve hours each day, till he has counted the whole, how long would he take in doing it?

Answer.   One hundred forty-eight years, one hundred nine days, and twenty-two hours.

Q.   2.   The whole of this sum being three thousand nine hundred millions of shillings, and the coinage standard being sixty-two in the Troy pound, what is the whole weight of this sum?

A.   Sixty-one millions, seven hundred fifty-two thousand, four hundred and seventy-six Troy pounds.

Q.   3.   How many ships would carry this weight, suppose one hundred tons each?

A.   Three hundred and fourteen ships.

Q.   4.   How many carts would carry this weight, suppose a ton in each?

A.   Thirty-one thousand, four hundred and fifty-two carts.

Q.   5.   The breadth of a shilling being one inch, if all these shillings were laid in a straight line, close to one another's edges, how long would that line be that would contain them?

A.   Sixty-one thousand, five hundred fifty-two miles; which is nine thousand, five hundred seventy-two miles more than twice round the whole circumference of the earth.

Q.   6.   Suppose the interest of this debt to be three and a half per cent per annum, what does the whole annual interest amount to?

A. Six millions, seven hundred and seventy thousand pounds.

Q. 7. How doth government raise this interest annually?

A. By taxing those who lent the principal, and others.

Q. 8. When will government be able to pay the principal?

A. When there is more money in England's treasury than there is in all Europe.

Q. 9. And when will that be?

A. Never.

Franklin discussed the French alliance and other matters in more homely fashion in this charming letter to Catherine Ray Greene.

Paris, Feb. 28, 1778.

My dear old Friend

Don't be offended at the Word *old;* I don't mean to call you an *old Woman;* it relates only to the Age of our Friendship; which on my part has always been a sincerely affectionate one, and I flatter myself the same on yours.

I received your kind Letter from Boston of Oct. 28. which gave me great Pleasure, as it inform'd me of the Welfare of you and your Family. I continue hearty, as do my two Grandsons, who present their Respects to you & Mr. Greene, being pleas'd with your Remembrance of them. We are all glad to hear of Ray, for we all love him. —I have been often much concern'd for my Friends at Warwick, hearing that the Enemy was so near them. I hope your Troubles will not be of much longer Duration: For tho' the Wickedness of the English Court, & its Malice against us is as great as ever, its Horns are shortened; its Strength diminishes daily; and we have formed an Alliance here, & shall form others, that will help to keep the Bull quiet and make him orderly. —I chat, you see as usual, any how, with you, who are kind enough never to *criticise* Improprieties in my Compositions or anything else. —I see by yours that my Sisters granddaughter is married. I wish the young Folks joy and Lasting Happiness. I pity my poor old Sister, to be so harassed & driven about by the enemy. For I feel a little myself the Inconvenience of being driven about by my friends. —I live here in great Respect and dine every day with great folks; but I still long for home & for

Liberté des Etats - Unis reconnue par la France.
février 1778.

Le Docteur Francklin & les Américains, recevant le Traité d'Alliance où leur liberté est reconnue.

In this French woodcut, the King gives Franklin and the Americans a paper on which is written "Liberty."

Repose; and should be happy to eat Indian Pudding in your Company & under your hospitable Roof.

Silas Deane became a political problem. Unstable and contentious, he was almost too ready to quarrel with the Lees and Ralph Izard. Both sides sought supporters in the Continental Congress. Finally Congress, distressed by the feud and alarmed at its potential harm to the American cause, recalled Deane to answer charges made by William and Arthur Lee that he had stolen millions from the money advanced to the United States by France. Franklin sent Deane on his way with the following letter of almost unqualified support, addressed to the president of the Continental Congress, Henry Laurens.

> Passy, near Paris, March 31, 1778.
> My colleague, Mr. Deane, being recall'd by Congress, and no Reasons given that have yet appear'd here, it is apprehended to be the Effect of some Misrepresentations from an Enemy or two at Paris or at Nantes. I have no doubt, that he will be able clearly to justify himself; but, having lived intimately with him now fifteen months, the greatest part of the time in the same House, and been a constant Witness of his public Conduct, I cannot omit giving this Testimony, tho' unask'd, in his Behalf, that I esteem him a faithful, active, and able Minister, who, to my knowledge, has done in various ways great and important Service to his Country, whose Interests I wish may always, by every one in her employ, be as much and as effectually promoted.

Arthur Lee became incensed when he discovered that Conrad Alexander Gérard had been appointed an ambassador to America and was to be escorted to Philadelphia by Deane, who would thus be traveling in an atmosphere of triumph. Lee declared himself insulted and blamed Franklin. He got the following reply.

> Passy, April 3, 1778
> It is true I have omitted answering some of your Letters. I do not like to answer angry Letters. I hate Disputes. I am old, cannot have long to live, have much to do and no time for Altercation. If I have often receiv'd and borne your Magisterial Snubbings and Rebukes without Reply, ascribe it to the right Causes, my Concern for the Honour & Success of our Mission, which would be hurt by our Quarrelling, my Love of Peace, my Respect for your good Qualities, and my Pity of your Sick Mind, which is forever tormenting itself, with its Jealousies, Suspicions &

Fancies that others mean you ill, wrong you, or fail in Respect for you.—If you do not cure your self of this Temper it will end in Insanity, of which it is the Symptomatick Forerunner, as I have seen in several Instances. God preserve you from so terrible an Evil: and for his sake pray suffer me to live in quiet.

A few days later, Franklin sent the following letter to Deane, who was waiting at Toulon to sail to America. "The Negociator" was William Pulteney, a member of Parliament sent by George III and Lord North with secret proposals for peace.

Passy, April 7, 1778

I have had a long and very angry Letter from Mr Lee, about your going without acquainting him with it, in which his Disorder seems to encrease, for he raves not only against you and me, but seems to resent the Court's sending a Minister to Congress without advising with him. I bear all his Rebukes with Patience, for the Good of the Service: but it goes a little hard with me.

The Negociator is gone back apparently much chagrin'd at his little Success. I have promis'd him faithfully that since his Propositions could not be accepted they should be buried in Oblivion. I therefore desire earnestly that you would put that Paper immediately in the Fire on the Receipt of this, without taking or suffering to be taken any Copy of it, or communicating its Contents.

At one point during these tense months, David Hartley warned Franklin that he was possibly in danger of being assassinated by British Government agents. "If tempestuous hours should come, take care of your own safety; events are uncertain, & men may be capricious," wrote Hartley. This was Franklin's reply.

[Passy, April, 1778]

I thank you for your kind caution, but having nearly finished a long life, I set but little value on what remains of it. Like a draper, when one chaffers with him for a remnant, I am ready to say, "As it is only the fag end, I will not differ with you about it; take it for what you please." Perhaps the best use such an old fellow can be put to, is to make a martyr of him.

While acting as America's chief spokesman in France, Franklin was also the unofficial admiral of the American navy in European waters. In this letter to John Paul Jones—following the thirty-year-old captain's sensationally successful twenty-eight-day foray in British home waters aboard the *Ranger* the previous April—the American minister discussed a variety of naval affairs.

Passy, June 10, 1778.

In consequence of the high Opinion the Minister of the Marine has of your Conduct and Bravery, it is now settled (observe, that this is to be a Secret between us, I being expressly enjoin'd not to communicate it to any other Person, not even to the other Gentlemen,) that you are to have the Frigate from Holland, which actually belongs to Government, and will be furnished with as many good French Seamen as you shall require. But you are to act under Congress' commission. As you may like to have a Number of Americans, and your own are homesick, it is proposed to give you as many as you can engage out of two hundred Prisoners, which the Ministry of Britain have at length agreed to give us in Exchange for those you have in your hands. They propose to make the exchange at Calais, where they are to bring the Americans. Nothing is wanting to this, but a List of yours, containing their Names and Rank; immediately on the Receipt of which, an equal Number are to be prepared and sent in a ship to that Port, where yours are to meet them. Pray send this List by the Return of the Post if possible. If by this means you can get a good new Crew, I think it will be best that you are quite free of the old, for a Mixture might introduce the Infection of that Sickness you complain of. But this may be left to your Discretion.

Perhaps we shall join you with the *Providence*, Captain Whipple, a new Continental Ship of 30 Guns, which in coming out of the river of Providence gave the two frigates that were posted to intercept her each of them so heavy a Dose of her 18 and 12 pounders, that they had not the courage, or were not able, to pursue her. The *Boston* is suppos'd to be gone from Bordeaux.

It seems to be desired by those concern'd in your future Ship that you should step up to Versailles, (where one will meet you,) in order to such a Settlement of Matters and Plans with those who have the Direction, as cannot well be done by Letter. I wish it may be convenient to you to do it directly. The project of giving you the Command of this Ship pleases me the more, as it is a probable Opening to the higher Preferment you so justly merit.

Franklin helped plan John Paul Jones's expedition in 1779, leading to America's first major naval victory.

John Adams replaced Silas Deane as American commissioner. From Franklin's point of view it was not the best possible change. Adams was temperamentally inclined to side with Arthur Lee, who had the backing in Congress of many New Englanders, in particular, Samuel Adams. But even Adams was appalled by Lee's manner and conduct. He was equally displeased by Franklin's easygoing style of running his side of the mission. Temple Franklin was not a very diligent private secretary. Many details, particularly on the accounting side, were left undone. Adams proposed to reorganize procedures. Franklin, eager to placate him, heartily concurred in this soothing letter.

Passy, Saturday, Sept. 26, 1778

I very much approve your Plan with regard to our future Accounts and wish it to be followed.

The Accounts that have been shown you, are only those of the Person we had entrusted with the receiving and paying our Money; and intended merely to show how he was discharged of it. We are to separate from that Account the Articles for which Congress should be charged, and those for which we should give Credit.

It has always been my Intention to pay for the Education of my Children, their Clothes &c. as well as for Books and other Things for my private Use; and whatever I spend in this Way, I shall give Congress Credit for, to be deducted out of the Allowance they have promis'd us. But as the Article of Clothes for ourselves here is necessarily much higher than if we were not in public Service, I submit it to your Consideration whether that Article ought not to be reckoned among Expences for the Publick. I know I had Clothes enough at home to have lasted me my Lifetime in a Country where I was under small Necessity of following new Fashions.

John Adams by Charles Willson Peale

INDEPENDENCE NATIONAL HISTORICAL PARK

American prisoners in England were never far from Franklin's mind. When several of them in Forton Prison charged in a bitter letter that American commissioners in France were guilty of neglect and indifference, Franklin immediately replied.

Passy, October 20, 1778

I have just received yours of the 2d. Instant. I beg that you will be assured that your long Detention, is not owing to any Neglect of you by the Commissioners. Our first Applications for exchanging you, were haughtily rejected. You were at that time consider'd as Rebels, committed for High Treason, who could only be delivered by course of Law. We then did every thing in our Power to make

Map of Plymouth showing the Old French Prison, where American captives were interned

your situation as comfortable as possible. When Time and Circumstances produced a Disposition to consider you in a more favourable light, we proposed that on your being all discharg'd, we would give up all we had here, and an Order to receive the Ballance of the number in America; this was refused, but good Mr. Hartley has finally by long solicitation obtain'd an Agreement of the Lords of the Admiralty to an exchange of Man for Man, and the Pass required for a Cartel Ship to bring over as many of you as we have here to give in Return, was sent to England in September. The Execution has been delay'd 'till a precise List could be sent of our Number. Of this we have only been a few days informed. By this Post I have written a Letter to Mr. Hartley, which I hope will remove that difficulty, and that those who have been longest in confinement to the number of 250. at least from the two Prisons of Forton and Plymouth will now soon be at liberty. Nothing in the Power of the Commissioners will be wanting to liberate the rest as soon as possible, for the Sufferings of so many of our brave Countrymen, affect us very sensibly.

A good idea of how Franklin's fame attracted to him people from all walks of French life, from high-level diplomats to crackpot would-be scientists, is provided by this fragment from a lost journal that he kept during 1778.

Passy, Sunday, December 13, 1778. A.M.
A man came to tell me he has invented a Machine, which would go of itself, without the help of a Spring, Weight, Air, Water, or any of the Elements, or the Labour of Man or Beast; and with force sufficient to work four Machines for cutting Tobacco; that he had experienc'd it, would shew it me if I would come to his House, and would sell the Secret of it for Two hundred Louis. I doubted it, but promis'd to go to him in order to see it.

A Monsieur Coder came with a Proposition in Writing, to levy 600 Men to be employ'd in landing on the Coast of England and Scotland, to burn and ransom Towns and Villages, in order to put a stop to the English proceeding in that Way in America. I thanked him, and told him I could not approve it, nor had I any Money at Command for such Purposes. Moreover that it would not be permitted by the Government here.

A Man came with a Request that I would patronize and

recommend to Government an Invention he had, whereby a Hussar might so conceal his arms and [habiliments], with Provision for 24 Hours, as to appear a common Traveller, by which Means a considerable Body might be admitted into a Town, one at a time unsuspected, and afterwards assembling, surprize it. I told him I was not a Military Man, of course no Judge of such Matters, and advised him to apply to the *Bureau de la Guerre.* He said he had no Friends and, so could procure no Attention. — The number of wild Schemes propos'd to me is so great, and they have heretofore taken so much of my time, that I begin to reject all, tho' possibly *some* of them may be worth Notice.

Received a parcel from an unknown Philosopher who submits to my Consideration a Memoir on the Subject of *Elementary fire,* containing Experiments in a dark Chamber. It seems to be well written, and is in English, with a little Tincture of French Idiom. I wish to see the Experiments, without which I cannot well judge of it.

The continuing acrimony in the American mission, and the angry debate that exploded in Congress over the charges against Silas Deane, convinced most Americans that there should be only one representative for the United States in France. The choice of Franklin was a foregone conclusion. In this letter, he informed the Count de Vergennes of his new title. The Count d'Estaing was the commander of the French fleet in American waters.

Passy, February 14, 1779.

I have the honour to acquaint your Excellency that I have received from the Congress their appointment to be their minister plenipotentiary at this Court, together with a letter of credence to be presented to his Majesty. I beg thereupon your Excellency's advice and direction.

I have need also of your counsel with regard to the trial and punishment of some conspirators on board our frigate, the *Alliance,* which is just arrived. I would have done myself the honour of waiting on your Excellency today, but am not quite well enough to go abroad in such weather.

I have received a number of letters from America, all expressing the highest esteem for the Count d'Estaing and the Marquis de la Fayette. As I think they will give you and M. de Sartine some pleasure, I send you the originals, praying only to have them returned.

As his comment on the *Alliance* suggests, Franklin's new title also meant that he now bore on his shoulders all the woes and worries of the American mission in France, from buying supplies to directing privateers and warships to maintaining good relations with the French. Nevertheless, he found time for the problems that had concerned him earlier, particularly the welfare of prisoners. In this letter, he replied to a group of British and Irish captives, notably one John Walsh, who had written to him complaining of harsh treatment.

Americans escaping from a British prison ship, nineteenth-century view

Passy March 2d. 1779.

I am sorry to understand by your Memorial of the 16. Past, which came to hand but Yesterday, that you are still in that uncomfortable Situation on board the Brigantine in Brest Road, having understood that Orders had been long since given for taking you on Shore. I write again this Day to the Minister of the Marine, to obtain a Renewal of those Orders; and I hope in consequence that you will soon be better accommodated. I imagine the Delay has been in Part occasioned by the constant Expectations given us from England, of sending over a Cartel Ship with a Number of Americans to exchange for you. The Passport for that Ship was sent from hence in September last: And we have been told from time to time these 3 Months past, that a Ship was actually taken up and victual'd for that Service; but as yet she has not appear'd. I shall be glad to receive the Account you mention of the Provisions that have been afforded to you. It was always the Desire and Intention of the Commissioners here that you should be well treated.

As the war dragged on, American finances became more and more disorganized. The paper money that Congress had printed in vast quantities began to depreciate sharply. Obtaining additional financing from France became one of Franklin's primary concerns, as this letter to Vergennes demonstrated. Ferdinand Grand was the Americans' banker in France.

Passy, March 9, 1779

It is with great Reluctance that I give your Excy any farther Trouble on the Subject of a Loan of Money. But the Bearer, Mr. Grand, who is much better acquainted with the Nature & Manner of such Operations than I am, being of Opinion that the sum we want might with your Permission & Countenance be procur'd in France, I beg you would be so good as to hear him upon the Subject, both of the Necessity of obtaining such a Loan, & of the Means of accomplishing it.

Franklin always sought for ways to mitigate the harsher practices of eighteenth-century warfare. As a scientist, too, he responded favorably to a plea from English friends to grant a safe passage to Captain Cook, who had sailed to the South Seas before the war began. Ironically, by the time Franklin wrote this generous message, Cook was dead, killed in a skirmish with the natives of the Hawaiian Islands.

[Passy, March 10, 1779]

To all Captains and Commanders of arm'd Ships acting by Commission from the Congress of the United States of America, now in War with Great Britain.

Gentlemen,

A Ship having been fitted out from England before the Commencement of this War, to make Discoveries of new Countries, in Unknown Seas, under the Conduct of that most celebrated Navigator and Discoverer Captain Cook; an Undertaking truely laudable in itself, as the Increase of Geographical Knowledge, facilitates the Communication between distant Nations, in the Exchange of useful Products and Manufactures, and the Extension of Arts, whereby the common Enjoyments of human Life are multiplied and augmented, and Science of other kinds encreased to the Benefit of Mankind in general. This is therefore most earnestly to recommend to every one of you; that in case the said Ship which is now expected to be soon in the European Seas on her Return, should happen to fall into your Hands, you would not consider her as an Enemy, nor suffer any Plunder to be made of the Effects contain'd in her, nor obstruct her immediate Return to England, by detaining her or sending her into any other Part of Europe or to America; but that you would treat the said Captain Cook and his People with all Civility and Kindness, affording them, as common Friends to Mankind, all the Assistance in your Power, which they may happen to stand in need of. In so doing you will not only gratify the Generosity of your own Dispositions, but there is no doubt of your obtaining the Approbation of the Congress, and your other American Owners.

Franklin's hearty sense of humor made him a congenial correspondent for sailors such as John Paul Jones. He mixed business and pleasure in this lively letter. Lord Selkirk was the Scottish nobleman whose house Jones had raided in his first voyage, aboard the *Ranger,* in the hope of seizing him as a hostage for the better treatment of American prisoners. Selkirk was away from home, and Jones contented himself with stealing his silver plate—which led to a long and acrimonious correspondence between them.

J. B. Nini made medallions of Franklin and his French hosts, Madame and Monsieur Leray de Chaumont, in 1778.

Passy, March 14. 1779

I yesterday rec'd your favour of the 4th inst. I did not understand from M. Alexander that Lord Selkirk had any particular Objection to receiving the Plate from you. It was general, that tho' he might refuse it if offer'd him by a public Body, as the Congress, he cou'd not accept it from any private Person whatever. I know nothing of M. Alexander's having any Enmity to you, nor can I imagine any Reason for it. But on the whole it seems to me not worth your while to give yourself any farther Trouble about Lord Selkirk. You have now the Disposal of what belongs to the Congress; and may give it with your own Share, if you think fit, in little Encouragements to your men on particular Occasions....

I have look'd over the Copy of my Letter to you of Feby 24, not being able to imagine what Part of it could give you the Idea that I hinted at an Affair I never knew. Not finding anything in the Letter, I suppose it must have been the Postscript of which I have no Copy, and which I know now that you could not understand—tho' I did not when I wrote it. The story I alluded to is this: L'Abbé Rochon had just been telling me & Madame Chaumont that the old Gardiner & his Wife had complained to the Curate, of your having attack'd her in the Garden about 7 o'clock the evening before your Departure, and attempted to ravish her relating all the Circumstances, some of which are not fit for me to write. The serious Part of it was yt three of her Sons were determin'd to kill you, if you had not gone off; the Rest occasioned some Laughing; for the old Woman being one of the grossest, coarsest, dirtiest & ugliest that we may find in a thousand, Madame Chaumont said it gave a high Idea of the Strength of Appetite & Courage of the Americans. A Day or two after, I learnt yt it was the femme de Chambre of Mademoiselle Chaumont who had disguis'd herself in a Suit, I think, of your Cloaths, to divert herself under that Masquerade, as is customary the last evening of Carnival: and that meeting the old Woman in the Garden, she took it into her Head to try her Chastity, which it seems was found Proof.

Franklin was an ideal ambassador to France. In this letter to Josiah Quincy, his old Boston friend, he told how much he enjoyed the French people. He then developed a theme that was to dominate many of his letters: Americans should do more for themselves.

Passy, April 22, 1779.

It is with great Sincerity I join you in acknowledging and admiring the Dispensations of Providence in our Favour. America has only to be thankful, and to persevere. God will finish his Work, and establish their Freedom; and the Lovers of Liberty will flock from all Parts of Europe with their Fortunes to participate with us of that Freedom, as soon as Peace is restored.

I am exceedingly pleas'd with your Account of the French Politeness and Civility, as it appeared among the Officers and People of their Fleet. They have certainly advanced in those Respects many degrees beyond the English. I find them here a most amiable Nation to live with. The Spaniards are by common Opinion suppos'd to be cruel, the English proud, the Scotch insolent, the Dutch Avaricious, &c., but I think the French have no national Vice ascrib'd to them. They have some Frivolities, but they are harmless. To dress their Heads so that a Hat cannot be put on them, and then wear their Hats under their Arms, and to fill their Noses with Tobacco, may be called Follies, perhaps, but they are not Vices. They are only the effects of the tyranny of Custom. In short, there is nothing wanting in the Character of a Frenchman, that belongs to that of an agreable and worthy Man. There are only some Trifles surplus, or which might be spared.

Will you permit me, while I do them this Justice, to hint a little Censure on our own Country People, which I do in Good will, wishing the Cause removed. You know the Necessity we are under of Supplies from Europe, and the Difficulty we have at present in making Returns. The Interest Bills would do a good deal towards purchasing Arms, Ammunition, Clothing, Sailcloth, and other Necessaries for Defence. Upon Enquiry of those who present these Bills to me for Acceptance, what the Money is to be laid out in, I find that most

Franklin was received cordially at the royal palace and found the French to be "a most amiable Nation."

of it is for Superfluities, and more than half of it for Tea. How unhappily in this Instance the Folly of our People, and the Avidity of our Merchants, concur to weaken and impoverish our Country. I formerly computed, that we consum'd before the War, in that single Article, the value of £500,000 Sterling annually. Much of this was sav'd by stopping the Use of it. I honoured the virtuous Resolution of our Women in foregoing that little Gratification, and I lament that such Virtue should be of so short Duration. Five Hundred Thousand Pounds Sterling, annually laid out in defending ourselves, or annoying our Enemies, would have great Effects. With what Face can we ask Aids and Subsidies from our Friends, while we are wasting our own Wealth in such Prodigality?

The moment Arthur Lee and Ralph Izard returned to America, they began a propaganda campaign to smear Franklin's reputation and get him fired. In a letter to Richard Bache, Franklin commented on their motives and tactics, which included nasty rumors about William Temple Franklin's loyalty.

Passy, June 2, 1779.

I am very easy about the efforts Messrs. Lee and Izard are using, as you tell me, to injure me on that side of the water. I trust in the justice of the Congress, that they will listen to no accusations against me, that I have not first been acquainted with, and had an opportunity of answering. I know those gentlemen have plenty of ill will to me, though I have never done to either of them the smallest injury, or given the least just cause of offence. But my too great reputation, and the general good will this people have for me, and the respect they show me, and even the compliments they make me, all grieve those unhappy gentlemen; unhappy indeed in their tempers, and in the dark, uncomfortable passions of jealousy, anger, suspicion, envy, and malice. It is enough for good minds to be affected at other people's misfortunes; but they, that are vexed at everybody's good luck, can never be happy. I take no other revenge of such enemies, than to let them remain in the miserable situation in which their malignant natures have placed them, by endeavouring to support an estimable character; and thus, by continuing the reputation the world has hitherto indulged me with, I shall continue

Mr. and Mrs. Ralph Izard by Copley

313

Imaginative French drawing of Franklin presenting his grandson Temple to Voltaire; the meeting actually took place in Voltaire's house and Temple was eighteen.

them in their present state of damnation; and I am not disposed to reverse my conduct for the alleviation of their torments.

I am surprised to hear, that my grandson, Temple Franklin, being with me, should be an objection against me, and that there is a cabal for removing him. Methinks it is rather some merit, that I have rescued a valuable young man from the danger of being a Tory, and fixed him in honest republican Whig principles; as I think, from the integrity of his disposition, his industry, his early sagacity, and uncommon abilities for business, he may in time become of great service to his country. It is enough that I have lost my *son;* would they add my *grandson?* An old man of seventy, I undertook a winter voyage at the command of Congress, and for the public service, with no other attendant to take care of me. I am continued here in a foreign country, where, if I am sick, his filial attention comforts me, and, if I die, I have a child to close my eyes and take care of my remains. His dutiful behaviour towards me, and his diligence and fidelity in business, are both pleasing and useful to me. His conduct, as my private secretary, has been unexceptionable, and I am confident the Congress will never think of separating us.

I have had a great deal of pleasure in Ben [Benjamin Franklin Bache] too. He is a good, honest lad, and will make, I think, a valuable man. He had made as much proficiency in his learning as the boarding school he was at could well afford him; and, after some consideration where to find a better for him, I at length fixed on sending him to Geneva. I had a good opportunity by a gentleman of that city; who had a place for him in his chaise, and has a son about the same age at the same school. He promised to take care of him, and enclosed I send you the letters I have since received relating to him and from him. He went very cheerfully, and I understand is very happy. I miss his company on Sundays at dinner. But, if I live, and I can find a little leisure, I shall make the journey next spring to see him, and to see at the same time *the old thirteen United States* of Switzerland.

Thanks be to God, I continue well and hearty. Undoubtedly I grow older, but I think the last ten years have made no great difference. I have sometimes the gout, but they say that is not so much a disease as a remedy. God bless you.

To nine-year-old Benjamin Franklin Bache at school in Geneva, Franklin wrote a series of charming letters, of which the following is a good example.

Passy, Augt 19, 1779.

My dear Child,

Do not think that I have forgotten you, because I have been so long without writing to you. I think of you every day, and there is nothing I desire more than to see you furnish'd with good Learning, that I may return you to your Father and Mother so accomplish'd with such Knowledge & Virtue as to give them Pleasure, and enable you to become an honourable Man in your own Country. I am therefore very willing you should have a Dictionary, and all such other Books as M. de Marignac or M. Cramer shall judge proper for you. Those Gentlemen are very good to you and you are I hope very thankful to them, and do everything chearfully they advise you to do; by so doing you will recommend yourself to me, and all good People as well as we will love & esteem you for your dutiful Behaviour.

Your Friends Cochran and Deane are well, Cochran gave me a Letter for you a long time since, which I mislaid, but having now found it, I send it inclos'd. The Small Pox is in that Pension, and 4 of the Scholars are dead of it. I will speak to Cochran to send you their Names. He has not yet had it. How happy it is for you that your Parents took care to have you inoculated when you were an Infant! Which puts you out of that Danger. ...I continue very well, Thanks to God; and I shall always love you very much if you continue to be a good Boy; being ever

Your affectionate Grandfather
B. F.

Let me know what you are learning, ⎫
   & whether you begin to draw. — ⎰

Dr. FRANKLIN, prefents his Compliments to and defires the honour of Company at Dinner, on Monday the 5th of *July*; in order to celebrate the ANNIVERSARY of the DECLARATION of AMERICAN INDEₜENDENCE.

Paffy, 1779.

An Anfwer if you pleaſe.

Franklin's invitation for the 5th of July, 1779, to celebrate Independence

Franklin seldom missed an opportunity to trouble the English in their home waters. This letter to Captain George Blackwell neatly solved the problem of a shortage of commissions from Congress, a solution that enabled Captain Blackwell to cruise in international waters as a legally constituted privateer.

Passy. Sept 14. 1779

I am Sorry I cannot give you the Commission you desire having none left. —But I see nothing amiss in your taking what you can, and carrying it in tho' without a Commission, for since the Congress, in reprisal, have immitated the government of England, and encourage sailors employ'd in ships to seize and bring them in giving them the whole as a Reward for their breach of Trust, I should think there is stronger Reason for allowing an honest Man the Prize he has openly taken from the Enemy and that resolution of Congress seems to me to be of the Nature of a General Commission. However, the taking particular Commissions is certainly the best and most regular and ought not to be dispenc'd with, unless in such Cases as yours, where Circumstances have made it at Present impracticable.

The Marquis de Lafayette had returned to France, after a highly successful military career in America. He was soon busy organizing a raid on the English coast, for which he sought Franklin's advice. Franklin suggested that he might make ransom demands on various English towns. In this letter, Franklin discussed other possibilities, as well as the Franco-American alliance.

Louis XVI and the Marquis de Lafayette painted on the top of a box

Passy, Aug. 19, 1779.

I have just now received your favour of the 17th. I wrote to you a Day or two ago, and have little to add. You ask my Opinion, what Conduct the English will probably hold on this Occasion, and whether they will not rather propose a Negociation for a Peace. I have but one Rule to go by in devining of those people, which is, that whatever is prudent for them to do, they will omit; and what is most imprudent to be done, they will do it. This like other general Rules, may some times have its Exceptions; but I think it will hold good for the most part at least while the present Ministry continues, or rather while the present Madman has the Choice of Ministers. You desire to know whether I am satisfied with the Ministers here? It is impossible for anybody to be more so. I see they exert themselves greatly in the Common Cause and do everything for us that they can. We can wish for nothing more, unless our great Want of Money should make us wish for a Subsidy, to enable us to act more vigorously, in expelling the enemy from their remaining Posts, and reducing Canada. But their own Expences are so great, that I cannot press such an Addition to it. I hope however that we shall get some Supplies of Arms and Ammunition, and perhaps when they can be spar'd some Ships to aid in reducing New York and Rhodeisland. At present I know of no good Opportunity of Writing to America. There are Marchant Ships continually going, but they are very uncertain Conveyances. I long to hear of your safe Arrival in England: but the Winds are adverse, and we must have Patience.

Franklin did not forget science, in spite of all he had to do, running the European side of the war. This letter to Joseph Priestley contains some of his most famous speculations about the future.

Passy, Feb. 8, 1780

Your kind Letter of September 27 came to hand but very lately, the Bearer having staied long in Holland. I always rejoice to hear of your being still employ'd in experimental Researches into Nature, and of the Success you meet with. The rapid Progress *true* Science now makes, occasions my regretting sometimes that I was born so soon. It is impossible to imagine the Height to which may be carried, in a thousand years, the Power of Man over Matter. We may perhaps learn to deprive large Masses of their Gravity, and give them absolute Levity, for the sake of easy Transport. Agriculture may diminish its Labour and double its Produce; all Diseases may by sure means be prevented or cured, not excepting even that of Old Age, and our Lives lengthened at pleasure even beyond the antediluvian Standard. O that moral Science were in as fair a way of Improvement, that Men would cease to be Wolves to one another, and that human Beings would at length learn what they now improperly call Humanity!

With talk of peace in the air, Franklin sent this sunny letter to George Washington, containing perhaps the most moving words he ever wrote about America's future.

Passy, March 5 1780.

Should peace arrive after another Campaign or two, and afford us a little Leisure, I should be happy to see your Excellency in Europe, and to accompany you, if my Age and Strength would permit, in visiting some of its ancient and most famous Kingdoms. You would, on this side of the Sea, enjoy the great Reputation you have acquir'd, pure and free from those little Shades that the Jealousy and Envy of a Man's Countrymen and Co-temporaries are ever endeavouring to cast over living Merit. Here you would know, and enjoy, what Posterity will say of Washington. For 1000 Leagues have nearly the same Effect with 1000 Years. The feeble Voice of those grovelling Passions cannot extend so far either in Time or Distance. At present I enjoy that Pleasure for you, as I frequently hear the old Generals of this martial Country, (who study the Maps of America, and mark upon them all your Operations,) speak with sincere Approbation and great Applause of your conduct; and join in giving you the Character of one of the greatest Captains of the Age.

I must soon quit this Scene, but you may live to see our Country flourish, as it will amazingly and rapidly after the War is over. Like a Field of young Indian Corn, which long Fair weather and Sunshine had enfeebled and discolored, and which in that weak State, by a Thunder Gust, of violent Wind, Hail, and Rain, seem'd to be threaten'd with absolute Destruction; yet the Storm being past, it recovers fresh Verdure, shoots up with double Vigour, and delights the Eye, not of its Owner only, but of every observing Traveller.

Franklin's mission to France, by this date, had already been extremely successful. He had negotiated treaties of alliance and commerce between his fledgling nation and Continental Europe's leading power, and he had repeatedly won grants to continue financing the American war effort. But he had five more years abroad, years that were to be capped by his most dramatic diplomatic achievement—the securing of peace.

A Picture Portfolio

An American Abroad

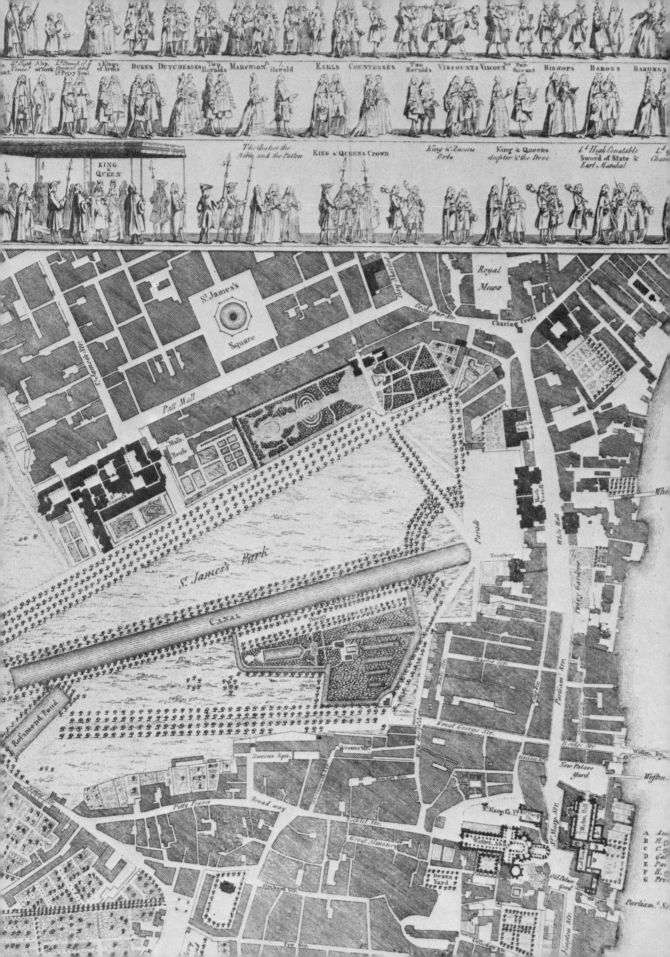

THE LONDON YEARS

Franklin spent nearly thirty years abroad. Eighteen of these were passed in London, where he had been sent as a Colonial agent for Pennsylvania in 1757 and whence he departed on the eve of the Revolution, his country's leading spokesman. As the splendid portrait of him painted in 1766 by David Martin attests, he was then in the prime of life, and at first he and England conducted a happy love affair. In 1761 he watched the coronation of George III, for which the map at left was printed, and soon after called him "the best King any nation was ever blessed with." But over the years he became sadly yet firmly convinced that the America Colonies must sever all ties with the mother country.

A SECOND HOME

For the long years Franklin lived in London away from his own family, he lodged in four rooms of the agreeable little house at left, No. 7 Craven Street, and later across the street at No. 36. His landlady was Mrs. Margaret Stevenson, whose daughter Polly (far left) named Franklin godfather of her first child and for whose delight and pleasure he wrote *The Craven Street Gazette*, a burlesque of contemporary British newspapers. Craven Street ran back from the Thames River, close to the tower in the painting above. It was wonderfully convenient for Franklin, within easy walking distance of the Government offices in Whitehall, seen at far left.

324

LONDON HAUNTS

Even before Franklin reached London, the distinguished Royal Society had awarded him its Copley Medal for his electrical experiments (below, far left). The society's house in Crane Court (below, left), became one of his favorite spots and many of its members his closest friends. He joined the Society of Antiquaries, also a senior learned society; the reception of a new member into that dignified company is depicted at left. The Royal Society of Arts was another congenial place. When James Barry painted the murals for its new Adams brothers' building (above), he sketched Franklin in his fur hat (below) but never actually painted him in. A detail of the actual mural (below, right) shows Franklin's friend William Shipley, founder, with his "plan."

Twyford at the Bishop
of St Asaph's,
1771

Dear Son,

I have ever had a Pleasure in obtaining any little Anecdotes of my Ancestors. You may remember the Enquiries I made among the Remains of my Relations when you were with me in England, and the Journey I took for this purpose. Now imagining it may be equally agreeable to you to know the Circumstances of my Life, many of which you are yet unacquainted with; and expecting a Weeks uninterrupted Leisure in my present Country Retirement, I set down to write them for you. To which I have besides some other Inducements. Having emerg'd from the Poverty & Obscurity in which I was born & bred, to a State of Affluence & some Degree of Reputation in the World, and having gone so far thro' Life with a considerable Share of Felicity, the conducing Means I made use of, which with the Blessing of God, so well succeeded, my Posterity may like to know, as they may find some of them suitable to their own Situations, & therefore fit to be imitated. That Felicity, when I reflected on it, has induced me sometimes to say, that were it offer'd to my Choice, I should have no Objection to a Repetition of the same Life from its Beginning, only asking the Advantages Authors have in a second Edition to correct some Faults of the first. So would I change some sinister Accidents & Events of it for others more favourable, but tho' this were deny'd, I should still accept the Offer. Since such a Repetition is not to be expected, the next Thing most like living one's

The Notes one of my Uncles (who had the same kind of Curiosity in collecting Family Anecdotes) once put into my Hands, furnish'd me with several Particulars relating to our Ancestors. From those Notes I learnt that the Family had liv'd in the same Village, Ecton in Northamptonshire, for 300 Years, & how much longer he knew not, (perhaps from the Time when the Name Franklin that before was the Name of an Order of People, was assum'd by them for a Surname, when others took Surnames all over the Kingdom) on a Freehold of about 30 Acres, aided by the Smith's Business which had continued in the Family till his Time, the eldest Son being always bred to that Business. When I search'd the Register at Ecton, I found an Account of their Births, Marriages and Burials, from the year 1555 only, there being no Register kept in that Parish at any time preceding. By that Register I perceiv'd that I was the youngest Son of the youngest Son for 5 Generations back. My Grandfather Thomas, who was born in 1598, lived at Ecton till he grew too old to follow Business longer, when he went to live with his Son John, a Dyer at Banbury in Oxfordshire, with whom my Father served an Apprenticeship. There my Grandfather died

"THE SWEET AIR OF TWYFORD"

It may have been William Shipley who introduced Franklin to his brother Jonathan, Bishop of St. Asaph (left). If so, it was a happy occurrence, for Franklin found the bishop a staunch friend of America and in his large and friendly home in the quiet village of Twyford (above) he found the time and inclination to write the first part of his renowned *Autobiography* (original manuscript page opposite). When Franklin returned to town he wrote his host: "I now breathe with reluctance the smoke of London, when I think of the sweet air of Twyford."

COUNTRY LIFE

Franklin's circle of friends was wide, and he wrote, not immodestly, to his son William that his company was "so much desired that I...could spend the whole summer in the country houses of inviting friends, if I choose it." One such house, whose "Gardens are a Paradise" (above, right), belonged to Lord and Lady le Despencer. The lord, better known as Sir Francis Dashwood, had had a checkered career before Franklin knew him as Postmaster General of England. He founded a rake's club of "monks" who conducted "rites of a nature subversive of all Decency." In the print above he is shown at these mock devotions. Franklin was also close to the young Earl of Shelburne (right), who as Secretary of State for the Colonies in 1767–68 was always a good friend to America. He was host to Franklin at his beautiful country home, Bowood (far right).

New-York, May 8, 1775.

Extract of a Letter
From Philadelphia,

To a Gentleman in this City, dated the 6th inst.

YESTERDAY evening Dr. FRANKLIN arrived here from London in six weeks, which he left the 20th of March, which has given great joy to this town, he says we have no favours to expect from the Ministry, nothing but submission will satisfy them, they expect little or no opposition will be made to their troops, those that are now coming are for *New-York*, where it is expected they will be received with cordiality. As near as we can learn there are about four thousand troops coming in this fleet, the men of war and transports are in a great measure loaded with dry goods, to supply *New-York*, and the country round it, agents are coming over with them. Dr. *Franklin* is highly pleased to find us arming and preparing for the worst events, he thinks nothing else can save us from the most abject slavery and destruction, at the same time encourages us to believe a spirited opposition, will be the means of our salvation. The Ministry are alarmed at every opposition, and lifted up again at every thing which appears the least in their favour, every letter and every paper from hence, are read by them.

N E W - Y O R K:
Printed by JOHN ANDERSON, at Beckman's-Slip.

FRIENDS AND ENEMIES

In his professional life as agent for four Colonies (Pennsylvania, Georgia, New Jersey, Massachusetts), Franklin made many friends and many enemies. Two men sympathetic to America's cause during the Stamp Act crisis were Lord Rockingham and his secretary Edmund Burke, seen at left in Sir Joshua Reynolds's fine unfinished portrait. Rockingham was then Prime Minister, and it was Burke who arranged for Franklin to testify in Parliament, working out with him the questions and answers of the interrogation that resulted in the Stamp Act's repeal. To Burke, Franklin was "the friend of the human race." When the understanding Earl of Shelburne was eliminated in a cabinet shuffle, Lord Hillsborough (above, far left) became Secretary of State for the Colonies. He and Franklin had little use for each other, and after one of their unsatisfactory conferences, Franklin described his character as "Conceit, Wrongheadedness, Obstinacy and Passion." Another bitter enemy was Alexander Wedderburn (above, left), Solicitor General in the North Ministry. It was Wedderburn who subjected Franklin to a degrading ordeal before the Privy Council, while he was supposedly defending Governor Hutchinson in the case arising from Franklin's disclosure of the "Hutchinson letters." After the attack, during which he remained entirely silent, Franklin commented: "Spots of Dirt thrown upon my character, I suffered while fresh to remain; I . . . rely'd on the vulgar adage, that they would all rub off when they were dry." During the last sad days of his eighteen-year-long sojourn in London, when war between England and her American Colonies seemed imminent, Franklin received overtures from Richard Lord Howe. Invited to Howe's sister's home to play chess (above), he held several talks with Howe only to realize that no solution was possible. A broadside (above, right) announced Franklin's return to Philadelphia and declared him "highly pleased to find us arming and preparing for the worst events. . . . "

ENVOY TO PARIS

Nine months after a bitter Franklin had returned to America from England, his country enlisted him to go abroad again, to persuade France to become an ally in the war against England. In his marten cap among the powdered heads of Paris, Franklin took the French by storm. He lived most comfortably in the mansion at left in the Parisian suburb of Passy—"about ½ an hours Drive from the City." From its terrace Franklin had a splendid view of the Seine and from here he was able to watch the balloon ascensions that later became all the rage (below, far left). Indeed, he was even satirized in an English cartoon of the period, which showed him in dark glasses (3) having cut the ropes of a balloon inscribed *America* with a knife inscribed *Sedition*, while George Washington goes aloft in the suspended basket.

INDÉPENDANCE DES ÉTATS-UNIS.

Le 4 Juillet 1776, les Treize Colonies Confédérées (connues depuis sous le nom d'États-Unis) sont déclarées, par le Congrès, libres et indépendantes. N. Gerard, porteur des pouvoirs de LOUIS XVI, Roi de France, Benjamin Franklin, pour les États-Unis, signent à Paris, le 6 Février 1777, un Traité d'amitié et de commerce, et un Traité d'alliance éventuelle, mis en vigueur par la déclaration de guerre survenue entre la France et l'Angleterre.

Le Comte d'Estaing, le Marquis de la Fayette, Comte de Rochambeau, &c. combattent pour la cause des Américains, soutenue avec tant de gloire par le Général Washington. Capitulation faite le 19 Octobre 1782 par le Lord Cornwallis, dont le

désastre accélère la Paix. L'indépendance des États-Unis est reconnue par les Traités de Paix. Pénétrés de reconnoissance pour les services que LOUIS XVI leur a rendus, les États-Unis ont depuis fait élever à Philadelphie un monument qui en éternisera le souvenir. Cet exemple est d'autant plus mémorable, que les Siècles passés n'offrent aucun exemple de monumens élevés par des Républiques à la gloire d'un Souverain. Les Traités de Paix ont rendu aux Nations la liberté des mers; bienfait dont l'Europe est redevable à la générosité de LOUIS XVI. Le Port de Cherbourg, ouvrage immortel du règne de ce grand Prince, doit affermir cette liberté si utile aux Peuples.

À Paris chez Blin, Imprimeur en Taille-Douce, Place Maubert; N° 17, vis-à-vis la rue des 3 Portes. A.P.D.R.

ROYAL ALLY

The painting above of Franklin's reception at the Court of France when Louis XVI (seated on the sofa with Marie Antoinette) avowed the treaties of alliance and commerce between France and America—although highly idealized—does reflect the esteem with which Franklin was regarded. When Franklin left France, the King gave him a miniature of himself (top left) in a frame studded with 408 diamonds (later sold by the family). At left, America pays homage to Louis, Franklin, and Washington, who worked together to secure her independence.

THE PEACEMAKER

In Paris, on September 3, 1783, the treaty signaling peace with England and recognition of American sovereignty was at long last signed (below). For Franklin—shown at center in Benjamin West's unfinished painting (opposite), surrounded by his fellow American commissioners, John Jay, John Adams, Henry Laurens, and his grandson and secretary William Temple Franklin—it was the capstone of a long and illustrious career, and to him the lion's share of the credit belongs. Franklin remained in Paris for two more years negotiating commercial treaties. As he prepared to leave for home, a venerable figure well into his eightieth year, he wrote to his English friend David Hartley, whose signature also appears on the treaty below: "We were long fellow labourers in the best of all works, the work of peace. I leave you still in the field, but having finished my day's task, I am going home *to go to bed!*" Happily, he lived another five years.

Chapter 11

Mr. Ambassador

There were times during his years in France when Benjamin Franklin almost gave up under the weight of his multiple harassments. In a letter to his nephew Jonathan Williams, Jr., who handled American business affairs at Nantes, the ambassador discussed another immense project that had fallen into his lap—buying and shipping to the American army fifteen thousand uniforms, fifteen thousand muskets, and two thousand barrels of powder. Some of it was supposed to go aboard the *Alliance* but was left onshore by the mutinous Captain Landais, who was supported and encouraged in this act of defiance by Arthur Lee.

Passy, June 27, 1780.

Dear Jonan:—

To get rid of all farther Projects and Propositions which I never understand relating to the Shiping of the Goods, I entrusted you with that Business and impower'd you to freight a Ship or Ships. But I have not succeeded, for in yours of the 23rd you send me new Schemes. No other Man-of-War to go under the Command of Comme Jones can at present be obtained: Assist him in getting out with the *Ariel*; after that you and M. de Chaumont may unite in finding some means of sending the rest of the Goods. You and he can agree and assist each other; but there never can be any Union of Counsels or Endeavors between the Commodore and him. I was told that if we would obtain the *Ariel*, she would do our Business; I join'd in the application and we obtained her. Now she is too Little and another is wanted. I will absolutely have nothing to do with any new Squadron Project. I have been too long in hot Water, plagu'd almost to Death with the Passions, Vagaries, and ill

Humours and Madnesses of other People. I must have a little Repose. This to yourself, and believe me ever,

Your affectionate Uncle,

B FRANKLIN

Franklin's relationship to his daughter was a strange mixture of affection and condescension. He seemed to find it difficult to recognize her many good qualities, perhaps identifying her too closely with his devoted though none too gifted wife, Deborah. The first letter below is a good example of the rather peremptory tone he often took with her, while the second has more of his natural sunshine in it.

Passy, March 16. 1780.

Dear Sally,

I received your kind Letters of Sept. 14. and 25th. You mention the Silk being in a Box with Squirrel Skins, but it is come to hand without them or the Box. Perhaps they were spoilt by the Salt Water and thrown away; for the Silk is much damag'd and not at all fit to be presented as you propose. Indeed I wonder how having yourself scarce Shoes to your Feet, it should come into your Head to give Cloathes to a Queen. I shall see if the Stains can be cover'd by Dyeing it, and make Summer Suits of it, for myself, Temple and Benny.

I send some of Ben's Letters inclosed to his Father. He is well taken Care of, and well contented. But I fancy you had rather he should be with me. Perhaps I may therefore recall him. Tho' I really think he is better at Geneva for his Learning. Many Persons of Quality here, send their Sons there, for the same Reason tho' the Religion is different.

I am glad to hear that Weaving Work is so hard to get done. Tis a Sign there is much Spinning. All the Things you Order will be sent, as you continue to be a good Girl, and spin and knit your Family Stockings.

My Health and Spirits continue and I am ever, Your affectionate Father

B FRANKLIN

Passy, June 27. 1780.

Dear Sally

I received your pleasing Letters of Nov. 14. Mr. Aston whom you recommended to me has been here, and I treated him with the Civilities you desired. I was glad to hear that William, Betsy and Louis, tho' the two latter

The Alliance *returning to America in 1780, where her captain, Pierre Landais, was court-martialed.*

are yet Strangers to me, were all well and lively. Will was always lively. Tell me what Improvement he makes in his Learning. He ought to read and begin to write by this time. I hope to have a Letter from him soon. Ben writes to me often. He is very glorious at present, having obtained the Prize of his School for a best Translation from the Latin into French; which was presented to him in the Cathedral Church by the first Magistrate of the City. I send you his Letter and his Masters containing the News of this Important Event. He gives a Treat on the Occasion to the rest of the Scholars for which I shall pay with much Pleasure.... The Congress have kept me in constant Expectation of being assisted by a Secretary; but he has not yet appeared, and Temple and I are absolute Drudges. I am ever My dear Child, Your affectionate Father

B Franklin

Temple presents his Duty.

To compound Franklin's problems, John Adams—who had returned to the United States in 1779 when he was relieved of his original commission—was now back in Europe. Although Adams had a new commission to negotiate peace, he had nothing to do. The British had renewed the war with vigor, capturing all of Georgia and most of South Carolina, including the key city of Charleston and its defending American army. Adams proceeded to pick a quarrel with the Count de Vergennes, which Franklin tried to smooth over in this letter.

Passy, August 3, 1780.

It was indeed with great Pleasure that I received the letter your Excellency did me the Honour of writing to me, communicating that of the President of Congress, and the Resolutions of that Body relative to the Succours then expected. For the Sentiments therein expressed are so different from the Language held by Mr. Adams in his late Letters to your Excellency as to make it clear that it was from his particular Indiscretion alone, and not from any Instructions received by him, that he has given such just Cause of Displeasure, and that it is impossible his Conduct therein should be approved by his Constituents. I am glad he has not admitted me to any Participation of those Writings, and that he has taken the Resolution he expresses, of not communicating with me, or making use of my Intervention in his future Correspondence; a Resolution that I believe he will keep, as he has never yet communicated to me more of his Business in Europe than I have seen in Newspapers. I live upon Terms of Civility with him, not of Intimacy. I shall as you desire lay before Congress the whole Correspondence which you have sent me for that purpose.

Franklin eventually found a fellow diplomat in whom he could confide, John Jay, who had been designated minister plenipotentiary to the Spanish court with instructions to negotiate a treaty with Spain and secure a loan. In this important letter, he advised Jay how to handle the Spaniards and discussed Jay's fear that the Spaniards were seeking to deprive Americans of the western territory along the Mississippi, as well as the right to use that river. But the overriding theme is the desperate condition of America's finances.

Passy, October. 2, 1780.

I received duly and in good Order the several Letters you have written to me of Augt. 16. 19. Sept. 8. and 22. The Papers that accompanied them of your writing, gave me the Pleasure of seeing the Affairs of our Country in such good Hands, and the Prospect from your Youth of its having the Service of so able a Minister for a great Number of Years: But the little Success that has attended your late Applications for Money mortified me exceedingly; and the Storm of Bills which I found coming upon us both, has terrified and vexed me to such a Degree that I have been deprived of Sleep, and so much indispos'd by continual Anxiety as to be render'd almost incapable of Writing.

At length I got over a Reluctance that was almost invincible, and made another Application to the Government here for more Money. I drew up and presented a State of Debts and newly expected Demands, and requested its Aid to extricate me. Judging from your Letters that you were not likely to obtain anything considerable from your Court, I put down in my Estimate the 25,000 Dollars drawn upon you with the same Sum drawn upon me, as what would probably come to me for Payment. I have now the Pleasure to acquaint you that my Memorial was received in the kindest and most friendly Manner; and tho' the Court here is not without its Embarrassments, on Account of Money, I was told to make myself easy, for that I should be assisted with what was necessary. Mr. Searle arriving about this Time, and assuring me there had been a plentiful Harvest, and

John Jay

Franklin had his own small printing press in Passy. This is a specimen of stencils made for him by Bery; the notations are in Franklin's hand.

great Crops of all Kinds; that the Congress had demanded of the several States, Contributions in Produce; which would be chearfully given; that they would therefore have Plenty of Provisions to dispose of; and I being much pleased with the generous Behavior just experienced, I presented another Paper, proposing in order to ease us, that the Congress might furnish their Army in America with Provisions in Part of Payment for the sums lent us. This Proposition I was told was well taken: But it being consider'd that the States having the Enemy in their Country and obliged to make great Expences for the present Campaign, the furnishing so much Provisions as the French Army would need might straiten and be inconvenient to the Congress; his Majesty did not at this time think it right to accept the Offer.

You will not wonder at my loving this good Prince: He will win the Hearts of all America:

If you are not so fortunate in Spain, continue however the even good Temper you have hitherto manifested. Spain owes us nothing, therefore whatever Friendship she shows us in lending Money or furnishing Cloathing, &ca. tho' not equal to our Wants and Wishes, is however *tant de gagné;* those who have begun to assist us are more likely to continue than to decline, and we are still so much obliged as their Aids amount to. But I hope and am confident that Court will be wiser, than to take Advantage of our Distress and insist on our making Sacrifices by an Agreement, which the Circumstances of such Distress would hereafter weaken, and the very Proposition can only give Disgust at present. Poor as we are, yet as I know we shall be rich, I would rather agree with them to buy at a great Price the whole of their Right on the Missisipi than sell a Drop of its Waters. A Neighbour might as well ask me to sell my Street Door.

I wish you could obtain an Account of what they have supplied us with already, in Money and Goods.

Mr. Grand informing me that one of the Bills drawn on you, having been sent from hence to Madrid, was come back unaccepted, I have directed him to pay it; and he has at my Request undertaken to write to the Marquis D'Yranda, to assist you with Money to answer such Bills as you are not otherwise enabled to pay, and to draw on him for the Amount, which Drafts I shall answer here, as far as the Sum above mentioned of twenty five thousand Dollars. If you expect more acquaint me. But pray write to Congress as I do to forbear this Practice, which is so extreamly hazardous and may some time or other prove very mischevous to their Credit and Affairs. I have undertaken too for all the Bills drawn on Mr. Laurens that have yet appear'd. He was to have sailed 3 Days after Mr. Searle, that is the 18th of July. Mr. Searle begins to be in pain for him, having no good Opinion of the little Vessel he was to embark in.

We have Letters from America to the 7th of August. The Spirit of our People was never higher. Vast Exertions making preparatory for some important Action. Great Harmony and Affection between the Troops of the two Nations. The New Money in good Credit &ca. &ca.

I will write to you again shortly and to Mr. Carmichael. I shall now be able to pay up your Salaries compleat for the Year. But as Demands unforeseen are continually coming upon me I still retain the Expectations you have given me of being reimbursed out of the first Remittances you receive.

If you find any Inclination to hug me for the good News of this Letter, I constitute and appoint Mrs. Jay my attorney to receive in my Behalf your Embraces.

Not even John Paul Jones gave Franklin any peace of mind at this time. The following letter chastised the commodore for spending money like a drunken sailor, which he seldom was.

Passy, Nov. 1. 1780.

I received duly yours of Oct. 13 and 20th. I am extreamly sorry for your Misfortune. The Storm was a terrible one, it was well you escaped with your Lives.

Since your Departure I have received the Acct. of Messrs. Gourlade and Moylan, and I am astonished to find that I am charged with so heavy a Sum as near 100,000 Livres for the Expences of the *Ariel.* After having twice entreated you for god Sake to consider my Circumstances, the Difficultyes I had to provide for so many Expences, and not take any thing but what was absolutely necessary, which you promised me fully you would attend to, I am surprised to find a charge of near 6000 Livres for Shot, which cannot be wanted in America where they are made in Plenty; 5566 Livres 16 for Drugs, an enormous Quantity, and more than 20000

Livres for Slops. &c. after all the officers and Sailors had had considerable Advances made them, without consulting me. Perhaps it will be said, that the Drugs and Slops may be wanted or useful in America. But you will easily conceive on Reflection that if every Person in office in a Ship of the States takes the Liberty of judging what is wanted in America, and in what Quantities, and to order those Quantities leaving me to pay for them, It may not only be involved in unexpected Debt and Demands as At Present, but very unnecessary and unproportioned Supplies may be sent over to the Damage of the Publick. I find myself therefore under the Necessity of putting Stop to this Proceeding: And I know no other way of doing it, than by absolutely refusing Payment of such Charges, made without my Orders or Consent first obtained. Some Medecins and some Slops may be necessary, but those Quantities appear to me enormous.

From America, with winter coming on, Lafayette frantically wrote, asking Franklin what had happened to the fifteen thousand uniforms supposed to have been purchased and shipped by then. Franklin replied to this question and discussed other matters, including a propaganda project on which he and Lafayette were collaborating.

Passy, Dec. 9. 1780.

There has been a kind of Fatality attending the affair of sending out the Cloathing. A Number of unforeseen and unaccountable Accidents have delay'd and prevented it from time to time. Part of it is however at length gone; and the Rest in a fair Way of going soon, with the Arms, Powder, &c. You may depend on my procuring and forwarding all I can, that is necessary for the Operations of our Army.

I congratulate you on the Escape from Arnold's Treachery. His Character is in the light of all Europe already on the Gibbet and will hang there in Chains for Ages.

I wish you had been more particular relating to the Plan you mention of the Eastern States; as I do not fully understand it.

You being now upon the Spot can easily obtain and send me all the authenticated Accounts of the Enemies Barbarity that are necessary for our little Book, or What is better get some body there to write it, and send me a Copy that I may adapt the Cuts to it. I have found an excellent Engraver for the Purpose.

In spite of the brave things Franklin said about the reviving American war effort, the opening of the year 1781 saw the American cause tottering. In desperation, Washington dispatched to France a special envoy of his own, Colonel John Laurens, to plead for more aid, and Congress asked Franklin to assist him. Before Laurens arrived, Franklin wrote this masterful letter to Vergennes, which obtained six million livres.

Passy, Feb. 13, 1781.

I have just received from Congress their Letter for the King, which I have the honour of putting herewith into the hands of your Excellency. I am charged, at the same time, to "represent, in the strongest Terms, the unalterable Resolution of the United States to maintain their Liberties and Independence; and inviolably to adhere to the Alliance at every hazard, and in every Event; and that the Misfortunes of the last Campaign, instead of repressing, have redoubled their Ardour; that Congress are resolved to employ every Resource in their Power to expel the Enemy from every Part of the United States, by the most vigorous and decisive Cooperation with Marine and other Forces of their illustrious Ally; that they have accordingly called on the several States for a powerful Army and ample Supplies of Provisions; and that the States are disposed effectually to comply with their Requisitions. That if, in Aid of their own Exertions, the Court of France can be prevailed on to assume a Naval Superiority in the American Seas, to furnish the Arms, Ammunition, and Clothing, specified in the Estimate heretofore transmitted, and to assist with the Loan mentioned in the Letter, they flatter themselves, that, under the divine Blessing, the War must speedily be terminated, with Glory and Advantage to both Nations."

Colonel John Laurens

By several Letters to me from intelligent Persons it appears, that the great and expensive Exertions of the last Year, by which a Force was assembled capable of facing the Enemy, and which accordingly drew towards New York, and lay long near that City, was rendred ineffectual by the Superiority of the Enemy at Sea; and that their Success in Carolina had been chiefly owing to that Superiority, and to the want of the necessary Means for furnishing, marching, and paying the Expence of Troops sufficient to defend that Province. The Marquis de la Fayette writes to me, that it is impossible to conceive, without seeing it, the Distress the Troops have suffer'd for want of Cloathing; and the following is a Paragraph of a Letter from General Washington, which I ought not to keep back from your Excellency, viz. "I doubt not you are so fully informed by Congress of our political and military State, that it would be superfluous to trouble you with any thing relative to either. If I were to speak on Topicks of the kind, it would be to shew that our present Situation makes one of two Things essential to us; a Peace, or the most vigorous Aid of our Allies, particularly in the Article of *Money.* Of their Disposition to serve us, we cannot doubt; their Generosity will do every thing their Means will permit." They had in America great Expectations, I know not on what Foundation, that a considerable Supply of Money would be obtained from Spain; but that Expectation has failed: And the Force of that Nation in those Seas has been employ'd to reduce small Forts in Florida, without rendring any direct Assistance to the United States; and indeed the long Delay of that Court, in acceding to the Treaty of Commerce, begins to have the Appearance of its not inclining to have any Connection with us; so that, for effectual Friendship, and for the Aid so necessary in the present Conjuncture, we can rely on France alone, and in the Continuance of the King's Goodness towards us.

I am grown old. I feel myself much enfeebled by my late long illness, and it is probable I shall not long have any more Concern in these Affairs. I therefore take this Occasion to express my Opinion to your Excellency, that the present Conjuncture is critical; that there is some Danger lest the Congress should lose its Influence over the people, if it is found unable to procure the Aids that are wanted; and that the whole System of the new Govern't in America may thereby be shaken; that, if the English are suffer'd once to recover that Country, such an Opportunity of effectual Separation as the present may not occur again in the Course of Ages; and that the Possession of those fertile and extensive Regions, and that vast SeaCoast, will afford them so broad a Basis for future Greatness, by the rapid growth of their Commerce, and Breed of Seamen and Soldiers, as will enable them to become the *Terror of Europe,* and to exercise with impunity that Insolence, which is so natural to their Nation, and which will increase enormously with the Increase of their Power.

LEWIS WALPOLE LIBRARY

LE ROI

Silhouette of Louis XVI, 1781

Eager as he was to use his reputation in France to forward the American cause, Franklin knew when to draw the line. He did so in this letter to French author Felix Nogaret.

Passy, March 8, 1781.

I received the Letter you have done me the honour of writing to me the 2d instant, wherein, after overwhelming me with a Flood of Compliments, which I can never hope to merit, you request my Opinion of your Translation of a Latin Verse, that has been apply'd to me. If I were, which I really am not, sufficiently skilled in your excellent Language, to be a proper Judge of its Poesy, the Supposition of my being the Subject, must restrain me from giving any Opinion on that Line, except that it ascribes too much to me, especially in what relates to the Tyrant; the Revolution having been the work of many able and brave Men, wherein it is sufficient Honour for me if I am allowed a small Share.

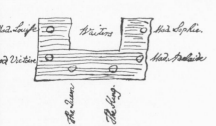

In 1767 Franklin had visited France, where he was presented to Louis XV; he made this sketch of the royal family seated at their Sunday supper.

From England came more bad news. Thomas Digges, a Marylander to whom David Hartley had entrusted the task of distributing money to American prisoners in British jails, had turned out to be an embezzler. In this scorching letter to William Hodgson, an Englishman who represented the Americans in the negotiations to exchange prisoners, Franklin passed judgment on Digges.

Passy, April 1, 1781.

I received your respected Favour of the 20th past, and am shock'd exceedingly at the Account you give me of Digges. He that robbs the Rich even of a single Guinea is a Villain; but what is he who can break his sacred Trust, by robbing a poor Man and a Prisoner of Eighteen Pence given charitably for his Relief, and repeat that Crime as often as there are Weeks in a Winter, and multiply it by robbing as many poor Men every Week as make up the Number of near 600? We have no Name in our Language for such atrocious Wickedness. If such a Fellow is not damn'd, it is not worth while to keep a Devil.

From America came news that Lee and Izard were now both in Congress, making ferocious attacks on Franklin. Although he professed to scorn their criticisms, Franklin knew too much about the vagaries of legislative bodies to feel that he could ignore them with impunity. He therefore decided to outmaneuver them, by handing in his resignation. He was also depressed and weakened by a very severe attack of the gout, which had all but crippled him for several months. In this postscript to a letter he wrote to Sally and Richard Bache about their son Benjamin, he dwelt on his age and health, and carefully avoided the political aspects of the resignation.

Passy, May. 14, 1781

P.S.   I have written to Congress requesting they would send somebody to supply my Place, and permit me to retire, for that I find the Business too heavy for me, and too confining, being oblig'd to perform all the Functions of Consul, Judge of Admiralty, Merchant, Banker, &c. &c. besides that of Minister. I have borne the Burthen as long as I could; but I find that Age requires Rest. Yet it is not my purpose to return immediately home, unless ordered; chusing rather to remain here till the Peace, among a People that love me and whom I love, than to hazard an English Prison. My proper Situation indeed would be in my own House, with my Daughter to take care of me and nurse me in case of Illness, and with her Children who amuse me; but as this cannot well be at present, we must manage as we can.

In the same disenchanted mood, Franklin wrote to Robert Morris, discussing Morris's decision to become superintendent of America's chaotic finances.

Passy, July 26, 1781.

I have just received your very friendly Letter of the 6th of June past, announcing your Appointment to the Super-intendence of our Finances. This gave me great Pleasure, as, from your Intelligence, Integrity, and Abilities, there is reason to hope every Advantage, that the Publick can possibly receive from such an Office. You are wise in estimating beforehand, as the principal Advantage you can expect, the consciousness of having done Service to your Country; for the Business you have undertaken is of so complex a Nature, and must engross so much of your Time and Attention, as necessarily to injure your private Interests; and the Publick is often niggardly, even of its Thanks, while you are sure of being censured by malevolent Criticks and Bug-writers, who will abuse you while you are serving them, and wound your Character in nameless Pamphlets; thereby resembling those little dirty stinking insects, that attack us only in the dark, disturb our Repose, molesting and wounding us, while our Sweat and Blood are contributing to their Subsist-ence. Every Assistance that my Situation here, as long as it continues, may enable me to afford you, shall certainly be given; for, besides my Affection for the glorious Cause we are both engaged in, I value myself upon your Friendship, and shall be happy if mine can be made of any Use to you.

Congress rejected Franklin's resignation. In this letter to William Carmichael, John Jay's secretary and later the American chargé d'affaires in Madrid, he showed little sign that the refusal distressed him.

Passy, Augt 24, 1781.

The Congress have done me the honour to refuse accepting my Resignation, and insist on my continuing in their Service till the Peace. I must therefore buckle again to Business, and thank God that my Health & Spirits are of late improved. I fancy it may have been a double Mortification to those Enemies you have mentioned to me, that I should ask as a Favour what they hop'd to vex me by taking from me; and that I should nevertheless be continued. But these sort of Considerations should never influence our Conduct. We ought always to do what appears best to be done, without much regarding what others may think of it. I call this Continuance an Honour, & I really esteem it to be a greater than my first Appointment, when I consider that all the Interest of my Enemies, united with my own Request, were not sufficient to prevent it. . . .

A contemporary Dutch cartoon about armed neutrality shows an American (2, with B. Franklin written on his hat) stealing England's clothes.

Mr Laurens's Business here was to solicit a large Aid in Money for the Army. It was thought that as he was a Witness of their Wants, he would be able to represent their Situation & Necessities more forcibly than I could do. He was indefatigable, while he staid, and took true Pains, but he *brusqu'd* the Ministers too much, and I found after he was gone that he had thereby given more Offence than I could have imagin'd. He obtain'd a Promise of a Loan of 10,000,000 to be borrowed in Holland: But as that Borrowing has not succeeded, he in fact obtained nothing. The Offence he gave will I hope have no durable Effects, tho' it produc'd me some Mortifications. Good humour and a kind Disposition towards us seems again to prevail. I had before his Arrival got the Grant of 6,000,000, and have since obtained more, or I could not have paid Mr Jay's Bills. . . .

I have accepted the Bill you last mentioned for 15,000 Dollars I had before accepted the Bill for 1700 Louis, being (with 50 left in my hands) the Amount of your half

Years Salaries, so that you are made easy on that head for the present; — but whether I shall have it in my Power to continue the Payments either to you or my self, is uncertain, and I would advise writing to Congress, as I shall do, for Remittances....

I have also just heard from Holland that the Affair of the Loan there is a good Train, & likely to succeed but this I do not depend on.

For a glimpse of history in the process of being made — or at least observed — by the leading participants, it is difficult to excel the following two letters that Franklin wrote to Vergennes.

The surrender at Yorktown

Passy Nov. 19. 1781.

I have the honour of sending to your Excellency some Advices I have just received. As the Letter from Virginia was received at New-Castle, a Town on the Delaware 40 Miles below Philadelphia, and probably after the Date of your Letters from thence, perhaps you may not have heard before, that M. DeBarras had joined M. deGrasse, and that the Northern Troops under the Generals Rochambeau and Washington, had joined the Marquis de la Fayette, and invested Cornwallis at York.

Passy. Novr. 20, 1781.

Your very obliging Letter communicating the News of the important Victory at York, gave me infinite Pleasure. The very powerful aid afforded by his Majesty to America this year, has rivetted the affections of that People, and the Success had made Millions happy. Indeed the King appears to me from this and another late Event, to be *le plus grand Faiseur d'heureux* that this World affords. May God prosper him, his Family and Nation to the End of Time!

As 1782 dawned, Yorktown seemed to have had no appreciable affect on Franklin's financial headaches. In fact, the French Government was almost bankrupt, and on January 28 Franklin wrote to Robert Morris, grimly informing him that there was no more money forthcoming from Louis XVI's treasury. Early in March, he sent Morris the following comments on hopeful signs of a peace movement in England.

Passy, March 7, 1782

You will see by the English Papers which I send to Mr. Secry. Livingston, that the Sense of the Nation is now fully against the Continuance of the America War. The Petitions of the Cities of London and Bristol were unanimous against it; Lord North muster'd all his Force, yet had a Majority against him of 19. It is said there were but two who voted with him, that are not Place men or Pensioners; and that even these in their private Conversations condemn the Prosecution of the War, and lay it all upon the King's Obstinacy. We must not however be lull'd by these Appearances. That Nation is changeable. And tho' some what humbled at Present, a little Success may make them as insolent as ever. I remember that when I was a boxing Boy, it was allow'd after an Adversary said he had enough, to give him a rising Blow. Let ours be a Douser.

A few months before Yorktown, Silas Deane, having returned to Europe full of bitterness over his cool reception from the Continental Congress, made a secret deal with the British Ministry and wrote a series of letters to America recommending a peace short of independence. He sent a copy of one of these letters to Franklin, and got the following reply.

Passy, April 19, 1782.

Sir,

I received the Letter you did me the honour to write to me the 30th. past, and will write to the purpose you desire respecting your Accounts. I hope the Method you propose for settling any disputable points in them will be approved and ordered. I received also your very long political Letter. The Multiplicity of Business on my Hands, on which Account you are so good as to excuse my not answering it, really makes it impossible for me to enter into the voluminous Discussions that would be necessary to do it fully. I can only say at present that I am not convinced; that perhaps my answer would not convince you; but that I think Time will. I am really sorry on your Account that you have written so much of the same kind to America. The Publication of those Letters has done great Prejudice to your Character there, and necessarily diminish'd much of the Regard your Friends had for you. You are now considered as having abandoned the Cause of your Country, and as having with Arnold espoused that of its Enemies. To me it appears that your Resentments and Passions have overcome your Reason and Judgment; and tho' my ancient Esteem and Affection for you induce me to make all the Allowances possible, in considering the Circumstances that have attended you since you first left France, yet the Lengths you have gone in endeavouring to discourage and diminish the Number of the Friends of our Country and Cause in Europe and America, and to encourage our Enemies, by those Letters, make it impossible for me to say with the same Truth & Cordiality as formerly that I am, Your affectionate Friend and humble Servant.

B Franklin

Toward the end of March, 1782, Franklin heard that the North Ministry had at last fallen, and his old friend from the Stamp Act crisis, Lord Rockingham, was now the King's First Minister. Another good friend, Lord Shelburne, had come in as Secretary of State for American Affairs. Shelburne immediately dispatched a representative, Richard Oswald, to discuss peace terms with Franklin. The American ambassador kept a journal of the early months of the negotiation, which is too lengthy to be included here in its entirety. But the following excerpt gives us a graphic look at Franklin the diplomat in action, moving toward a goal that he had already suggested to David Hartley and other English friends—the British surrender of Canada.

[Franklin's record of a conversation with Richard Oswald, April 19, 1782]

I then remarked, that his Nation seem'd to desire Reconciliation with America; that I heartily wish'd the same thing, that a mere Peace would not produce half its Advantages if not attended with a sincere Reconciliation; that to obtain this the Party which had been the Aggressor and had cruelly treated the other, should show some Mark of Concern for what was past, and some Disposition to make Reparation; that perhaps there were things, which America might demand by way of Reparation, and which England might yield, and that the Effect would be vastly greater, if they appeared to be voluntary, and to spring from returning Good will; that I therefore wish'd England would think of offering something to relieve those who had suffer'd by its Scalping and Burning Parties. Lives indeed could not be restor'd nor compensated, but the Villages and Houses wantonly destroy'd might be rebuilt, &c. I then touch'd upon the Affair of Canada, and as in a former Conversation he had mention'd his Opinion, that the giving up of that Country to the English at the last Peace had been a politic Act in France, for that it had weaken'd the Ties between England and her Colonies, and that he himself had predicted from it the late Revolution, I spoke of the

Occasions of future Quarrel that might be produc'd by her continuing to hold it; hinting at the same time but not expressing too plainly that such a Situation, to us so dangerous, would necessarily oblige us to cultivate and strengthen our Union with France. He appear'd much struck with my Discourse.

In this letter to John Jay, written a few days after Franklin had seen Oswald, the ambassador announced the final triumph of his long struggle to free American sailors from British prisons.

Passy, April 24, 1782.

The Prince de Massaran being so good as to desire carrying a letter to you, I sit down to write you a few lines, though I hope soon to see you. . . .

In consequence of a proposition I sent over, the Parliament of Britain have just passed an act for exchanging American prisoners. They have near eleven hundred in the jails of England and Ireland, all committed as charged with high treason. The act is to empower the King, notwithstanding such commitments, to consider them as prisoners of war, according to the law of nations, and exchange them as such. This seems to be giving up their pretensions of considering us as rebellious subjects, and is a kind of acknowledgment of our independence. Transports are now taking up, to carry back to their country the poor, brave fellows, who have borne for years their cruel captivity, rather than serve our enemies, and an equal number of English are to be delivered in return. I have, upon desire, furnished passports for the vessels.

Our affairs in Holland are *en bon train;* we have some prospect of another loan there; and all goes well here.

The proposal to us of a separate peace with England has been rejected in the manner you wish, and I am pretty certain they will now enter into a general treaty.

Victor Hugo made this drawing of Franklin's residence in Passy.

Franklin was soon joined by Jay and John Adams. All had been appointed by Congress as commissioners to negotiate peace. A fourth commissioner, Henry Laurens, remained in England, ill from his long imprisonment in the Tower, where he had been put when he was captured en route to Europe. Negotiations did not progress as smoothly as Franklin hoped. Jay insisted that Britain recognize the independence of the United States before negotiations began. This delayed serious bargaining for almost two months. Franklin himself came down with a severe attack of the gout and a bladder stone ailment, and in the meantime the English stiffened their stand considerably as a result of victories in the West Indies and at Gibraltar. Franklin's hope for a peace of reconciliation, which would have included the acquisition of Canada and Nova Scotia, vanished. In this letter to Robert R. Livingston, the American Secretary for Foreign Affairs, he discussed the situation.

Paris, October 14, 1782.

I have but just received information of this opportunity, and have only time allowed to write a few lines.

In my last of the 26th past, I mentioned that the negotiation for peace had been obstructed by the want of due form in the English commissions appointing their plenipotentiaries. In that for treating with us, the mentioning our States by their public name had been avoided, which we objected to; another is come, of which I send a copy enclosed. We have now made several preliminary propositions, which the English minister, Mr. Oswald, has approved, and sent to his court. He thinks they will be approved there, but I have some doubts. In a few days, however, the answer expected will determine. By the first of these articles, the King of Great Britain renounces, for himself and successors, all claim and pretension to dominion or territory within the Thirteen United States; and the boundaries are described as in our instructions, except that the line between Nova Scotia and New England is to be settled by commissioners after the peace. By another article, the fishery in the American seas is to be freely exercised by the Americans, wherever they might formerly exercise it while united with Great Britain. By another, the citizens and subjects of each nation are to enjoy the same protection and privileges in each others' ports and countries, respecting commerce, duties, &c., that are enjoyed by native subjects. The articles are drawn up very fully by Mr. Jay, who I suppose sends you a copy; if not, it will go by the next opportunity. If these articles are agreed to, I apprehend little difficulty in the rest. Something has been mentioned about the refugees and English debts, but not insisted on; as we declared at once, that, whatever confiscations had been made in America, being in virtue of the laws of particular States, the Congress had no authority to repeal those laws, and therefore could give us none to stipulate for such repeal....

The different accounts given of Lord Shelburne's

character, with respect to sincerity, induced the ministry here to send over M. de Rayneval, Secretary to the Council, to converse with him, and endeavour to form by that means a more perfect judgment of what was to be expected from the negotiations. He was five or six days in England, saw all the ministers, and returned quite satisfied, that they are sincerely desirous of peace, so that the negotiations now go on with some prospect of success. But the court and people of England are very changeable. A little turn of fortune in their favour sometimes turns their heads; and I shall not think a speedy peace to be depended on, till I see the treaties signed.

After more wrangling over the compensation for the loyalists, which Franklin fiercely opposed although his son William would have been one of the chief gainers, and some equally hot arguments over American fishing rights off Newfoundland, the Americans and British agreed to preliminary articles of peace. The Americans made this decision without consulting the French, who had only begun negotiating with the British. The Americans thus violated the strict letter of their instructions from Congress, which stipulated they were to consult their allies throughout the negotiations. Jay and Adams had urged this separate course on a reluctant Franklin, because they no longer trusted French intentions and feared that the French would join with the Spanish, in an attempt to deprive the United States of the lands between the Alleghenies and the Mississippi. Franklin now had the unpleasant task of informing the French Foreign Minister, the Count de Vergennes, that America had signed a separate treaty of peace. Vergennes was not happy with the news. Tartly, he accused Franklin of holding out "a certain hope of peace to America, without even informing yourself on the state of the negotiation on our part." He demanded to know how Franklin could do this with "propriety." Franklin replied in a letter that masterfully soothed the angry Frenchman, and simultaneously asked him for one more loan. He got it.

Passy, December 17, 1782

I received the letter your Excellency did me the honour of writing to me on the 15th instant. The proposal of having a passport from England was agreed to by me the more willingly, as I at that time had hopes of obtaining some money to send in the *Washington,* and the passport would have made its transportation safer, with that of our despatches, and of yours also, if you had thought fit to make use of the occasion. Your Excellency objected, as I understood it, that the English ministers, by their letters sent in the same ship, might

A passport issued by Franklin in 1782
bears the Franklin coat of arms.

convey inconvenient expectations into America. It was therefore I proposed not to press for the passport till your preliminaries were also agreed to. They have sent the passport without being pressed to do it, and they have sent no letters to go under it, and ours will prevent the inconvenience apprehended. In a subsequent conversation, your Excellency mentioned your intention of sending some of the King's cutters, whence I imagined, that detaining the *Washington* was no longer necessary; and it was certainly incumbent on us to give Congress as early an account as possible of our proceedings, who will think it extremely strange to hear of them by other means, without a line from us. I acquainted your Excellency, however, with our intention of despatching that ship, supposing you might possibly have something to send by her.

Nothing has been agreed in the preliminaries contrary to the interests of France; and no peace is to take place between us and England, till you have concluded yours. Your observation is, however, apparently just, that, in not consulting you before they were signed we have been guilty of neglecting a point of *bienséance*. But as this was not from want of respect for the King, whom we all love and honour, we hope it will be excused, and that the great work, which has hitherto been so happily conducted, is so nearly brought to perfection, and is so glorious to his reign, will not be ruined by a single indiscretion of ours. And certainly the whole edifice sinks to the ground immediately if you refuse on that account to give us any further assistance.

We have not yet despatched the ship, and I beg leave to wait upon you on Friday for your answer.

It is not possible for any one to be more sensible than I am, of what I and every American owe to the King, for the many and great benefits and favours he has bestowed upon us. All my letters to America are proofs of this; all tending to make the same impressions on the minds of my countrymen, that I felt in my own. And I believe, that no Prince was ever more beloved and respected by his own subjects, than the King is by the people of the United States. *The English, I just now learn, flatter themselves they have already divided us.* I hope this little misunderstanding will therefore be kept a secret, and that they will find themselves totally mistaken.

A few weeks later, Franklin received sad news from England. Margaret Stevenson had died on January 1, 1783. In this moving letter to her daughter Polly, he wrote of his grief, and recalled his deep affection for Mrs. Stevenson, and for England.

Passy, Jan. 27. 1783.

—The Departure of my dearest Friend, which I learn from your last Letter, greatly affects me. To meet with her once more in this Life was one of the principal Motives of my proposing to visit England again, before my Return to America. The last Year carried off my Friends Dr. Pringle, and Dr. Fothergill, Lord Kaims, and Lord de Despencer. This has begun to take away the rest, and strikes the hardest. Thus the Ties I had to that Country, and indeed to the World in general, are loosened one by one, and I shall soon have no Attachment left to make me unwilling to follow.

I intended writing when I sent the 11 Books, but I lost the Time in looking for the 12th. I wrote with that; and hope it came to hand. I therein ask'd your Counsel about my coming to England. On Reflection, I think I can, from my Knowledge of your Prudence, foresee what it will be, viz. not to come too soon, lest it should seem braving and insulting some who ought to be respected. I shall, therefore, omit that Journey till I am near going to America, and then just step over to take Leave of my Friends, and spend a few days with you. I purpose bringing Ben with me, and perhaps may leave him under your Care.

At length we are in Peace, God be praised, and long, very long, may it continue. All Wars are Follies, very expensive, and very mischievous ones. When will Mankind be convinced of this, and agree to settle their Differences by Arbitration? Were they to do it, even by the Cast of a Dye, it would be better than by Fighting and destroying each other.

Spring is coming on, when Travelling will be delightful. Can you not, when your children are all at School, make a little Party, and take a Trip hither? I have now a large House, delightfully situated, in which I could accommodate you and two or three Friends, and I am but half an Hour's Drive from Paris.

In looking forward, Twenty-five Years seems a long Period, but, in looking back, how short! Could you imagine, that 'tis now full a Quarter of a Century since

we were first acquainted? It was in 1757. During the
greatest Part of the Time, I lived in the same House
with my dear deceased Friend, your Mother; of course
you and I saw and convers'd with each other much and
often. It is to all our Honours, that in all that time we
never had among us the smallest Misunderstanding.
Our Friendship has been all clear Sunshine, without the
least Cloud in its Hemisphere. Let me conclude by saying to you, what I have had too frequent Occasions to
say to my other remaining old Friends, "The fewer we
become, the more let us love one another."

Finally, France and Spain agreed to terms and signed
preliminary peace treaties. In this letter to Robert R. Livingston, Franklin
drew down the curtain on the great drama of the Revolution.

Passy, January 21, 1783.

I have just received your letters of November 9th and
December 3d. This is to inform you, and to request you to
inform the Congress that the preliminaries of peace between France, Spain, and England, were yesterday signed,
and a cessation of arms agreed to by the ministers of those
powers, and by us in behalf of the United States, of which
act, so far as relates to us, I enclose a copy. I have not
yet obtained a copy of the preliminaries agreed to by the
three crowns, but hear, in general, that they are very
advantageous to France and Spain. I shall be able, in a
day or two, to write more fully and perfectly. Holland
was not ready to sign preliminaries, but their principal
points are settled. Mr. Laurens is absent at Bath, and Mr.
Jay in Normandy, for their healths, but will both be here
to assist in forming the definitive treaty. I congratulate
you and our country on the happy prospects afforded us
by the finishing so speedily this glorious revolution.

Thanks to Franklin's efforts, relations between France
and the United States remained good. In this letter to Robert Morris, Franklin
demonstrated, once more, the positive results of his approach. The "certain
mischievous madman" referred to in the second paragraph was John Adams,
who had become paranoid on the subject of France and French influence
over the new American nation.

Passy, March 7, 1783.

With this I send you a copy of the last contract I made
with this court, respecting the late loan of six millions,
the terms of the loan, and the times of repayment. It

From his first audience with King Louis, depicted above in a German engraving, until the signing of the peace treaty, Franklin worked diligently to maintain the "Kings Goodness towards us."

was impossible for me to obtain more, and, indeed, considering the state of finances and expenses here, I wonder I have obtained so much. You will see by the enclosed Gazette, that the government is obliged to stop payment for a year of its own bills of exchange, drawn in America and the East Indies; yet it has advanced six millions to save the credit of ours. You will, I am sure, do all in your power to avoid drawing beyond your funds here; for I am absolutely assured, that no farther aid for this year is to be expected; and it will not be strange, that they should suffer your bills to take the same fate with their own.

You will also see in the contract fresh marks of the King's goodness towards us, in giving so long a term for payment, and forgiving the first year's interest. I hope the ravings of a certain mischievous madman here against France and its ministers, which I hear of every day, will not be regarded in America, so as to diminish in the least the happy union that has hitherto subsisted between the two nations, and which is indeed the solid foundation of our present importance in Europe.

Meanwhile, Franklin continued to write grandfatherly letters to Benjamin Franklin Bache. A few weeks after Franklin wrote this letter, he brought Benny back from Geneva, and kept him with him at Passy for the rest of his stay in France.

Passy, May 2. 1783

My dear Child,

I have receiv'd several Letters from you, and in the last a Specimen of your Drawing, which I was pleas'd with, as well as with your Letters. I am not going yet to England, as you supposed. When I do go there, I shall certainly take you with me. I send you the Medal you desire; but I cannot afford to give Gold Watches to Children. When you are more of a Man, perhaps, if you have behaved well, I may give you one or something that is better. You should remember that I am at a great Expence for your Education, to pay for your Board and Cloathing and Instruction in Learning that may be useful to you when you are grown up, and you should not tease me for expensive things that can be of little or no Service to you. Your Father and Mother and Brothers and Sisters were all well when I last heard from them: and I am ever Your affectionate Grandfather

B FRANKLIN

359

In September, 1783, the definitive treaty of peace was signed. It consisted of nothing more than the preliminary articles agreed to by the negotiators in the fall of 1782. But Franklin's enemies continued to harass him. In this letter to John Jay, he tried to defend himself against their latest slander. He wrote an identical letter to John Adams, on the same day. Both men responded with letters affirming their belief in Franklin's honesty and loyalty—but Jay wrote in far more friendly terms than did the often sour and cantankerous Adams.

Passy, September 10, 1783.

I have received a letter from a very respectable person in America, containing the following words, viz.

"It is confidently reported, propagated, and believed by some among us, that the Court of France was at the bottom against our obtaining the fishery and territory in that great extent, in which both are secured to us by the treaty; that our minister at that court favoured, or did not oppose, this design against us; and that it was entirely owing to the firmness, sagacity, and disinterestedness of Mr. Adams, with whom Mr. Jay united, that we have obtained these important advantages."

It is not my purpose to dispute any share of the honour of that treaty, which the friends of my colleagues may be disposed to give them; but, having now spent fifty years of my life in public offices and trusts, and having still one ambition left, that of carrying the character of fidelity at least to the grave with me, I cannot allow that I was behind any of them in zeal and faithfulness. I therefore think, that I ought not to suffer an accusation, which falls little short of treason to my country, to pass without notice, when the means of effectual vindication are at hand. You, Sir, were a witness of my conduct in that affair. To you and my other colleagues I appeal, by sending to each a similar letter with this, and I have no doubt of your readiness to do a brother Commissioner justice, by certificates that will entirely destroy the effect of that accusation.

In Paris, interest in war was soon replaced by a passion for ballooning. Although Franklin was still troubled by gout and a bladder stone, he roused himself from Passy and jouneyed to Paris to see one of these experiments. He then proceeded to write the following scientifically detailed report to Sir Joseph Banks, president of the Royal Society. On another occasion, questioned about the usefulness of balloons, Franklin replied to scoffers, "What good is a new-born baby?"

Passy, December 1. 1783.

In mine of yesterday I promised to give you an account of Messrs. Charles & Robert's experiment, which was to have been made this day, and at which I intended to be present. Being a little indisposed, and the air cool, and the ground damp, I declined going into the garden of the Tuileries, where the balloon was placed, not knowing how long I might be obliged to wait there before it was ready to depart, and chose to stay in my carriage near the statue of Louis XV., from whence I could well see it rise, and have an extensive view of the region of air through which, as the wind sat, it was likely to pass. The morning was foggy, but about one o'clock the air became tolerably clear, to the great satisfaction of the spectators, who were infinite, notice having been given of the intended experiment several days before in the papers, so that all Paris was out, either about the Tuileries, on the quays and bridges, in the fields, the streets, at windows, or on the tops of houses, besides the inhabitants of all the towns and villages of the environs. Never before was a philosophical experiment so magnificently attended. Some guns were fired to give notice that the departure of the balloon was near, and a small one was discharged, which went to an amazing height, there being but little wind to make it deviate from its perpendicular course, and at length the sight of it was lost. Means were used, I am told, to prevent the great balloon's rising so high as might endanger its bursting. Several bags of sand were taken on board before the cord that held it down was cut, and the whole weight being then too much to be lifted, such a quantity was discharged as to permit its rising slowly. Thus it would sooner arrive at that region where it would be in equilibrio with the surrounding air, and by discharging more sand afterwards, it might go higher if desired. Between one and two o'clock, all eyes were gratified with seeing it rise majestically from among the trees, and ascend gradually above the buildings, a most beautiful spectacle. When it was about two hundred feet high, the brave adventurers held out and waved a little white pennant, on both sides their car, to salute the spectators, who returned loud claps of applause. The wind was very little, so that the object though moving to the northward, continued long in view; and it was a great while before the admiring people began to dis-

Franklin watched this balloon ascension with his pocket glass.

Franklin was too ill to attend the launching of this balloon from Versailles, but he nonetheless gathered data and wrote a report.

perse. The persons embarked were Mr. Charles, professor of experimental philosophy, and a zealous promoter of that science; and one of the Messieurs Robert, the very ingenious constructors of the machine. When it arrived at its height, which I suppose might be three or four hundred toises, it appeared to have only horizontal motion. I had a pocket-glass, with which I followed it, till I lost sight first of the men, then of the car, and when I last saw the balloon, it appeared no bigger than a walnut. I write this at seven in the evening. What became of them is not yet known here. I hope they descended by daylight, so as to see and avoid falling among trees or on houses, and that the experiment was completed without any mischievous accident, which the novelty of it and the want of experience might well occasion. I am the more anxious for the event, because I am not well informed of the means provided for letting themselves down, and the loss of these very ingenious men would not only be a discouragement to the progress of the art, but be a sensible loss to science and society.

I shall enclose one of the tickets of admission, on which the globe was represented, as originally intended, but is altered by the pen to show its real state when it went off. When the tickets were engraved the car was to have been hung to the neck of the globe, as represented by a little drawing I have made in the corner.

I suppose it may have been an apprehension of danger in straining too much the balloon or tearing the silk, that induced the constructors to throw a net over it, fixed to a hoop which went round its middle, and to hang the car to that hoop.

Tuesday morning, December 2d. —I am relieved from my anxiety by hearing that the adventurers descended well near L'Isle Adam before sunset. This place is near seven leagues from Paris. Had the wind blown fresh they might have gone much farther....

P.S.   Tuesday evening. —Since writing the above I have received the printed paper and the manuscript containing some particulars of the experiment, which I enclose. I hear further that the travellers had perfect command of their carriage, descending as they pleased by letting some of the inflammable air escape, and rising again by discharging some sand; that they descended over a field so low as to talk with the labourers in passing, and mounted again to pass a hill. The little balloon falling at Vincennes shows that mounting higher it met with a current of air in a contrary direction, an observation that may be of use to future aerial voyagers.

Although peace was a reality, Franklin was not inclined to drop his guard against an obviously hostile England. In this excerpt from his letter to Thomas Mifflin, the president of Congress, he explained why he remained suspicious of the former mother country.

Passy, January 25. 1784.

With respect to the British Court we should I think be constantly on our guard and impress strongly on our minds that tho it has made peace with us it is not in truth reconciled to us or to its loss of us but flatters itself with hopes that some change in the affairs of Europe or some disunion among ourselves may afford them an opportunity of recovering their dominion, punishing those who have most offended and recuring our future dependence. It is easy to see by the general turn of y Ministerial news papers (light things indeed as straws or feathers but like them they shew which way the wind blows) and by the malignant improvement their ministers make in all the foreign courts of every little accident or dissention among us, the rise of a few Soldiers in Philadelphia, the resolves of some town meetings, the reluctance to pay taxes &c. all which are exaggerated to represent our governments as so many anarchies of which the people themselves are weary, the Congress as having lost its influence being no longer respected. I say that is easy to see by this conduct that they bear us no good will and that they wish the reality of what they are pleased to imagine. They have too numerous a royal progeny to provide for some of whom are educated in the military line. In these circumstances we cannot be too carefull to preserve the friendships we have acquired abroad & the union we have established at home, to secure our credit by a punctual discharge of our obligations of every kind & our reputation by the wisdom of our councils since we know not how soon we may have a fresh occasion for friends for credit and for reputation.

Among his English friends, Franklin easily forgave and forgot. This cheerful letter to William Strahan demonstrates how easily he picked up the mood and the tone of their old friendship.

Passy, Feb. 16, 1784.

I receiv'd and read with Pleasure your kind Letter of the first Inst, as it inform'd me of the Welfare of you and yours. I am glad the Accounts you have from your Kinswoman at Philadelphia are agreable, and I shall be happy if any Recommendations from me can be serviceable to Dr. Ross, or any other friend of yours, going to America.

Your arguments, persuading me to come once more to England, are very powerful. To be sure, I long to see again my Friends there, whom I love abundantly; but there are difficulties and Objections of several kinds, which at present I do not see how to get over.

I lament with you the political Disorders England at present labours under. Your Papers are full of strange Accounts of Anarchy and Confusion in America, of which we know nothing, while your own Affairs are really in a Situation deplorable. In my humble Opinion, the Root of the Evil lies not so much in too long, or too unequally chosen Parliaments, as in the enormous Salaries, Emoluments, and Patronage of your great Offices; and that you will never be at rest till they are all abolish'd, and every place of Honour made at the same time, instead of a Place of Profit, a place of Expence and burthen.

Ambition and avarice are each of them strong Passions, and when they are united in the same Persons, and have the same Objects in view for their Gratification, they are too strong for Public Spirit and Love of Country, and are apt to produce the most violent Factions and Contentions. They should therefore be separated, and made to act one against the other. Those Places, to speak in our old stile (Brother Type), may be for the good of the *Chapel,* but they are bad for the Master, as they create constant Quarrels that hinder the Business. For example, here are near two Months that your Government has been employed in *getting its form to press;* which is not yet fit to *work on,* every Page of it being *squabbled,* and the whole ready to fall into *pye.* The Founts too must be very scanty, or stangely *out of sorts,* since your *Compositors* cannot find either *upper* or *lower case Letters* sufficient to set the word ADMINISTRATION, but are forc'd to be continually *turning for them.* However, to return to common (tho' perhaps too saucy) Language, don't despair; you have still one resource left, and that

Frederick Mesmer had exploited his cult of animal magnetism successfully for several years before Franklin (at left in this cartoon) and a board of eminent French scientists exposed him as a fraud in 1784.

not a bad one, since it may reunite the Empire. We have some Remains of Affection for you, and shall always be ready to receive and take care of you in Case of Distress. So if you have not Sense and Virtue enough to govern yourselves, e'en dissolve your present old crazy Constitution, and *send members to Congress.*

You will say my *Advice* "smells of *Madeira."* You are right. This foolish Letter is mere chitchat *between ourselves* over the *second bottle.*

In his final summer in Europe, Franklin received a letter from his son, who had retreated to England with a very ugly moral cloud over his head. He was wanted for murder. As head of the Board of Associated Loyalists, a guerrilla organization, William had ordered the hanging of a captive American. Congress ordered Washington to hang a British officer in retaliation, and only the intervention of Louis XVI prevented it. William expressed no repentance in his letter for this or any other aspect of the course he had chosen. Franklin struggled to meet his plea for reconciliation, but even in this guarded letter, it is obvious how difficult it was for him. The letter also contains a reference to the papers that helped form the present — and earlier — editions of Franklin's writings.

Passy, Aug. 16, 1784.

Dear Son,

I received your Letter of the 22d past, and am glad to find that you desire to revive the affectionate Intercourse, that formerly existed between us. It will be very agreable to me; indeed nothing has ever hurt me so much and affected me with such keen Sensations, as to find myself deserted in my old Age by my only Son; and not only deserted, but to find him taking up Arms against me, in a Cause, wherein my good Fame, Fortune and Life were all at Stake. You conceived, you say, that your Duty to your King and Regard for your Country requir'd this. I ought not to blame you for differing in Sentiment with me in Public Affairs. We are Men, all subject to Errors. Our Opinions are not in our own Power; they are form'd and govern'd much by Circumstances, that are often as inexplicable as they are irresistible. Your Situation was such that few would have censured your remaining Neuter, *tho' there are Natural Duties which precede political ones, and cannot be extinguish'd by them.*

This is a disagreable Subject. I drop it. And we will endeavour, as you propose mutually to forget what has

A drawing of the reception of the American Loyalists in Great Britain included William Franklin (center, behind man with long wig).

happened relating to it, as well as we can. I send your Son over to pay his Duty to you. You will find him much improv'd. He is greatly esteem'd and belov'd in this Country, and will make his Way anywhere. It is my Desire, that he should study the Law, as a necessary Part of Knowledge for a public Man, and profitable if he should have occasion to practise it. I would have you therefore put into his hands those Law-books you have, viz. Blackstone, Coke, Bacon, Viner, &c. He will inform you, that he received the Letter sent him by Mr. Galloway, and the Paper it enclosed, safe.

On my leaving America, I deposited with that Friend for you, a Chest of Papers, among which was a Manuscript of nine or ten Volumes, relating to Manufactures, Agriculture, Commerce, Finance, etc., which cost me in England about 70 Guineas; eight Quire Books, containing the Rough Drafts of all my Letters while I liv'd in London. These are missing. I hope you have got them, if not, they are lost. Mr. Vaughan has publish'd in London a Volume of what he calls my Political Works. He proposes a second Edition; but, as the first was very incompleat, and you had many Things that were omitted, (for I used to send you sometimes the Rough Drafts, and sometimes the printed Pieces I wrote in London,) I have directed him to apply to you for what may be in your Power to furnish him with, or to delay his Publication till I can be at home again, if that may ever happen.

I did intend returning this year; but the Congress, instead of giving me Leave to do so, have sent me another Commission, which will keep me here at least a Year longer; and perhaps I may then be too old and feeble to bear the Voyage. I am here among a People that love and respect me, a most amiable Nation to live with; and perhaps I may conclude to die among them; for my Friends in America are dying off, one after another, and I have been so long abroad, that I should now be almost a Stranger in my own Country.

I shall be glad to see you when convenient, but would not have you come here at present. You may confide to your son the Family Affairs you wished to confer upon with me, for he is discreet. And I trust, that you will prudently avoid introducing him to Company, that it may be improper for him to be seen with. I shall hear from you by him and any letters to me afterwards, will come safe under Cover directed to Mr. Ferdinand Grand, Banker at Paris. Wishing you Health, and more Happiness than it seems you have lately experienced, I remain your affectionate father,

B FRANKLIN

Temple went to England equipped with letters of introduction to many Franklin friends. In this one to Bishop Shipley, Franklin revealed the failure of William's attempt to become reconciled.

Passy, Augt. 22. 1784

Nous Benjamin Franklin,
Ecuyer , Ministre Plénipotentiaire des
Etats-Unis de l'Amérique , près Sa
Majesté Très-Chrétienne,

PRIONS *tous ceux qui sont à prier*
de vouloir laisser surement & librement
passer Mr. Harmar, Colonel au service
des dits Etats allant à L'Orient pour s'embarquer.

sans lui donner ni permettre qu'il lui soit
donné aucun empêchement , mais au contraire
de lui accorder toutes sortes d'aide & d'assis-
tance , comme nous ferions en pareil cas , pour
tous ceux qui nous seroient recommandés.
EN FOI DE QUOI *nous lui avons*
délivré le présent Passeport , valable pour trois
Semaines signé de notre main , contresigné
par l'un de nos Secretaires , & au bas
duquel est l'empreinte de nos Armes.
DONNÉ *à Passy, en notre Hôtel , le*
17 Juin mil sept cent quatre-vingt-
Quatre. —

Par ordre du Ministre Plénipotentiaire.

GRATIS.

A passport issued to Colonel Josiah Harmar of the American army carries signatures of Franklin and Temple.

When I am long without hearing from you I please my self with re-perusing some of your former Letters. In your last of April 24. 83. you mention the Departure of Anna Maria with her Husband for Bengal. I hope you have since heard often of their Welfare there. When you next favour me with a Line, please to be particular in letting me know how they do. My Grandson, a good Young Man, (who as a Son makes up to me my Loss by the Estrangement of his Father) will have the Honour of delivering you this Line, and will bring me I trust good Accounts of your Health and that of the rest of the Family. I beg leave to recommend him to your Civilities and Counsels. As to my self I am at present well and hearty, the Stone excepted, which however gives me but little Pain and not often, its chief Inconvenience being that it prevents my using a Carriage on the Pavement; but I can take some Exercise in Walking, am chearful & enjoy my Friends as usual. God be thanked!

Your kind Invitation to spend some time at Twyford with the Family I love, affects me sensibly. Nothing would make me happier. I have solicited the Congress to discharge me, but they have sent me another Commission, that will employ me another Year at least; and it seems my Fate, constantly to wish for Repose, and never to obtain it.

Franklin finally enticed Polly Stevenson Hewson to join him in Paris for the winter of 1784–85. Not content with that triumph, he immediately began attempting to persuade her to join him in America. In this letter he continued his campaign, which was eventually successful.

Passy, May 5, 1785.

My dear, dear Friend,

I receiv'd your little Letter from Dover, which gave me great Pleasure, as it inform'd me of your happy Progress

367

Before Franklin left Paris he was invited to dine with Lafayette.

so far in your way home. I hope the rest of your Journey was as prosperous.

You talk of Obligations to me, when in fact I am the Person oblig'd. I pass'd a long Winter, in a manner that made it appear the shortest of any I ever past. Such is the Effect of pleasing Society, with Friends one loves.

I have now receiv'd my Permission to return, and am making my Preparations. I hope to get away in June. I promise myself, or rather flatter myself, that I shall be happy when at home. But, however happy that Circumstance may make me, your joining me there will surely make me happier, provided your Change of Country may be for the advantage of your dear little Family. When you have made up your Mind on the Subject, let me know by a Line, that I may prepare a House for you as near me, and otherwise as convenient for you, as possible.

My neighbours begin to come out from Paris, and replace themselves in their Passy Houses. They enquire after you, and are sorry you are gone before they could make themselves known to you. For those who did know you speak well of you. M. le Veillard, in particular, has told me at different times, what indeed I knew long since, *C'est une bien digne Femme, cette Madame Hewson, une très aimable Femme.* I would not tell you this if I thought it would make you vain—er than you are; but that is impossible; you have too much good Sense.

So wish me a good Voyage, and, when you pray at Church for all that travel by Land or Sea, think of your ever affectionate Friend,

B. FRANKLIN

Franklin's departure from France was like a royal progress. Because his bladder stone made riding in a jouncing carriage impossible, he traveled in a litter drawn by the King's mules. The person from whom he parted with keenest regret was Mme. Helvétius, who will be introduced in Chapter 12. This letter is translated from the French.

Le Havre, July 19, '85

We arrived here, my very dear friend, safely yesterday evening. I was not at all tired. I felt even better than before my departure. We will stay here for a few days to wait for our baggage and our traveling companion, Mr. Houdon. When they come, we will leave France, the country *I love most in the world;* and I will leave *my dear Helvetius* there. She can be happy there. I am *not sure I will be happy* in America; but I must return. It seems to me that things are arranged badly in this world, when I see beings so very much made to be happy *together forced* to separate.

I encountered so many difficulties with my plan to come here from Rouen through Eau, that I was very pleased to receive permission from the good Duc de Coigny to continue via litter. Tell the Fathers, the good Fathers, (nice) things for me, things full of friendship. I am not telling you that I love you. I would be told that there is nothing extraordinary and no merit at all in that, because everyone loves you. I only hope that you will always love me a little.

At Southampton, Franklin had brief reunions with several English friends. In these excerpts from his journal, he cryptically recounted this happy gathering of Franklinophiles, and also the cold formal meeting with his son, William. All hope of reconciliation had vanished on both sides by now, and nothing was discussed except outstanding business matters, such as the purchase of William's farm in New Jersey for Temple's benefit.

[1785]

[Sunday,] *July 24th.* We had a fair wind all night, and this morning at seven o'clock, being off Cowes, the captain represented to me the difficulty of getting in there against the flood; and proposing that we should rather run up to Southampton, which we did, and landed there between eight and nine. Met my son, who had arrived from London the evening before, with Mr. Williams and Mr. J. Alexander. Wrote a letter to the bishop of St. Asaph, acquainting him with my arrival, and he came with his lady and daughter, Miss Kitty, after dinner to see us; they talk of staying here as long as we do. Our meeting was very affectionate....

[Monday,] *July 25th.* The Bishop and family lodging in the same inn, the Star, we all breakfast and dine together. I went at noon to bathe in Martin's salt-water hot-bath, and, floating on my back, fell asleep, and slept near an hour by my watch without sinking or turning! a thing I never did before, and should hardly have thought possible. Water is the easiest bed that can be. Read over the writings of conveyance, &c., of my son's lands in New Jersey and New York to my grandson. Write to M. Ruellan, M. Limosin, M. Holker, and M.

Grand. Southampton a very neat, pretty place. The two French gentlemen, our friends, much pleased with it. The Bishop gives me a book in 4to, written by Dean Paley, and the family dine with us. Sundry friends came to see me from London....Mr. Williams brought a letter from Mr. Nepean, secretary to Lord Townshend, addressed to Mr. Vaughan, expressing that orders would be sent to the customhouse at Cowes not to trouble our baggage, &c. It is still here on board the packet that brought it over....

[Tuesday,] *July 26th.* Deeds signed between W. Franklin and W. T. Franklin.

Mr. Williams, having brought sundry necessaries for me, goes down with them to Cowes, to be ready for embarking. Captain Jennings carries down our baggage that he brought from Havre. My dear friend, M. Le Veillard, takes leave to go with him. Mr. Vaughan arrives from London, to see me.

[Wednesday,] *July 27th.* Give a power to my son to recover what may be due to me from the British government. Hear from J. Williams that the ship is come.

We all dine once more with the Bishop and family, who kindly accept our invitation to go on board with us. We go down in a shallop to the ship. The captain entertains us at supper. The company stay all night.

[Thursday,] *July 28th.* When I waked in the morning found the company gone, and the ship under sail.

From France, as one of his last letters, Franklin had sent the following note to his fellow peacemaker, David Hartley. It is a near-perfect curtain line for his career in Europe.

Passy, July 5, 1785.

I cannot quit the coasts of Europe without taking leave of my ever dear Friend Mr. Hartley. We were long fellow labourers in the best of all works, the work of peace. I leave you still in the field, but having finished my day's task, I am going home *to go to bed!* Wish me a good night's rest, as I do you a pleasant evening. Adieu! and believe me ever yours most affectionately,

B FRANKLIN,

in his 80th year

Chapter 12

The Ladies of France

As he had done at Craven Street, and almost everywhere else he had lived, Franklin swiftly converted those around him at Passy into a kind of family—over which he presided as a combination father, lover, brother, and sage. He was also friendly with Frenchwomen outside the small Passy circle, such as the Countess d'Houdetot, once the beloved of Rousseau and heroine of his novel, *La nouvelle Héloïse,* and mistress of the highly touted poet of the day, Jean François de Saint-Lambert; and the Duchess d'Anville, mother of the Duke de la Rochefoucauld. But these were more formal relationships. Far more interesting were his friendships with two of his Passy neighbors, Mme. Brillon de Jouy and Anne-Catherine de Ligniville Helvétius, widow of a well-known philosopher. Many of the letters Franklin wrote to and received from these charming friends were undated. It therefore seems best to tell their story in this separate chapter. Most of the following letters have been newly translated from the French in which they were written. This letter to his niece Elizabeth Partridge gives us a cheerful picture of Franklin's reaction to the ladies of France— and a sad note on the vision of a man nearly seventy-four.

Passy, Oct. 11. 1779.

Your kind Letter, my dear Friend, was long in coming; but it gave me the Pleasure of knowing that you had been well in October and January last. The Difficulty, Delay & Interruption of Correspondence with those I love, is one of the great Inconveniencies I find in living so far from home: but we must bear these & more, with Patience, if we can; if not, we must bear them as I do with Impatience.

You mention the Kindness of the French Ladies to me. I must explain that matter. This is the civilest nation upon Earth. Your first Acquaintances endeavour

371

Countess d'Houdetot

to find out what you are like, and they tell others. If 'tis understood that you like Mutton, dine where you will you find Mutton. Somebody, it seems, gave it out that I lov'd Ladies; and then every body presented me their Ladies (or the Ladies presented themselves) to be *embrac'd*, that is to have their Necks kiss'd. For as to kissing the Lips or Cheeks it is not the Mode here, the first, is reckon'd rude, & the other may rub off the Paint. The French Ladies have however 1000 other ways of rendering themselves agreable; by their various Attentions and Civilities, & their sensible Conversation. 'Tis a delightful People to live with.

I thank you for the Boston Newspapers, tho' I see nothing so clearly in them as that your Printers do indeed want new Letters. They perfectly blind me in endeavouring to read them. If you should ever have any Secrets that you wish to be well kept, get them printed in those Papers.

Far deeper than this playful gamesmanship was Franklin's relationship to Mme. Brillon. She was a talented musician, considered one of the finest harpsichordists in Europe, and equally esteemed for her talent on the piano. She was also a composer, and numerous famous composers of the era dedicated works to her. But she had no desire for a public career. She was married to a man twenty-four years older than she, and was the mother of two daughters. She had a sensitive, very artistic temperament, and had been deeply devoted to her father, recently dead. Instinctively, she came to regard Franklin as a foster father on whom she could depend. But Mme. Brillon was also very French. She loved to sit on Franklin's lap and hug and kiss him, and responded wittily to the erotic badinage he loved. At first there was very little of the father in the role Franklin espoused. In this letter he discussed a bargain that he had just made with Mme. Brillon —she was to be his spiritual guide and assist him to save his soul.

Passy, Mar. 10

I am charm'd with the Goodness of my Spiritual Guide, and resign myself implicitly to her Conduct, as she promises to lead me to Heaven on so delicious a Road, when I could be content to travel thither even in the roughest of all ways with the Pleasure of her Company. How kindly partial to her Penitent in finding him, on examining his conscience, guilty of only one capital Sin, and to call that by the gentle Name of a *Foible!*

I lay fast hold of your promise to absolve me of all Sins past, present, & future, on the easy & pleasing

Condition of loving God, America and my Guide above all things. I am in Rapture when I think of being absolv'd of the *future*.

People commonly speak of *Ten* Commandments.—I have been taught that there are *twelve*. The first was *Increase & multiply* & replenish the Earth. The *Twelfth* is, A new Commandment I give unto you, *That ye love one another*. It seems to me they are a little misplac'd, And that the last should have been the first. However I never made any Difficulty about that, but was always willing to obey them both whenever I had an opportunity.

Pray tell me my dear Casuist, whether my keeping religiously these two Commandments tho' not in the Decalogue, may not be accepted in Compensation for my breaking so often one of the Ten I mean that which forbids Coveting my Neighbour's Wife, and which I *confess* I break constantly God forgive me, as often as I see or think of my lovely Confessor. And I am afraid I should never be able to repent of the Sin even if I had the full Posession of her.

And now I am consulting you upon a Case of Conscience I will mention the Opinion of a certain Father of the Church which I find myself willing to adopt, tho' I am not sure it is orthodox. It is this, that the most effectual Way to get rid of a certain Temptation is, as often as it returns, to comply with and satisfy it. Pray instruct me how far I may venture to practice upon this Principle?

Manuscript page for the second violin part of Mme. Brillon's composition "Marche des Insurgents," which was to be played "vivement et fièrement"

Mme. Brillon replied that she would not advise him without "consulting that neighbor whose wife you covet, because he is a far better casuist than I am. And then, too, as Poor Richard would say, in weighty matters two heads are better than one." Though she declined to yield, Mme. Brillon was as covetous as Franklin. She was extremely jealous of the time and attention he gave other French ladies and scolded him for it. He replied by donning his diplomat's role to propose a treaty of peace.

What a difference, my dear friend, between you and me: you find innumerable faults in me, while I see only one in you (but that might be the fault of my glasses)—I mean this kind of avarice which leads you to seek a monopoly of all my affections; and does not allow me any for the lovely ladies of your country. You suppose that it is impossible for my Affection (or my tenderness) to be divided without being diminished. You are wrong; and you forget the playful manner in which you have stopped me. You renounce and totally exclude all the sensuality that our love could have by only allowing me a few civil and honest Kisses, like the kind you would give to some little cousins: then, what am I getting that is so special, so that I can't give a little of it to others without a lessening of what belongs to you? The Workings of the Spirit, Esteem, Admiration, Respect and even Affection! (for an object) can multiply in so far as worthy objects present themselves; and nevertheless have the same thoughts for the first Object which has, as a result, no grounds to complain of an injury. They are by nature just as divisible as the sweet sounds of the piano produced by your skilful hands, twenty people can derive pleasure from them at the same time, without diminishing that which you kindly mean for me and (with as little reason) I can claim from your friendship, that these sweet sounds can neither reach or charm ears other than mine.

You see, then, how unjust you are in your demands, and in the open war you are declaring on me, if I do not capitulate; in fact, it is I who have the most Grounds to complain! My poor little love, that you, it seems to me, should have cherished, instead of being fat and pretty (like those of your elegant paintings) is thin and ready to die of hunger! from a lack of substantial food, which its mother inhumanely refuses. And now she wants to clip its little wings so that it won't be able to go look elsewhere! I think that neither of us can gain a single thing in this war; since I feel I am the weaker, I will offer a plan for peace (even though it should be done by the wisest).

For a peace to be durable the articles of the treaty must be governed by the most perfect principles of equity and equality: with this point of view in mind I have drawn up the following articles.

Article 1. That there ought to be peace, friendship, eternal love between Madame B. and Mr. Franklin.

Article 2. In order to maintain this inviolable peace, Madame B. on her side Stipulates and agrees that Mr. F. comes to her house every time she asks him to.

Article 3. That he stay at her house as much and as long as she wishes.

Article 4. That when he is at her house, he is obliged

This charming aquatint was painted by Mme. Brillon and shows the view from Franklin's terrace in Passy.

to drink tea, play chess, listen to music or do anything she may wish to ask.[1]

Article 5.   And that he love no woman other than her.

Article 6.   And the said Mr. F. on his side stipulates and agrees to go to Madame B.'s house as often as she wishes.

Article 7.   That he will stay there as long as she wishes.

Article 8.   That as long as he is with her, he will do everything he wants to.

Article 9.   And that he will love no other woman, as long as he finds her lovable.[2]

What do you think of those preliminaries? It seems to me they express the true manner of thinking and the real intention of each party more clearly than in many treaties.

I rest strongly, first, on the 8th Article, even though I am without much hope for your consent in the execution; and on the 9th also even though I despair of ever finding any other woman I could love with a tenderness equal to that I always feel for my dear, dear Friend.

[1] What he will be able to do is well understood.

[2] The women can go drown themselves.

When Mme. Brillon declined to sign the treaty, an undaunted Franklin returned with this impromptu parable.

A Beggar asked for a Louis from a wealthy Bishop. "You are foolish. One doesn't give Louis to Beggars." "How about a sou?" "No. That's too much." "A Liard then or your Blessing." "My Blessing! Yes. I will give you that." "I shall not accept it because you don't want to give its value in Liards." That was how much this Bishop loved his Neighbour. That was his Charity! And if I look at your charity, I don't find it much more admirable. I was very hungry and you didn't feed me; I was a Foreigner and almost as sick as Colin of your Song and you neither received me nor cured me, nor even helped me.

You who are as rich as an Archbishop in all the moral and Christian Virtues, and who could share a little portion of some of them with me without noticeable loss; you tell me that such a sacrifice is too much and that you don't want to make it. This is the kind of Charity you display toward a poor, miserable fellow who used to be affluent and who is now reduced to begging from you!

You say, however, that you love him but you would not give him your Friendship if it required spending the smallest little Piece of the Worth of a Liard, of your Virtues.

Franklin's deepening friendship with Mme. Brillon inspired him to write one of his most charming light essays — or bagatelles as they came to be called. It was prompted by a visit to the Moulin Joli, a small island in the Seine where mutual friends had a country house. Part of Franklin's purpose was to please Mme. Brillon, of course. The ostensible reason for the essay was to practice his French. He wrote it first in English, then translated it into French and allowed Mme. Brillon to correct it. But Franklin being Franklin, he transformed this practice session into a fascinating discussion of contemporary artistic and philosophical concerns in France. Paris at the time was torn by a dispute about the music of Gluck and Piccini. The scientists and philosophers, not yet in possession of the great principles of the conservation of energy, were locked in argument about how and when the world would end.

"The Ephemera," 1778

You may remember, my dear friend, that when we lately spent that happy day in the delightful garden and sweet society of the Moulin Joli. I stopped a little in one of our walks, and stayed some time behind the company. We had been shown numberless skeletons of a kind of little fly, called an ephemera, whose successive generations, we were told, were bred and expired within the day. I happened to see a living company of them on a leaf, who appeared to be engaged in conversation. You know I understand all the inferior animal tongues: my too great application to the study of them is the best excuse I can give for the little progress I have made in your charming language. I listened through curiosity to the discourse of these little creatures; but as they, in their national vivacity, spoke three or four together, I could make but little of their conversation. I found, however, by some broken expressions that I heard now and then, they were disputing warmly on the merit of two foreign musicians, one a *cousin,* the other a *moscheto;* in which dispute they spent their time, seemingly as regardless of the shortness of life as if they had been sure of living a month. Happy people! thought I; you are certainly under a wise, just, and mild government, since you have no public grievances to complain of, nor any subject of contention but the perfections and imperfections of foreign music. I turned my head from them to an old grey-headed one, who was single on another leaf, and talking to himself. Being amused with his soliloquy, I put it down in writing, in hopes it will likewise amuse her to whom I am so much indebted for the most pleasing of all amusements, her delicious company and heavenly harmony.

"It was," said he, "the opinion of learned philosophers of our race, who lived and flourished long before my time, that this vast world, the Moulin Joli, could not itself subsist more than eighteen hours; and I think there was some foundation for that opinion, since, by the apparent motion of the great luminary that gives life to all nature, and which in my time has evidently declined considerably towards the ocean at the end of the earth, it must then finish its course, be extinguished in the waters that surround us, and leave the world in cold and darkness, necessarily producing universal death and destruction. I have lived seven of those hours, a great age, being no less than four hundred and twenty minutes of time. How very few of us continue so long! I have seen generations born, flourish, and expire. My present friends are the children and grandchildren of the friends of my youth, who are now, alas, no more! And I must soon follow them; for, by the course of nature, though still in health, I cannot expect to live above seven or eight minutes longer. What now avails all my toil and labor, in amassing honey-dew on this leaf, which I cannot live to enjoy! What the political struggles I have been engaged in for the good of my compatriot inhabitants of this bush, or my philosophical studies for the benefit of our race in general! for, in politics, what can laws do without morals? Our present race of ephemerae will in a course of minutes become corrupt, like those of other and older bushes, and consequently as wretched. And in philosophy how small our progress! Alas! art is long, and life is short! My friends would comfort me with the idea of a name, they say, I shall leave behind me; and they tell me I have lived long enough to nature and to glory. But what will fame be to an ephemera who no longer exists? And what will become of all history in the eighteenth hour, when the world itself, even the whole Moulin Joli, shall come to its end and be buried in universal ruin?"

To me, after all my eager pursuits, no solid pleasures

Engraving of an English garden on the island of Moulin Joli, which Franklin visited with Mme. Brillon

now remain but the reflection of a long life spent in meaning well, the sensible conversation of a few good lady ephemerae, and now and then a kind smile and a tune from the ever amiable *Brillante.*

During this weekend at Moulin Joli, Mme. Brillon asked Franklin in all seriousness to become her adopted father. She told him, "You have taken in my heart the place of that father whom I loved and respected so much." Franklin, though declining to abandon completely the role of suitor, accepted the paternal role in this tender letter. Mme. Brillon had remained in the country, and Franklin was writing to her from Passy.

I accept with infinite pleasure, my dear friend, your very kind offer to adopt me as your father. I would be most happy to be the parent of such a good child; and since in coming and establishing myself here, I have lost the sweet Company and respectful Attention of an affectionate Daughter, this Loss will be made up, and I will have the Satisfaction of confidently reflecting that, if I spend my few remaining days here, another affectionate daughter will care for me during my lifetime, and will tenderly close my eyes when I must take my final Repose. Yes, my very dear child, I love you as a Father, with all my Heart. It's true that I sometime suspect this Heart of wanting to go further, but I try to hide this from myself.

I cannot stop recalling the memory of that hospitality where I was so often happy in your Company, and your friendship, without experiencing painful Regrets because of your Absence here. Your good Neighbours are very obliging, and they try to make Wednesday and Saturday evenings without you as nice as possible for me: But the Sight of those people that I was accustomed to seeing with you, constantly makes me aware that you are not there: this draws Sighs from me, for which I do not reproach myself, because even though at my age it is not becoming to say that I am in love with a young woman, there is nothing which prevents me from confessing that I admire and love a Collection of all feminine virtues and all admirable Talents; I love my Daughter because she is truly lovable, and because she loves me.

When Franklin came down with an attack of the gout, Mme. Brillon composed a poem in which M. Gout and the Sage, whom he was tormenting, discussed the Sage's many faults. Franklin was inspired to reply with one of his wittiest essays, "The Dialogue with the Gout."

A French cartoon of 1778 depicts a headdress saluting the ideal of American independence and the "Triumph of Liberty."

Midnight, October 22, 1780.

FRANKLIN.   Eh! Oh! Eh! What have I done to merit these cruel sufferings?

GOUT.   Many things; you have ate and drank too freely, and too much indulged those legs of yours in their indolence.

FRANKLIN.   Who is it that accuses me?

GOUT.   It is I, even I, the Gout.

FRANKLIN.   What! my enemy in person?

GOUT.   No, not your enemy.

FRANKLIN.   I repeat it; my enemy; for you would not only torment my body to death, but ruin my good name; you reproach me as a glutton and a tippler; now all the world, that knows me, will allow that I am neither the one nor the other.

GOUT.   The world may think as it pleases; it is always very complaisant to itself, and sometimes to its friends; but I very well know that the quantity of meat and drink proper for a man, who takes a reasonable degree of exercise, would be too much for another, who never takes any.

FRANKLIN.   I take—Eh! Oh!—as much exercise—Eh!—as I can, Madam Gout. You know my sedentary state, and on that account, it would seem, Madam Gout, as if you might spare me a little, seeing it is not altogether my own fault.

GOUT.   Not a jot; your rhetoric and your politeness are thrown away; your apology avails nothing. If your situation in life is a sedentary one, your amusements, your recreations, at least, should be active. You ought to walk or ride; or, if the weather prevents that, play at billiards. But let us examine your course of life. While the mornings are long, and you have leisure to go abroad, what do you do? Why, instead of gaining an appetite for breakfast, by salutary exercise, you amuse yourself, with books, pamphlets, or newspapers, which commonly are not worth the reading. Yet you eat an inordinate breakfast, four dishes of tea, with cream, and one or two buttered toasts, with slices of hung beef, which I fancy are not things the most easily digested. Immediately afterward you sit down to write at your desk, or converse with persons who apply to you on business. Thus the time passes till one, without any kind of bodily exercise. But all this I could pardon, in regard, as you say, to your sedentary condition. But what is your practice after dinner? Walking in the beautiful gardens of those friends, with whom you have dined, would be the choice of men of sense; yours is to be fixed down to chess, where you are found engaged for two or three hours! This is your perpetual recreation, which is the least eligible of any for a sedentary man, because, instead of accelerating the motion of the fluids, the rigid attention it requires helps to retard the circulation and obstruct internal secretions. Wrapt in the speculations of this wretched game, you destroy your constitution. What can be expected from such a course of living, but a body replete with stagnant humours, ready to fall a prey to all kinds of dangerous maladies, if I, the Gout, did not occasionally bring you relief by agitating those humours, and so purifying or dissipating them? If it was in some nook or alley in Paris, deprived of walks, that you played awhile at chess after dinner, this might be excusable; but the same taste prevails with you in Passy, Auteuil, Montmartre, or Sanoy, places where there are the finest gardens and walks, a pure air, beautiful women, and most agreeable and instructive conversation; all which you might enjoy by frequenting the walks. But these are rejected for this abominable game of chess. Fie, then Mr. Franklin! But amidst my instructions, I had almost forgot to administer my wholesome corrections; so take that twinge,— and that....

FRANKLIN.   Oh! Ehhh!—It is not fair to say I take no exercise, when I do very often, going out to dine and returning in my carriage.

GOUT.   That, of all imaginable exercises, is the most slight and insignificant, if you allude to the motion of a carriage suspended on springs. By observing the degree of heat obtained by different kinds of motion, we may form an estimate of the quantity of exercise given by each. Thus, for example, if you turn out to walk in winter with cold feet, in an hour's time you will be in a glow all over; ride on horseback, the same effect will scarcely be perceived by four hours' round trotting; but if you loll in a carriage, such as you have mentioned, you may travel all day, and gladly enter the last inn to warm your feet by a fire. Flatter yourself then no longer, that half an hour's airing in your carriage deserves the name of exercise. Providence has appointed few to roll in carriages, while he has given to all a pair of legs....

FRANKLIN. How can you so cruelly sport with my torments?

GOUT. Sport! I am very serious. I have here a list of offences against your own health distinctly written, and can justify every stroke inflicted on you.

FRANKLIN. Read it then.

GOUT. It is too long a detail; but I will briefly mention some particulars.

FRANKLIN. Proceed. I am all attention.

GOUT. Do you remember how often you have promised yourself, the following morning, a walk in the grove of Boulogne, in the garden de la Muette, or in your own garden, and have violated your promise, alleging, at one time, it was too cold, at another too warm, too windy, too moist, or what else you pleased; when in truth it was too nothing, but your insuperable love of ease?

FRANKLIN. That I confess may have happened occasionally, probably ten times in a year.

GOUT. Your confession is very far short of the truth; the gross amount is one hundred and ninety-nine times.

FRANKLIN. Is it possible?

GOUT. So possible, that it is fact; you may rely on the accuracy of my statement. You know M. Brillon's gardens, and what fine walks they contain; you know the handsome flight of an hundred steps, which lead from the terrace above to the lawn below. You have been in the practice of visiting this amiable family twice a week, after dinner, and it is a maxim of your own, that "a man may take as much exercise in walking a mile, up and down stairs, as in ten on level ground." What an opportunity was here for you to have had exercise in both these ways! Did you embrace it, and how often?

FRANKLIN. I cannot immediately answer that question.

GOUT. I will do it for you; not once.

FRANKLIN. Not once?

GOUT. Even so. During the summer you went there at six o'clock. You found the charming lady, with her

This small sketch of Franklin was enclosed in a letter received by Abbé de la Roche, a friend Franklin made at the home of Mme. Helvétius.

lovely children and friends, eager to walk with you, and entertain you with their agreeable conversation; and what has been your choice? Why to sit on the terrace, satisfying yourself with the fine prospect, and passing your eye over the beauties of the garden below, without taking one step to descend and walk about in them. On the contrary, you call for tea and the chess-board; and lo! you are occupied in your seat till nine o'clock, and that besides two hours' play after dinner; and then, instead of walking home, which would have bestirred you a little, you step into your carriage....

FRANKLIN.   What then would you have me do with my carriage?

GOUT.   Burn it if you choose; you would at least get heat out of it once in this way; or, if you dislike that proposal, here's another for you; observe the poor peasants, who work in the vineyards and grounds about the villages of Passy, Auteuil, Chaillot, &c.; you may find every day, among these deserving creatures, four or five old men and women, bent and perhaps crippled by weight of years, and too long and too great labour. After a most fatiguing day, these people have to trudge a mile or two to their smoky huts. Order your coachman to set them down. This is an act that will be good for your soul; and, at the same time, after your visit to the Brillons, if you return on foot, that will be good for your body.

FRANKLIN.   Ah! how tiresome you are!

GOUT.   Well, then, to my office; it should not be forgotten that I am your physician. There.

FRANKLIN.   Ohhh! what a devil of a physician!

GOUT.   How ungrateful you are to say so! Is it not I who, in the character of your physician, have saved you from the palsy, dropsy, and apoplexy? one or other of which would have done for you long ago, but for me.

FRANKLIN.   I submit, and thank you for the past, but entreat the discontinuance of your visits for the future; for, in my mind, one had better die than be cured so dolefully .... Oh! oh!—for Heaven's sake leave me! and I promise faithfully never more to play at chess, but to exercise daily, and live temperately.

GOUT.   I know you too well. You promise fair; but, after a few months of good health, you will return to your

French salons of the eighteenth century were lively and elegant.

old habits; your fine promises will be forgotten like the forms of last year's clouds. Let us then finish the account, and I will go. But I leave you with an assurance of visiting you again at a proper time and place; for my object is your good, and you are sensible now that I am your *real friend*.

A few days later he returned the draft of Mme. Brillon's poem about the sage and the gout with the following wry note.

I am returning the rough draft of your pretty story to you, my very dear daughter, since you insist on getting it back. I thought that in offering you a more attractive edition, which your work certainly deserved, I could convince you to let me keep the original, something I wanted, because I love what comes from your hand so much....

One of the characters in your story, i.e. The Gout, strikes me as reasoning well enough, except for her assumption that mistresses played some part in causing this painful ailment. I, personally, think the contrary, and here is my reasoning. When I was a young man and enjoyed more favours of the [fair] Sex than at present, I had no gout at all. Thus if the Ladies of Passy had had more of the kind of Christian charity which I have so often vainly recommended to you, I would not have gout now. I think this is very logical.

I feel much better. I have little pain, but I am very weak. As you can see, I can joke a little, but I can't be really gay until I hear that your precious health is restored.

Franklin soon found himself playing a father's role with Mme. Brillon in an unexpected way. She discovered that her husband was having an affair with the governess of her children. In a frenzy of emotion, she fled to Franklin for advice. After listening to her tearful story, he sent her this wise letter.

[May 10, 1782?]

You told me, my dear daughter, that your heart is too sensitive. I see clearly in your letters that this is too true. To be very sensitive to our faults is good because that leads us to avoid them in the future; but to be very sensitive to and afflicted by the faults of others is not good. It is up to them to be sensitive and to be afflicted by what they did badly; for us, we must preserve the tranquility which is the just portion of innocence and virtue. But you say: "Ingratitude is a frightful evil." It is true for the

Engraving after Rosalie Filleul's
portrait of Franklin made in 1778

ungrateful—but not for their benefactors. You have conferred acts of kindness on those people you have thought worthy of them; you have thus done your duty, since it is our duty to do good and you should be satisfied by it and happy in the thought. If they are ungrateful it is their crime and not yours; and it is up to them to be unhappy when they reflect on the baseness of their conduct toward you. If they insult you, think that although they could formerly have been your equals, they have, in this manner, placed themselves below you; if you take revenge by punishing them, you thereby restore them to their state of equality which they lost. But if you forgive them with no punishment, you keep them fixed in that low state into which they have fallen and from which they can never escape without repentance and full reparation. Then follow, my very dear daughter, the good resolution which you so wisely made, to continue to fulfill all your duties as a good mother, good wife, good friend, good neighbour, good Christian, etc. and ignore and forget, if possible, the insults you receive at present; and be assured that in time, the rectitude of your conduct will prevail upon the minds of even the worst people and even more on the minds of the individuals who are basically good and who also have common sense, even though for the present they are led astray by the artifices of other people. Then, everyone will quickly ask you for the return of your friendship and will become in the future, some of your most loyal friends.

I am sensitive to the fact that I have just written some very bad French; that could disgust you, you who write this charming language with so much purity and elegance. But, if you can, finally, decipher my awkward and improper expressions, you will have, at least the kind of pleasure derived from explaining riddles or discovering secrets.

Finally Franklin abandoned all hope of winning Mme. Brillon in this world. He accepted—or at least pretended to accept—her assurance that they would be happy together in heaven. But he had his own wry comments to make on their sojourn in Paradise, in this letter. Mme. d'Hardancourt was Mme. Brillon's mother. Father Pagin was Mme. Brillon's music teacher. The others were members of the Passy circle.

Since you assured me that we shall meet and recognize each other in Heaven, I have been thinking continually about the settlement of our Affairs in that land: because I have great confidence in your assurances and I believe implicitly in what you believe.

Probably more than forty years will elapse after my arrival there, before you follow me: I am a little afraid that during such a long period of time, you may forget me —I have therefore considered asking you to give me your word of honour not to renew your contract with Mr. B. I shall then give you mine to wait for you. But this gentleman is so kind and so generous toward us—he loves you—and we him—so much—that I cannot contemplate this idea without some scruples of conscience. Yet, the thought of an Eternity in which I would not be favoured with more than occasional permission to kiss your hands or your cheeks, or to spend more than two or three hours on Wednesday and Saturday evenings in your sweet company, is frightful. Finally, I cannot make this proposal, but since (along with everyone who knows you) I wish to see you happy in every way, we can agree not to talk about it anymore now and to leave it up to you, when we all meet: there to determine what you will judge best for your happiness and ours. Decide as you wish, I feel that I will love you eternally. If you reject me, maybe I will address myself to Madame D'Hardancourt, and maybe she will want to keep house with me; then I will spend my domestic hours agreeably with her; and I will be more within reach of seeing you, I will have enough time during those 40 years, to practice the Harmonica, and maybe I will be able to play well enough to be worthy to accompany your piano(forte), and from time to time we will have little concerts: the good Father Pagin will be one of the party, your neighbour and his dear family (Mr. Jupin), Mr. de Chaumont, Mr. B., Mr. Jourdon, Mr. Grammont, Madame du Tartre, the little mother and other chosen friends will be our audience, and the dear good girls, accompanied by some other young angels of whom you have already given me portraits, will sing Alleluia with us, all together we will eat roasted apples of paradise with butter and nutmeg; and we will have pity on those who are not dead.

With Mme. Helvétius, Franklin had an entirely different relationship. She was the opposite of Mme. Brillon in almost every way. An aristocrat, she lived at Auteuil, the village next to Passy, in a highly uncon-

Self-portrait of Mme. Filleul, another member of the Passy circle

ventional ménage that consisted of herself, two free-thinking former priests —Abbé Martin Lefebre de la Roche and Abbé André Morellet—and a young physician, Pierre Georges Cabanis. Although at fifty-seven she was no longer beautiful—her enemies called her the Ruins of Palmyra—Mme. Helvétius fascinated Franklin and he plunged cheerfully into the hectic life of Auteuil. He saw that Madame was a kind of goddess in her special world, and quickly gave her a slightly sacrilegious nickname, Notre Dame d'Auteuil. In this letter he tried to analyze the fascination she held for him and other men.

PRIVATE COLLECTION

Louis-Michel Van Loo's elegant portrait of the fascinating, still attractive Mme. Helvétius.

I have in my way been trying to form some hypothesis to account for your having so many friends and of such various kinds. I see that statesmen, philosophers, historians, poets, and men of learning attach themselves to you as straws to a fine piece of amber.

It is not that you make pretensions to any of their sciences, and, if you did, similarity of studies does not always make people love one another. It is not that you take pains to engage them: artless simplicity is a striking part of your character. I would not attempt to explain it by the story of the ancient, who, being asked why philosphers sought the acquaintance of kings, and kings not that of philosophers, replied that philosophers knew what they wanted, which was not always the case with kings.

Yet thus far the comparison may go, that we find in your sweet society that charming benevolence, that amiable attention to oblige, that disposition to please and be pleased, which we do not always find in the society of one another. It springs from you; it has its influence on us all; and in your company we are not only pleased with you, but better pleased with one another and with ourselves.

The cheerful disorder that reigned at Auteuil was admirably described by Franklin in this letter to another French lady friend, Mme. de la Frete.

My goodness, Madame, you did the right thing not to come so far, in such a bad season for such a sad lunch. My son and I were not so wise. I'll give you an account of it.

Since the invitation was for eleven o'clock, and since you were among the group, I thought to find a breakfast in the manner of a dinner; that there would be many people; that we would have not only tea, but also coffee, chocolate, maybe ham and several other good things. I decided to go on foot; my shoes were a little too tight; I arrived

386

almost lame. Entering the courtyard, I was a little surprised to find it so empty of carriages, and to see that we [Franklin and Temple] were the first to arrive. We went upstairs. No noise at all. We went into the dining room. No one except M. l'Abbé and Mr. C—breakfast finished and eaten! Nothing on the table except some scraps of bread and a little butter. They exclaim; they run to tell Madame H. that we had come for breakfast. She leaves her toilette, and comes with her hair half-combed. They are surprised that I came since you wrote me that you weren't coming....

Finally another breakfast is ordered. One of them runs for fresh water, another for coal. They blow vigorously to make a fire. I was very hungry; it was so late; "A watched pot never boils," as Poor Richard says. Madame leaves for Paris and abandons us. We begin to eat. The butter is soon finished. M. l'Abbé asks if we want some more. Yes, certainly. He rings. No one comes. We talk, he forgets the butter. I scrape the plate; he understood why and ran to the kitchen to look for some. After a time he slowly returns, saying sadly, there is no more in the house. For my amusement, M. l'Abbé suggests a walk; my feet refuse to do it. As a result, we leave the breakfast there; and go upstairs to his room to find books with which to finish our meal.

Franklin was soon quite candidly in love with Mme. Helvétius. He used the abbés to carry notes for him, and wooed her with ingenious essays, such as this one.

The Flies of the Apartments of M. F. request Permission to present their Respects to Madame H., and to express in their best language their Gratitude for the Protection she has been kind enough to give them,

Bizz, izzz ouizz a ouizzz izzzzzzzzz, etc.

We have long lived under the hospitable Roof of the said bonhomme F. He has given us free Lodgings; we have also eaten and drunk the whole Year at his Expense without its having cost us anything. Often, when his Friends and himself have used up a Bowl of Punch, he has left a sufficient Quantity to intoxicate a hundred of us Flies.

We have drunk freely from it, and after that we have made our Sallies, our Circles and our Cotillions very prettily in the Air of his Bedroom, and have gaily consummated our little Loves under his Nose.

Finally, we would have been the happiest People in the World, if he had not permitted to remain over the top of his Wainscoting a Number of our declared Enemies, who stretched their Nets to capture us, and who tore us pitilessly to pieces. People of a Disposition both subtle and fierce, abominable Combination!

You, very excellent Lady, had the goodness to order that all these Assassins with their Habitations and their Snares be swept; and your Orders, as they always ought to be, were carried out immediately. Since that Time we have lived happily, and have enjoyed the Beneficence of the said bonhomme F. without fear.

There only remains one Thing for us to wish in order to assure the Stability of our Fortune; permit us to say it,

Bizz izzz ouizz a ouizzzz izzzzzz etc.,

It is to see both of you forming at last but one Ménage.

Finally, Franklin proposed to Mme. Helvétius. When she refused him, he went back to Passy and composed one of his most famous bagatelles, "The Elysian Fields."

Saddened by your barbarous resolution, stated so positively last night, to remain single the rest of your life, in honor of your dear husband, I went home, fell on my bed, believing myself dead, and found myself in the Elysian Fields.

I was asked if I had a wish to see some Important Persons—Take me to the Philosophers.—There are two who reside quite near here, in this Garden: they are very good neighbors and very good friends of each other.—Who are they?—Socrates and H——. I have prodigious esteem for both of them; but let me see H—— first, for I understand some French and not a word of Greek.

He received me with great courtesy, having known me by reputation, he said, for some time. He asked me a thousand questions on War, and on the present state of Religion, of Liberty, and of the Government in France.—But you are not enquiring at all about your dear Friend Madame H——; yet, she is excessively in love with you, and I was with her but an hour ago.

Ah! said he, you are reminding me of my former felicity. But one must forget, in order to be happy in this place. For several of the first years, I thought of nobody but her. Well, now I am consoled. I have taken another

With a letter in praise of wine that Franklin sent to his friend Abbé Morellet, he included this drawing by Temple, proving that God —since He gave man elbows— intended him to drink.

Wife. One as similar to her as I could find. She is not, to be sure, quite as beautiful, but she has just as much common sense, a little more wisdom, and she loves me infinitely. Her continuous endeavor is to please me; and she has gone out right now to search for the best Nectar and Ambrosia to regale me with tonight; Stay with me and you shall see her.

I notice, said I, that your former Friend is more faithful than you: For several good Matches have been offered her, and she has turned them all down. I confess that I, for one, loved her madly; but she was harsh toward me and rejected me absolutely for love of you.

I pity you, said he, for your misfortune; for she is truly a good and lovely woman, and most amiable....

As he was saying this, the new Madame H. came in with the Nectar. I recognized her instantly as Madame F., my former American Friend. I claimed her. But she said coldly, I have been a good Wife to you for forty-nine years and four months, almost half a century; be content with that. I have formed a new Connection here, that will last for Eternity.

Grieved by this Rebuke from my Euridyce, I resolved there and then to abandon those ungrateful Shadows, and to come back to this good World, to see the Sun again, and you. Here I am! Let's take our revenge.

The deep affection that existed between Franklin and his French ladies is nowhere better summed up than in this brief note, which he wrote to Mme. Brillon toward the close of his stay in France. It could have been written just as readily to Mme. Helvétius.

Saturday in Passy

Since one day, my dear friend, I will have to leave for America, with no hope of ever seeing you again, I have sometimes had the thought that it would be wise to cut myself off from you by degrees, first to see you just once a week, after that, only once every two weeks, once a month, etc., etc. so as to lessen little by little the inordinate desire that I always feel for your enchanting company, and in this way to avoid the great hurt that I must otherwise suffer at the final separation. But, in testing the experience, I find that instead of diminishing this desire, absence augments it. The hurt that I fear is, thus, incurable, and I will come to visit you this evening.

Chapter 13

The Nation's Patriarch

Although Franklin vowed that he was through with politics, he permitted himself to be elected President of Pennsylvania's Executive Council almost as soon as he reached America. He knew it was a mistake. When his sister Jane reproached him, he replied. "We have all of us wisdom enough to judge what others ought to do, or not to do in the management of their affairs; and 'tis possible that I might blame you as much if you were to accept the offer of a young husband." In this letter to Jonathan Shipley, he discussed his decision to take on a new duty at the age of eighty, and went on to tell the good bishop a little about affairs in America and the present state of the Franklin family.

Philadelphia, Feb. 24th, 1786.
I received lately your kind letter of Nov. 27th. My Reception here was, as you have heard, very honourable indeed; but I was betray'd by it, and by some Remains of Ambition, from which I had imagined myself free, to accept of the Chair of Government for the State of Pennsylvania, when the proper thing for me was Repose and a private Life. I hope, however, to be able to bear the Fatigue for one Year, and then to retire.

I have much regretted our having so little Opportunity for Conversation when we last met. You could have given me Informations and Counsels that I wanted, but we were scarce a Minute together without being broke in upon. I am to thank you, however, for the Pleasure I had after our Parting, in reading the new Book you gave me, which I think generally well written and likely to do good; tho' the Reading Time of most People is of late so taken up with News Papers and little periodical Pamphlets, that few now-a-days venture to attempt reading a

Quarto Volume. I have admir'd to see, that, in the last Century, a Folio, *Burton on Melancholly*, went through Six Editions in about Twenty Years. We have, I believe, more Readers now, but not of such large Books.

You seem desirous of knowing what Progress we make here in improving our Governments. We are, I think, In the right Road of Improvement, for we are making Experiments. I do not oppose all that seem wrong, for the Multitude are more effectually set right by Experience, than kept from going wrong by Reasoning with them. And I think we are daily more and more enlightened; so that I have no doubt of our obtaining in a few Years as much public Felicity, as good Government is capable of affording.

Your NewsPapers are fill'd with fictitious Accounts of Anarchy, Confusion, Distrsses, and Miseries, we are suppos'd to be involv'd in, as Consequences of the Revolution; and the few remaining Friends of the old Government among us take pains to magnify every little Inconvenience a Change in the Course of Commerce may have occasion'd. To obviate the Complaints they endeavour to excite, was written the enclos'd little Piece, from which you may form a truer Idea of our Situation, than your own public Prints would give you. And I can assure you, that the great Body of our Nation find themselves happy in the Change, and have not the smallest Inclination to return to the Domination of Britain. There could not be a stronger Proof of the general Approbation of the Measures, that promoted the Change, and of the Change itself, than has been given by the Assembly and Council of this State, in the nearly unanimous Choice for their Governor, of one who had been so much concern'd in those Measures; the Assembly being themselves the unbrib'd Choice of the People, and therefore may be truly suppos'd of the same Sentiments. I say nearly unanimous, because, of between 70 and 80 Votes, there were only my own and one other in the negative.

As to my Domestic Circumstances, of which you kindly desire to hear something, they are at present as happy as I could wish them. I am surrounded by my Offspring, a Dutiful and Affectionate Daughter in my House, with Six Grandchildren, the eldest of which you have seen, who is now at a College in the next Street, finishing the learned Part of his Education; the others promising, both

Armorial bearings of the State of Pennsylvania, from a 1787 magazine

for Parts and good Dispositions. What their Conduct may be, when they grow up and enter the important Scenes of Life, I shall not live to *see,* and I cannot *foresee.* I therefore enjoy among them the present Hour, and leave the future to Providence.

He that raises a large Family does, indeed, while he lives to observe them, *stand,* as Watts says, *a broader Mark for Sorrow;* but then he stands a broader Mark for Pleasure too. When we launch our little Fleet of Barques into the Ocean, bound to different Ports, we hope for each a prosperous Voyage; but contrary Winds, hidden Shoals, Storms, and Enemies come in for a Share in the Disposition of Events; and though these occasion a Mixture of Disappointment, yet, considering the Risque where we can make no Insurance, we should think ourselves happy if some return with Success. My Son's Son, Temple Franklin, whom you have also seen, having had a fine Farm of 600 Acres convey'd to him by his Father when we were at Southampton, had drop'd for the present his Views of acting in the political Line, and applies himself ardently to the Study and Practice of Agriculture. This is much more agreable to me, who esteem it the most useful, the most independent, and therefore the noblest of Employments. His Lands are on navigable water, communicating with the Delaware, and but about 16 Miles from this City. He has associated to himself a very skillful English Farmer lately arrived here, who is to instruct him in the Business, and partakes for a Term of the Profits; so that there is a great apparent Probability of their Success.

You will kindly expect a Word or two concerning myself. My Health and Spirits continue, Thanks to God, as when you saw me. The only complaint I then had, does not grow worse, and is tolerable. I still have Enjoyment in the Company of my Friends; and, being easy in my Circumstances, have many Reasons to like Living. But the Course of Nature must soon put a period to my present Mode of Existence. This I shall submit to with less Regret, as, having seen during a long Life a good deal of this World, I feel a growing Curiosity to be acquainted with some other; and can chearfully, with filial Confidence, resign my Spirit to the conduct of that great and good Parent of Mankind, who created it, and who has so graciously protected and prospered me from my Birth to

The Franklin coat of arms, embossed on one of Temple Franklin's books

the present Hour. Wherever I am, I hope always to retain the pleasing remembrance of your Friendship, being with sincere and great Esteem, my dear Friend, yours most affectionately,

B FRANKLIN

P.S.   We all join in Respects to Mrs. Shipley, and best wishes for the whole amiable Family.

The separation from Mme. Helvétius was something Franklin felt most keenly in America. In this tender letter, he carried himself in his imagination back to Auteuil. "The Stars" was a nickname Franklin invented for Mme. Helvétius's daughters.

Philadelphia, 20 Oct. 1785

Yesterday was Wednesday. At 10 in the Morning, I thought of you, of your House, of your Table, of your Friends, etc. At this hour, I said, they are all at dinner, M. le Roy, M. Hennin, Abbés de la Roche & Morellet, M. Cabbanis, perhaps one of the little Stars. Madame is serving the whole Company, with as much Ease as Pleasure. But, alas, I was not there, to share in the gay conversation marked by good Sense, Wit, & Friendship, which season all her Meals.

You will be Pleased to Know that I am here in good Health and happy in the Bosom of my Family. But I failed to find the Rest I had hoped for; I have been asked to become Governor, & I have had the weakness to agree; so there I am busier than ever.—If I can do some good for my People, that will console me. Otherwise, I would wish that I had accepted your friendly Invitation to spend the rest of my days at your home.

Good-by, my good Friend, love me always, as I love you. Embrace for me all my Friends of your Circle, and always remember that I am bound to you with Feelings of greatest affection.

In this chatty letter to Jane Mecom, Franklin not only continued to demonstrate the affection he felt for his favorite sister, but also provided a good glimpse of himself, late in 1786. "That Soap" was the soap Franklin's father used to make, according to his private formula, which the family had preserved.

Philada, Sept. 21, 1786.

My dear Sister:

I received your kind Letter of the 25th past, by our Cousin Williams, who, besides, informs me of your Welfare, which gives me great Pleasure.

Your Grandson having finished all the Business I had to employ him in, set out for Boston a few Days before Cousin Williams arrived. I suppose he may be with you before this time.

I had begun to build two good Houses next the Street, instead of three old Ones which I pull'd down, but my Neighbour disputing my Bounds, I have been obliged to postpone till that Dispute is settled by Law. In the meantime, the Workmen, and Materials being ready, I have ordered an Addition to the House I live in, it being too small for our growing Family. There are a good many Hands employ'd, and I hope to see it cover'd in before Winter. I propose to have in it a long Room for my Library and Instruments, with two good Bedchambers and two Garrets. The Library is to be even with the Floor of my best old Chamber; and the Story under it will for the present be employ'd only to hold Wood, but may be made into Rooms hereafter. This Addition is on the Side next the River. I hardly know how to justify building a library at an Age that will so soon oblige me to quit it; but we are apt to forget that we are grown old, and Building is an Amusement.

I think you will do well to instruct your Grandson in the Art of making that Soap. It may be of use to him, and 'tis pity it should be lost.

Some knowing Ones here in Matters of Weather predict a hard Winter. Permit me to have the Pleasure of helping to keep you warm. Lay in a good Stock of Firewood, and draw upon me for the Amount. Your Bill shall be paid upon Sight by your affectionate Brother,

B FRANKLIN

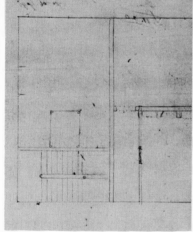

Franklin's sketch of the second floor of his house in Philadelphia, with his double bed drawn in

Although Franklin continued to assure his friends in Europe that all was well in the United States, he reacted like most Americans to Shays' Rebellion, the revolt of a group of destitute farmers in western Massachusetts. His old friend James Bowdoin was Governor of Massachusetts, and this sharpened Franklin's hostility to the violence. In this letter to Bowdoin, he stated his sentiments clearly. The proclamation offered a reward of 150 pounds for the capture of the four ringleaders.

Philada. March 6, 1787

I received the Letter you did me the honour lately to write me respecting the Proclamation for apprehending several Promoters of the Rebellion in your State. The

Proclamation was immediately printed in our News-papers; and the Matter being laid before the Council and Assembly, it was thought fit to make an Addition to the Rewards your Government had offered, which will be done, tho' the usual Forms of Proceeding have occasioned some Delay. I congratulate your Excellency most cordially on the happy Success attending the wise and vigorous Measures taken for the Suppression of that dangerous Insurrection, and I pray most heartily for the future Tranquility of the State which you so worthily and happily govern. Its Constitution is I think one of the best in the Union, perhaps I might say in the World. And I persuade my self that the good Sense and sound Understanding predominant among the great Majority of your People, will always secure it from the mad Attempts to overthrow it, which can only proceed chiefly from the Wickedness, or from the Ignorance of a few who while they enjoy it are insensible of its Excellence.

James Bowdoin

Shays' Rebellion played a part, perhaps exaggerated by some historians, in awakening Americans to the defects of their Federal Government. The decision to reform it soon gathered momentum, and the Constitutional Convention met in Philadelphia on May 14, 1787. Franklin was an inevitable choice as one of Pennsylvania's delegates. Recognizing the crucial importance of the occasion, Franklin attended the Convention almost daily. It was his last outpouring of energy, a final expression of commitment to the American nation he had done so much to create. During the often bitter debates, he played his favorite role of conciliator and compromiser. Many of the compromises were achieved by very thin margins, and when the document was ready for a final vote, there was strong concern among many of the delegates that a substantial minority of those who had lost the arguments would vote against the final document. This would almost certainly guarantee its rejection by the states. The leaders of the Convention turned to Franklin and asked him to make a final plea for unanimity. He responded with this famous speech—which because of his growing infirmity he had to ask James Wilson to read for him—on the final day of the Convention. He next agreed to make a motion—actually drafted by the unpopular Gouverneur Morris—recommending members to sign as witnesses of the "unanimous consent of the states."

[September 17, 1787]

Mr. President,

I confess, that I do not entirely approve of this Constitution at present; but, Sir, I am not sure I shall never approve it; for, having lived long, I have experienced many

*A land grant and a commission
appointing justices of the peace, both
signed by Franklin in 1787 as the
President of Pennsylvania's Supreme
Executive Council, an office
equivalent to Governor*

instances of being obliged, by better information or fuller consideration, to change my opinions even on important subjects, which I once thought right, but found to be otherwise. It is therefore that, the older I grow, the more apt I am to doubt my own judgment of others. Most men, indeed, as well as most sects in religion, think themselves in possession of all truth, and that wherever others differ from them, it is so far error. Steele, a Protestant, in a dedication, tells the Pope, that the only difference between our two churches in their opinions of the certainty of their doctrine, is, the Romish Church is *infallible,* and the Church of England is *never in the wrong.* But, though many private Persons think almost as highly of their own infallibility as that of their Sect, few express it so naturally as a certain French Lady, who, in a little dispute with her sister, said, "But I meet with nobody but myself that is *always* in the right." *"Je ne trouve que moi qui aie toujours raison."*

In these sentiments, Sir, I agree to this Constitution, with all its faults,—if they are such; because I think a general Government necessary for us, and there is no *form* of government but what may be a blessing to the people, if well administered; and I believe, farther, that this is likely to be well administered for a course of years, and can only end in despotism, as other forms have done before it, when the people shall become so corrupted as to need despotic government, being incapable of any other. I doubt, too, whether any other Convention we can obtain, may be able to make a better constitution; for, when you assemble a number of men, to have the advantage of their joint wisdom, you inevitably assemble with those men all their prejudices, their passions, their errors of opinion, their local interest, and their selfish views. From such an assembly can a *perfect* production be expected? It therefore astonishes me, Sir, to find this system approaching so near to perfection as it does; and I think it will astonish our enemies, who are waiting with confidence to hear, that our councils are confounded like those of the builders of Babel, and that our States are on the point of separation, only to meet hereafter for the purpose of cutting one another's throats. Thus I consent, Sir, to this Constitution, because I expect no better, and because I am not sure that it is not the best. The opinions I have had of its *errors* I sacrifice to the public good. I have never whispered a syllable of them abroad. Within these walls they were born, and here they shall die. If every one of us, in returning to our Constituents, were to report the objections he has had to it, and endeavour to gain Partisans in support of them, we might prevent its being generally received, and thereby lose all the salutary effects and great advantages resulting naturally in our favour among foreign nations, as well as among ourselves, from our real or apparent unanimity. Much of the strength and efficiency of any government, in procuring and securing happiness to the people, depends on *opinion,* on the general opinion of the goodness of that government, as well as of the wisdom and integrity of its governors. I hope, therefore, for our own sakes, as a part of the people, and for the sake of our posterity, that we shall act heartily and unanimously in recommending this Constitution, wherever our Influence may extend, and turn our future thoughts and endeavours to the means of having it *well administered.*

On the whole, Sir, I cannot help expressing a wish, that every member of the Convention who may still have objections to it, would with me on this occasion doubt a little of his own infallibility, and, to make *manifest* our *unanimity,* put his name to this Instrument.

In another letter to his sister Jane, written three days after the Convention adjourned, Franklin discussed the conclave, and then turned to an interesting disquisition on war and its alternatives.

Philadelphia, Sept. 20, 1787.

Dear Sister,

I received your kind Letter of the 16th past, which gave me the great Pleasure of learning that you were well. I thought I had before acknowledged the Receipt of yours per Colonel Sergeant.

The Convention finish'd the 17th Instant. I attended the Business of it 5 Hours in every Day from the Beginning, which is something more than four Months. You may judge from thence, that my Health continues; some tell me I look better, and they suppose the daily Exercise of going and returning from the Statehouse has done me good. You will see the Constitution we have propos'd in the Papers. The Forming of it so as to accommodate all the different Interests and Views was a difficult

INDEPENDENCE NATIONAL HISTORICAL PARK

View of the public buildings in Philadelphia during Franklin's time

Task; and perhaps, after all, it may not be received with the same Unanimity in the different States, that the Convention have given the Example of in delivering it out for their Consideration. We have, however, done our best, and it must take its chance.

I agree with you perfectly in your disapprobation of war. Abstracted from the inhumanity of it, I think it wrong in point of human prudence; for, whatever advantage one nation would obtain from another, whether it be part of their territory, the liberty of commerce with them, free passage on their rivers, &c. &c., it would be much cheaper to purchase such advantage with ready money than to pay the expense of acquiring it by war. An army is a devouring monster, and, when you have raised it, you have, in order to subsist it, not only the fair charges of pay, clothing, provisions, army, and ammunition, with numberless other contingent and just charges to answer and satisfy, but you have all the additional knavish charges of the numerous tribe of contractors to defray, with those of every other dealer who furnishes the articles wanted for your army, and takes advantage of that want to demand exorbitant prices. It seems to me, that, if statesmen had a little more arithmetic, or were more accustomed to calculation, wars would be much less frequent. I am confident, that Canada might have been purchased from France for a tenth part of the money England spent in the conquest of it. And if, instead of fighting with us for the power of taxing us, she had kept us in good humour by allowing us to dispose of our own money, and now and then giving us a little of hers, by way of donation to colleges, or hospitals, or for cutting canals, or fortifying ports, she might have easily drawn from us much more by our occasional voluntary grants and contributions, than ever she could by taxes. Sensible people will give a bucket or two of water to a dry pump, that they may afterwards, get from it all they have occasion for. Her ministry were deficient in that little point of common sense. And so they spent one hundred millions of her money, and after all lost what they contended for.

I lament the loss your town has suffered this year by fire. I sometimes think men do not act like reasonable creatures when they build for themselves combustible dwellings, in which they are every day obliged to use

In this detail of a 1787 cartoon, the Pennsylvania Constitution is symbolically pictured as a rocky citadel whose defenders brandish a banner inscribed with the words "Franklin & Liberty."

fire. In my new buildings, I have taken a few precautions, not generally used; to wit, none of the wooden work of one room communicates with the wooden work of any other room; and all the floors, and even the steps of the stairs, are plastered close to the boards, besides the plastering on the laths under the joists. There are also trap-doors to go out upon the roofs, that one may go out and wet the shingles in case of a neighbouring fire. But, indeed, I think the staircases should be stone, and the floors tiled as in Paris, and the roofs either tiled or slated....

I sent you lately a Barrel of Flour, and I blame myself for not sooner desiring you to lay in your Winter's Wood, and drawing upon me for it as last Year. But I have been so busy. To avoid such Neglect in Future, I now make the Direction general, that you draw on me every Year for the same purpose.

Adieu, my dear Sister, and believe me ever your affectionate brother,

B FRANKLIN

Franklin accepted a third one-year term as President of Pennsylvania. "This universal and unbounded confidence of a whole people flatters my vanity much more than a peerage could do," he told his sister Jane. At the same time, he gave much of his dwindling strength and energy to another presidency—that of the Pennsylvania Society for Promoting the Abolition of Slavery and the Relief of Free Negroes. In this fascinating letter, Franklin neatly needled the Governor of Rhode Island for the part his fellow citizens played in the continuation of the slave trade. Similar letters went to the governors of other northern states.

Philda Jany 12th, 1788

The Pennsylvania Society for promoting the abolition of Slavery, and the relief of free negroes unlawfully held in bondage have taken the liberty to request your Excellencys acceptance of a few Copies of their Constitution, and of the Laws of Pennsylvania which relate to one of the objects of their Institution, also of a Copy of Thomas Clarksons excellent essay upon the Commerce and Slavery of the Africans.

The Society have heard with great distress that a considerable part of the Slaves who have been sold in the Southern States since the establishment of the Peace have been imported in vessels fitted out in the State over which your Excellency presides. From your Excellencys Station they hope your influence will be exerted hereafter to prevent a practice which is so evidently repugnant to the political principles and forms of Government lately adopted by the Citizens of the United States, and which cannot fail of delaying the enjoyment of the blessings of peace and liberty by drawing down the displeasure of the great and impartial ruler of the Universe upon our Country.

Numerous friends urged Franklin to finish his *Autobiography.* He had added a few pages while he was in France. One of the most importunate pleaders was his Passy neighbor, Louis-Guillaume Le Veillard. In this friendly letter, Franklin responded to him, and mentioned, among other things, the heartening progress of the Constitution.

Philadelphia, June 8, 1788.

I received a few days ago your kind letter of the 3d of January. The *arrêt* in favour of the *non-catholiques* gives pleasure here, not only from its present advantages, but as it is a good step towards general toleration, and to the abolishing in time all party spirit among Christians, and the mischiefs that have so long attended it. Thank God, the world is growing wiser and wiser; and as by degrees men are convinced of the folly of wars for religion, for dominion, or for commerce, they will be happier and happier.

Eight States have now agreed to the proposed new constitution; there remain five who have not yet discussed it; their appointed times of meeting not being yet arrived. Two are to meet this month, the rest later. One more agreeing, it will be carried into execution. Probably some will not agree at present, but time may bring them in; so that we have little doubt of it becoming general, perhaps with some corrections. As to your friend's taking a share in the management of it, his age and infirmities render him unfit for the business, as the business would be for him. After the expiration of his presidentship, which will now be in a few months, he is *determined* to engage no more in public affairs, even if required; but his countrymen will be too reasonable to require it. You are not so considerate; you are a hard taskmaster. You insist on his writing *his life,* already a long work, and at the same time would have him continually employed in augmenting the subject, while the time shortens in which the work is to be executed. Gen-

A slave cameo Wedgwood sent to Franklin when he was the President of the Pennsylvania Abolition Society

eral Washington is the man that all our eyes are fixed on for *President,* and what little influence I may have, is devoted to him.

Unfortunately, Franklin's health broke down almost completely not long after he wrote the following letter. The bladder stone was giving him so much pain that he had had to take opium, which made it difficult for him to write. Sensing that death was near, he began to write farewells to close friends. One of the most tender letters went to Catherine Ray Greene.

Philadelphia, March 2, 1789.

Dear Friend,

Having now done with public affairs, which have hitherto taken up so much of my time, I shall endeavour to enjoy, during the small remainder of life that is left to me, some of the pleasures of conversing with my old friends by writing, since their distance prevents my hope of seeing them again.

I received one of the bags of sweet corn you were so good as to send me a long time since, but the other never came to hand. Even the letter mentioning it, though dated December 10th, 1787, has been above a year on its way; for I received it but about two weeks since from Baltimore in Maryland. The corn I did receive was excellent, and gave me great pleasure. Accept my hearty thanks.

I am, as you suppose in the abovementioned old letter, much pleased to hear, that my young friend Ray is "smart in the farming way," and makes such substantial fences. I think agriculture the most honourable of all employments, being the most independent. The farmer has no need of popular favour, nor the favour of the great; the success of his crops depending only on the blessing of God upon his honest industry. I congratulate your good spouse, that he, as well as myself, is now free from public cares, and that he can bend his whole attention to his farming, which will afford him both profit and pleasure; a business which nobody knows better how to manage with advantage.

I am too old to follow printing again myself, but, loving the business, I have brought up my grandson Benjamin to it, and have built and furnished a printing-house for him, which he now manages under my eye. I have great pleasure in the rest of my grandchildren, who are now in number eight, and all promising, the youngest only six months old, but shows signs of great good nature. My friends here are numerous, and I enjoy as much of their conversation as I can reasonably wish; and I have as much health and cheerfulness, as can well be expected at my age, now eighty-three. Hitherto this long life has been tolerably happy; so that, if I were allowed to live it over again, I should make no objection, only wishing for leave to do, what authors do in a second edition of their works, correct some of my *errata.* Among the felicities of my life I reckon your friendship, which I shall remember with pleasure as long as that life lasts, being ever, my dear friend yours most affectionately,

B FRANKLIN

In September, Franklin wrote sadly to Le Veillard that he had abandoned all hope of finishing his *Autobiography.* Opium had, he said, "taken away my Appetite and so impeded my Digestion that I am become totally emaciated, and little remains of me but a Skeleton covered with a Skin." A few days later, he wrote the following letter of farewell to George Washington, who had been inaugurated first President of the United States the previous April 30.

Philada, Sept. 16, 1789.

My Malady renders my Sitting up to write rather painful to me; but I cannot let my Son-in-law Mr. Bache part for New York, without congratulating you by him on the Recovery of your Health, so precious to us all, and on the growing Strength of our New Government under your Administration. For my own personal Ease, I should have died two Years ago; but, tho' those Years have been spent in excruciating Pain, I am pleas'd that I have lived with them, since they have brought me to see our present Situation. I am now finishing my 84th [year], and probably with it my Career in this Life; but in whatever State of Existence I am plac'd hereafter, if I retain any Memory of what has pass'd here, I shall with it retain the Esteem, Respect, and Affection, with which I have long been, my dear Friend, yours most sincerely,

B FRANKLIN

In France, another revolution was brewing. Franklin followed it as well as he could, but he was more concerned about the fate of his individual friends than anything else. In this letter to another Passy neighbor, Jean Baptiste Le Roy, he reflected this concern, and passed on the mournful news of his decline.

French print showing the "terrible night" of October 5, 1789, when angry women marched on the royal palace at Versailles

Philadelphia, November 13, 1789

It is now more than a year, since I have heard from my dear friend Le Roy. What can be the reason? Are you still living? Or have the mob of Paris mistaken the head of a monopolizer of knowledge, for a monopolizer of corn, and paraded it about the streets upon a pole.

Great part of the news we have had from Paris, for near a year past, has been very afflicting. I sincerely wish and pray it may all end well and happy, both for the King and the nation. The voice of *Philosophy* I apprehend can hardly be heard among those tumults. If any thing material in that way had occurred, I am persuaded you would have acquainted me with it. However, pray let me hear from you a little oftener; for, though the distance is great, and the means of conveying letters not very regular, a year's silence between friends must needs give uneasiness.

Our new Constitution is now established, and has an appearance that promises permanency; but in this world nothing can be said to be certain, except death and taxes.

My health continues much as it has been for some time, except that I grow thinner and weaker, so that I cannot expect to hold out much longer.

My respects to your good brother, and to our friends of the Academy, which always has my best wishes for its prosperity and glory. Adieu, my dear friend, and believe me ever yours most affectionately,

B FRANKLIN

In this letter to David Hartley, Franklin commented on the French Revolution and tossed off one of his most memorable lines.

Philada, Decr 4, 1789.

I received your Favor of August last. Your kind Condolences on the painful State of my Health are very obliging. I am thankful to God, however, that, among the numerous Ills human Life is subject to, one only of any Importance is fallen to my Lot; and that so late as almost to insure that it can be but of short Duration.

The Convulsions in France are attended with some disagreable Circumstances; but if by the Struggle she obtains and secures for the Nation its future Liberty, and a good Constitution, a few Years' Enjoyment of those Blessings will amply repair all the Damages their Acquisition may have occasioned. God grant, that not only the Love of Liberty, but a thorough Knowledge of the Rights of Man, may pervade all the Nations of the Earth, so that a Philosopher may set his Foot anywhere on its Surface, and say, "This is my Country."

Ezra Stiles, the president of Yale and an old friend, wrote to the philosopher, asking for a confidential statement of his religious beliefs. Franklin's reply contained an interesting combination of candor and caution.

Philada, March 9, 1790.

Reverend and dear Sir,

You desire to know something of my Religion. It is the first time I have been questioned upon it. But I cannot take your Curiosity amiss, and shall endeavour in a few Words to gratify it. Here is my Creed. I believe in one God, Creator of the Universe. That he governs it by his Providence. That he ought to be worshipped. That the most acceptable Service we render to him is doing good to his other Children. That the soul of Man is immortal, and will be treated with Justice in another Life respecting its Conduct in this. These I take to be the fundamental Principles of all sound Religion, and I regard them as you do in whatever Sect I meet with them.

As to Jesus of Nazareth, my Opinion of whom you particularly desire, I think the System of Morals and his Religion, as he left them to us, the best the World ever saw or is likely to see; but I apprehend it has received various corrupting Changes, and I have, with most of the present Dissenters in England, some Doubts as to his Divinity; tho' it is a question I do not dogmatize upon, having never studied it, and think it needless to busy myself with it now, when I expect soon an Opportunity of knowing the Truth with less Trouble. I see no harm, however, in its being believed, if that Belief has the good Consequence, as probably it has, of making his Doctrines more respected and better observed; especially as I do not perceive, that the Supreme takes it amiss, by distinguishing the Unbelievers in his Government of the World with any peculiar Marks of his Displeasure.

I shall only add, respecting myself, that, having experienced the Goodness of that Being in conducting me prosperously thro' a long life, I have no doubt of its Continuance in the next, though without the smallest Conceit of meriting such Goodness. My Sentiments on this Head you will see in the Copy of an old Letter enclosed, which I wrote in answer to one from a zealous Religionist, whom I had relieved in a paralytic case by electricity, and who, being afraid I should grow proud upon it, sent me his serious though rather impertinent Caution. I send you also the Copy of another Letter, which will shew something of my Disposition relating to Religion. With great and sincere Esteem and Affection, I am, Your obliged old Friend and most obedient humble Servant

B FRANKLIN

P.S. Had not your College some Present of Books from the King of France? Please to let me know, if you had an Expectation given you of more, and the Nature of that Expectation? I have a Reason for the Enquiry.

I confide, that you will not expose me to Criticism and censure by publishing any part of this Communication to you. I have ever let others enjoy their religious Sentiments, without reflecting on them for those that appeared to me unsupportable and even absurd. All Sects here, and we have a great Variety, have experienced my good will in assisting them with Subscriptions for building their new Places of Worship; and, as I have never opposed any of their Doctrines, I hope to go out of the World in Peace with them all.

Ezra Stiles by Nathaniel Smibert

A last letter went to Jane Mecom.

Philadelphia, 24 March, 1790

My dear Sister,

I received your kind letter by your ever good neighbor, Captain Rich. The information it contained, that you continue well, gave me, as usual, great pleasure. As to myself, I have been quite free from pain for near three weeks past, and therefore not being obliged to take any laudanum, my appetite has returned, and I have recovered some part of my strength. Thus I continue to live on, while all the friends of my youth have left me, and gone to join the majority. I have, however, the pleasure of continued friendship and conversation

French print announcing Franklin's death to the country he loved

with their children and grandchildren. I do not repine at my malady, though a severe one, when I consider how well I am provided with every convenience to palliate it, and to make me comfortable under it; and how many more horrible evils that human body is subject to; and what a long life of health I have been blessed with, free from them all.

You have done well not to send me any more fish at present. These continue good, and give me pleasure.

Do you know anything of our sister Scott's daughter; whether she is still living, and where? This family join in love to you and yours, and to cousins Williams, with your affectionate brother,

B. FRANKLIN

P.S. It is early in the morning, and I write in bed. The awkward position has occasioned the crooked lines.

Finally, there was one more joust with the British Government. The new Secretary of State, Thomas Jefferson, asked Franklin to help him settle the Maine boundary.

Philadelphia, April 8, 1790.
I received your letter of the 31st of last past, relating to encroachments made on the eastern limits of the United States by settlers under the British Government, pretending that it is the *western,* and not the *eastern* river of the Bay of Passamaquoddy which was designated by the name of St. Croix in the treaty of peace with that nation; and requesting of me to communicate any facts which my memory or papers may enable me to recollect, and which may indicate the true river, which the commissioners on both sides had in their view, to establish as the boundary between the two nations.

Your letter found me under a severe fit of my malady, which prevented my answering it sooner, or attending, indeed, to any kind of business. I now can assure you that I am perfectly clear in the remembrance that the map we used in tracing the boundary, was brought to the treaty by the commissioners from England, and that it was the same that was published by Mitchell above twenty years before. Having a copy of that map by me in loose sheets, I send you that sheet which contains the Bay of Passamaquoddy, where you will see that part of the boundary traced. I remember, too, that in that part of the boundary we relied much on the opinion of Mr. Adams, who had been concerned in some former disputes concerning those territories. I think, therefore, that you may obtain still further light from him.

That the map we used was Mitchell's map, Congress were acquainted at the time by a letter to their Secretary for Foreign Affairs, which I suppose may be found upon their files.

A few days later Franklin suffered an attack of pleurisy. After several days of agonizing pain, he seemed, momentarily, to recover. He rose from his bed. But he explained to his daughter Sally that he simply wanted the bed made, so that he might "die in a decent manner." Sally replied that she was praying that he would get well and live many more years. "I hope not," Franklin replied. A few hours later, an abscess in his lungs burst. He died at eleven o'clock at night on April 17, 1790. In Paris, the French Chamber of Deputies, at the suggestion of the Comte de Mirabeau, seconded by Lafayette and La Rochefoucauld, went into mourning for three days. Eulogies poured from French and American presses. Perhaps the most touching comment was made by Jane Mecom, when she heard the sad news. To her niece Sally Franklin Bache, she wrote, "He while living was to me every enjoyment. Whatever other pleasures were, as they mostly took their rise from him, they passed like little streams from a beautiful fountain. They remind me of two lines of a song Mr. Peters used to sing at your house: 'But now they are withered and waned all away.'"

French drawing inscribed "Au Génie de Franklin," with a motto composed by Turgot: "Eripuit caelo fulmen, sceptrumque tyrannis." (He snatched the lightning from heaven, and the scepter from tyrants.)

YALE UNIVERSITY LIBRARY

Selected Bibliography

Aldridge, Alfred O. *Benjamin Franklin, Philosopher and Man.* Philadelphia: Lippincott, 1965.
———. *Franklin and his French Contemporaries,* New York: New York University Press, 1957.

Bowen, Catherine D. *Miracle at Philadelphia: The Story of the Constitutional Convention, May to September 1787,* Boston: Atlantic Monthly Press, Little Brown, 1966.

Bridenbaugh, Carl and Bridenbaugh, Jessica B. *Rebels and Gentlemen: Philadelphia in the Age of Franklin.* New York: Oxford University Press, 1965.

Burnett, Edmund C. *The Continental Congress.* New York: Norton, 1964.

Cohen, I. Bernard, *Benjamin Franklin: His Contribution to the American Tradition.* Indianapolis: Bobbs-Merrill, 1953.

Conner, Paul W. *Poor Richard's Politicks: Benjamin Franklin and His New American Order.* New York: Oxford University Press, 1965.

Fleming, Thomas. *The Man who Dared the Lightning: A New Look at Benjamin Franklin.* New York: Morrow, 1971.

Franklin, Benjamin. *The Autobiography of Benjamin Franklin.* Edited by Leonard W. Labaree *et al.* New Haven: Yale University Press, 1964.

———. *Benjamin Franklin's Autobiographical Writings.* Edited by Carl Van Doren. New York: Viking, 1945.

———. *The Complete Works of Benjamin Franklin.* Edited by John Bigelow, 10 vols. New York: Putnam, 1887-89.

———. *The Papers of Benjamin Franklin.* Vols. 1-14, Edited by Leonard W. Labaree *et al.* Vol. 15 —, Edited by William B. Willcox *et al.* New Haven: Yale University Press, 1959-

———. *The Works of Benjamin Franklin.* Edited by Jared Sparks. 10 vols. Boston: Hilliard, Gray: 1836-40.

———. *The Writings of Benjamin Franklin.* Edited by Albert H. Smyth. 10 vols. New York: Macmillan, 1905-7.

Granger, Bruce I. *Benjamin Franklin, an American Man of Letters.* Ithaca: Cornell University Press, 1964.

Hall, Max. *Benjamin Franklin & Polly Baker: The History of a Literary Deception.* Chapel Hill: University of North Carolina Press, 1960.

Hanna, William S. *Benjamin Franklin and Pennsylvania Politics,* Stanford: Stanford University Press, 1964.

Hays, I. Minis, ed. *Calendar of the Papers of Benjamin Franklin in the Library of the American Philosophical Society,* 5 vols. Philadelphia: American Philosophical Society, 1908.

Lopez, Claude-Anne. *Mon Cher Papa: Franklin and the Ladies of Paris.* New Haven: Yale University Press, 1966.

Morris, Richard B. *The Peacemakers: The Great Powers and American Independence.* New York: Harper & Row, 1965.

Nolan, James Bennett, *Benjamin Franklin in Scotland and Ireland: 1759 and 1771.* Philadelphia: University of Pennsylvania Press, 1956.

———. *General Benjamin Franklin: The Military Career of a Philosopher.* Philadelphia: University of Pennsylvania Press, 1956.

Rossiter, Clinton, *1787: The Grand Convention.* New York: Macmillan, 1966.

Roelker, William G., ed. *Benjamin Franklin and Catharine Ray Greene: Their Correspondence 1755-1790.* Philadelphia: American Philosophical Society, 1949.

Stourzh, Gerald. *Benjamin Franklin and American Foreign Policy.* Chicago: University of Chicago Press, 1954.

Van Doren, Carl, *Benjamin Franklin.* New York: Viking, 1938.

Van Doren, Carl, ed. *Letters and Papers of Benjamin Franklin and Richard Jackson 1753 – 1785,* Philadelphia: American Philosophical Society, 1947.

Van Doren, Carl, ed. *The Letters of Benjamin Franklin and Jane Mecom.* Princeton: Princeton University Press, 1950.

Wright, Esmond, ed. *Benjamin Franklin: A Profile.* New York: Hill & Wang. 1970.

Acknowledgments

The Editors are particularly grateful to the American Philosophical Society in Philadelphia for permission to reprint documents in its possession, the greatest collection of Benjamin Franklin papers in existence. The selections from the *Autobiography* have been taken from *The Autobiography of Benjamin Franklin,* edited by Leonard W. Labaree, *et al.* (New Haven and London: Yale University Press, 1964); the original manuscript of the *Autobiography* is at the Henry E. Huntington Library and Art Gallery in San Marino, California. In addition the Editors would like to thank the following individuals and institutions for permission to reprint documents in their possession:

Adams Manuscript Trust, Massachusetts Historical Society, page 306 (top)
Archives des Affaires Etrangères, Paris, pages 296 (top) and 350 (center)
Archivo Historico Nacional, Madrid, pages 292-93
Blumhaven Library and Gallery, Philadelphia, page 304 (center)
Mugar Library, Boston University, pages 351-52
Bristol Historical Society, Rhode Island, pages 267-68
Cornell University Library, Ithaca, page 234 (top)
Mr. Albert F. Greenfield, Philadelphia, page 222 (top)
Haverford College Library, Haverford, Penna., page 277 (bottom)
Historical Society of Pennsylvania, pages 278-79
David C. Holland, Esq., London, pages 285-86 and 294 (top)
Indiana University Library, Bloomington, pages 257-58
Mrs. Martin H. Kendig, Chicago, pages 339-40
Manuscript Division, Library of Congress, Washington, D.C., pages 282-83, 298-99, 306-7, 307-8, 309 (top), 316 (top), 316-17, 343-45, 394-95
Mrs. Arthur Loeb, Philadelphia, page 264 (top)
Mr. Albert E. Lownes, Providence, pages 339-40
Manuscripts and History Division, New York State Library, Albany, page 221
Princeton University Library, Princeton, page 348 (top)
Sheffield Central Library, England, pages 258-59 and 264 (bottom)
The Collection of Edward Wanton Smith, Philadelphia, page 359 (bottom)
William L. Clements Library, University of Michigan, Ann Arbor, page 363
Benjamin Franklin Collection, Sterling Memorial Library, Yale University, New Haven, pages 259-60, 367 (center), 376-78, 387-88, and 388-89

The Editors also wish to express their appreciation to the many institutions and individuals who made available their pictorial materials for use in this volume. In particular the Editors are grateful to:

The American Philosophical Society, Philadelphia—Whitfield J. Bell, Jr., Librarian
The Papers of Benjamin Franklin, Yale University, New Haven—William B. Willcox, Editor; Dorothy W. Bridgwater, Mary L. Hart, Claude A. Lopez, G.B. Warden, Assistant Editors
Benjamin Franklin Collection, Sterling Memorial Library, Yale University (credited as Yale University Library)
Bibliothèque Nationale, Paris
British Museum, London
Historical Society of Pennsylvania, Philadelphia
Henry E. Huntington Library, San Marino, California
Library of Congress, Washington, D.C.
Library Company of Philadelphia
Musée de Blerancourt, France
National Portrait Gallery, London
New York Public Library
Lewis Walpole Library, Farmington, Conn.

Finally, the Editors thank Susan Storer in New York and Russell Ash, John Harris, Peter Stockham, and Ben Weinreb in London for advice and assistance in obtaining pictorial material; Sylvia J. Abrams in Washington for copyediting and proofreading; and Mary-Jo Kline in New York for compiling the chronology and bibliography.

Index

412

413